D1287898

By Lillian Ross

PICTURE
PORTRAIT OF HEMINGWAY
THE PLAYER (WITH HELEN ROSS)
VERTICAL AND HORIZONTAL
REPORTING
ADLAI STEVENSON
TALK STORIES

TALK STORIES

by Lillian Ross

SIMON AND SCHUSTER · NEW YORK

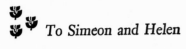 To Simeon and Helen

CONTENTS

8   CONTENTS

TALK STORIES

❦ MOVEMENT

FAWCETT PUBLICATIONS invited us to a party last week to celebrate the publication of a paperback anthology entitled *The Beats* and containing poems, essays, and stories by a couple of dozen writers who are now leading (according to Fawcett) the Beat (with, according to Fawcett, a capital *B*) movement. The party was held in the lobby of the Living Theatre, a second-floor walkup at Fourteenth Street and Sixth Avenue, a couple of hours before curtain time of that conspicuously living play called *The Connection*, which is housed there. As we climbed the stairs, we found copies of *The Beats* pasted to the walls. Some displayed the front cover, which has on it a photograph of a pretty young girl and a bearded young man wearing shell-rimmed eyeglasses, plus warnings that read, "Here are the most vital and controversial writers on the American scene," and "Raw, penetrating stories, poems and social criticism by JACK KEROUAC, NORMAN MAILER, ALLEN GINSBERG, LAWRENCE FERLINGHETTI, and many others. Edited by Seymour Krim." Other copies of the book showed the back cover, which added, "The drive, the fury, the frankness they bring to their writing has made the Beat Generation the most hotly discussed literary movement of this century."

Upstairs, the party seemed slow in getting started. Several lovely young ladies, all of them wearing conservative black dresses, were putting up more copies of *The Beats* at the corners of a square bar in the middle of the lobby and helping bartenders open bottles of whiskey. We approached a young man, impeccable in Ivy League oxford gray and a knitted black tie, who was putting up still more copies of *The Beats* on the walls. "Nobody here yet who's authentic Beat," he told us. "All of us are from Fawcett. We're here to inspire confidence. How do you like the girl on the cover? She's an associate editor on our books. She's not Beat at all. We put her on because she looked so typical." He paused. "Ah, at last! Seymour Krim!"

With this, the Fawcett man turned us over to Mr. Krim, a tall, skinny young man, friendly and wide-eyed, who was sporting a dark-maroon shirt, a black four-in-hand, a brown V-necked pullover, dark-gray trousers, and a silvery coat.

"I'm so nervous," Mr. Krim told us. "I never presided over a cock-tail party before. What am I supposed to do? Introduce people? Mix drinks? Offer them cheese crackers? I wish I didn't feel so nervous. Would you like some Scotch? I think it's real."

We moved over to the bar, and the bartender poured Krim and us some Scotch. "Tell me something, will you, kid?" the bartender said to Krim. "What are you kids calling this a *movement* for? You make it sound like the Communists, when all you are, you're a bunch of not too brainy, warmhearted kids."

"*Fawcett* calls it a movement," Krim said. "Actually, it's sort of a *wave*. Actually, it's sort of an *attitude* in anybody who's young or young in heart. It's a posture of rebellion. It's for anybody unwilling to put up with older compromises."

"O.K., O.K., kid," said the bartender. "I only thought any writer worth his salt, he stuck to his attic all by himself and *wrote*."

"We're like the French Impressionist painters, that whole group, although the analogy is a little square," Krim said. "Actually, there's less competitiveness among us than you find among most other writers. The wave brings ideas useful to all of us interchangeably. We turn each other on."

"A writer should be like an island," the bartender said. "Alone."

The party was warming up, with a number of informally attired youthful guests arriving in twos and threes. We were joined by a young man wearing chino trousers, a wrinkled khaki shirt open at the collar, and brand-new white sneakers, who had a small, childlike face and shining eyes. "Where's Norman Mailer?" he asked Krim. "I want to meet Norman Mailer. He's the only really good writer in the whole room."

"He's not here yet," said Krim.

"He's the only writer here with major talent," the young man said.

"What about yourself?" Krim asked, plucking a copy of *The*

Beats from the wall, introducing the young man to us as Dan Propper, and opening the book to a page headed "Dan Propper—'The Fable of the Final Hour.'"

"I don't regard myself as a great writer," said Propper. "Norman Mailer has made it; he's there. This is my wife, Eunice," he added, introducing a little, round-faced, black-haired girl wearing a black shirt, black pants, and white sneakers as clean as her husband's.

"Where's Norman Mailer?" Eunice asked.

Another young man, handsome and confident, came by and waved a manuscript packed between black hard covers at us.

"Got a carbon copy?" Krim asked.

"I never make carbons," said the young man.

"You'll regret it someday," said Krim.

"I don't even belong here," said the young man. "I'm a senior at Harvard. This party looks like any old party at Harvard."

"Is that Norman Mailer?" Eunice asked Krim, standing on her toes and pointing to a nearby man of at least thirty.

"That's Leonard Bishop," Krim said, loudly enough for Bishop to hear. "He's sort of a William Styron type."

"I'm only a sicknik!" Leonard Bishop called over.

"What's Herbert Gold doing in your book? What's the idea?" asked the Harvard man.

"Well, he's really anti-Beat," said Krim. "He's still finding his way. He'll get there."

"You've got hope here," said the Harvard man. "That's more than we've got at Harvard."

"Where's Jack Kerouac?" a chic, attractive lady asked. "My son told me if I came to this party I'd see Jack Kerouac."

"He plays hard to get," said Krim. "Too bad Ginsberg is in Chile, or we'd have had ten good arguments already. Nobody has opened up yet. The party's tame. Anyway, here's Ted Joans."

We shook hands with a bearded young Negro who had a Midwestern accent and was wearing a heavy sweater with brown and gray horizontal stripes. "I'm splitting Friday," Joans told us. "That means leaving town. Going on a trip around the world. Getting on a boat. Going to read my poems in the middle of the Atlantic. Going to read all over the world—in Liverpool, London, and Brussels. No matter where I am, I always find a place to read."

"You make a lot of money getting rented?" Krim asked him.

"Enough to get me on that boat to Liverpool," Joans said, and held us by the sleeve. "My friend put this ad in the *Village Voice* offering to rent Beatniks for your party," he said. "I'm the one got rented. People always ask me don't I feel commercial letting myself get rented? What I always reply is 'There's nothing wrong with a Cadillac if you don't let it drive you.' I tell them it's the same as renting yourself out as a capitalist. Nothing wrong with that, long as you get paid."

As we made our way back to the bar, we ran into Mr. and Mrs. Propper. "Norman Mailer is here!" they said happily. Sure enough, in a few seconds we came upon Norman Mailer, looking very conservative in a business suit and very much the elder statesman. We introduced him to the Proppers, whose beaming faces were a joy to see.

"Boy!" said Propper. "I read the scenes from your play! It's a groovy play."

"I read your fable," Mailer said, a fatherly twinkle in his eye. "I liked your fable."

"I was young, rebellious, and adolescent when I wrote that fable," said Propper.

"His current stuff is much better," said Eunice.

Mailer gave them a fatherly nod. "It's a good fable," he said.

"Your play is a groovy play," said Eunice. "That part where the atom bomb goes off."

"That part's all right," said Mailer. "Then I've got two more scenes after that, they're even better."

Ted Joans joined us. "Norman Mailer!" he said. "In one of my poems, I tell them to buy your book."

"Say, thanks," Mailer said, looking bashful.

"I'm splitting Friday," said Joans. "Leaving on a trip around the world. Going to tell everybody, all over, to buy your book."

"I've never heard so many non sequiturs in my life," the bartender told us when we got back to him. "What kind of writers are they, they all talk the same? These kids, they are not Tolstoy."

"Kerouac isn't here yet," the chic, attractive lady said to us. "But I met this cute little Dan Propper. He gave me a copy of the book. I asked him for his autograph. I told him, 'I'm going to take it home, where I can read it *properly*.' He didn't get it."

We came upon Propper and Eunice a few minutes later.

"Nobody asked Norman Mailer for *his* autograph," Eunice said.

"That's a mark of his skill," said Propper.

We started to shove off, and, on our way to the door, passed Krim. "Fawcett is putting water in the drinks," he told us. "But the party is opening up."

❀ ANNIVERSARY

DURING the recent sultry weekend that marked the fifteenth anniversary of the atomic bombing of Hiroshima, we went over to the United Nations Headquarters, where Secretary-General Dag Hammarskjöld, who had just flown back from the Congo, was calling the Security Council together to decide what to do about Katanga Premier Moise Tshombe's Belgian-forces-in-and-U.N.-forces-out policy, Congo Premier Patrice Lumumba's U.N.-forces-in-and-Belgian-forces-out policy, Ghana Premier Kwame Nkrumah's offer-of-independent-military-assistance-to-get-Belgian-forces-out policy, and other matters pertaining to the keep-another-bomb-from-going-off-anywhere-in-the-world policy.

With twenty-three hours to go before the Security Council met, we made our way to the fourth floor of the Secretariat Building, where a bulletin board was covered with notices of doings that were being planned by U.N. personnel: an announcement of meetings of the U.N. Folk Dance Club on folk dances of France, with instruction by Mme. Olga Tarassova; an announcement of the U.N. Ski Club's charter flights to Zurich next February; invitations to join the U.N. Golf Club, the U.N. Gym Club, the U.N. Bowling League; and notices of an astonishing number of other extracurricular activities, future events, and future plans that reminded us of our college days. We stopped in at the cafeteria, where U.N. workers sat in groups of two and three talking quietly, or, carrying sandwich-and-black-coffee-laden trays, moved quickly out on their way to offices throughout the building. We grabbed a hamburger on roll with French fries, lettuce and tomato, strawberry jello, and black coffee, for seventy cents, and sat down at a table facing a picture window that looked out on slow-moving tugs, barges, and sightseeing boats on the East River. At a table near us, a young Indian was eating

prune yoghurt from a white-and-purple container and listening to a
pocket-sized radio tuned to a baseball game.

"What's the score?" we asked.

"Two to one, Kansas City," he said, looking gloomy.

On our other side, a couple of Oxford-accented gentlemen, pink-
cheeked, tweedy, and as ageless as happy professors, were giving
deep, serious consideration to how the S.-G., having flown 14,118
miles to Léopoldville and back, and having gone directly from Idlewild to his desk upstairs after twenty-one flying hours and, apparently, no sleep in two days, was holding up.

"Extraordinary man, the S.-G.," one professor said to the other.
"A superhuman person."

"A human dynamo," the other said. "At midnight, he received
the Italian Ambassador, who had just arrived. The S.-G. didn't go
home until two-thirty in the morning. I got in at nine and found
him back at his desk, smiling, cheerful, healthy, in remarkably good
humor. In excellent condition. Most heroic."

They looked relieved, and we, feeling reassured, got up to go. The
young Indian's pocket radio was clattering tinnily with yells and
cheers. "Moose Skowron hit a home run with Maris aboard. Three
to two, New York," he said to us, and smiled.

We took an escalator down to the second floor, where the sound
of working typewriters drew us to the office of Norman Ho, a gentle-
voiced, clear-eyed man of Scotch-Chinese parentage, who is chief of
the central news desk. He was in shirtsleeves and looked wilted, but
told us it was perfectly natural for him to be working on a weekend.
"I've accumulated ninety-five and a half hours of free time to make
up someday, perhaps, for the overtime, but almost everybody around
here can say the same," he went on. "We're used to working around
the clock. Excuse me while I see about the translation of this cable
we just received from Léopoldville. It's about a statement made by
Dr. Ralph Bunche, the S.-G.'s personal representative in the Congo.
Dr. Bunche is correcting a misrepresentation made by the Congo's
Deputy Prime Minister. Let's see . . ."

He handed us the cable, and we read from the middle, ". . . JE
ME SUIS LIMITE STRICTEMENT AU MANDAT DEFINI PAR M HAMMAR-
SKJOLD CMA CEST-A-DIRE CMA A SUBQUOTE PREPARER LE TERRAIN POUR
LE RETRAIT DES TROUPES BELGES ET LENTREE DES TROUPES DE L ONU

UNSUBQUOTE STOP JE NAI ENGAGE AUCUNE NEGOCIATION AVEC QUI QUE
CE SOIT A ELISABETHVILLE STOP . . ."

"The translation now goes to my secretary, Mrs. Han," Ho told
us. "Margaret! Please," he called to an attractive Chinese girl in an
adjoining office, waving his papers at her. She came in, followed by a
two-year-old Chinese boy wearing a yellow seersucker play suit and
chattering away in Chinese. "I had to bring Eddie with me, Norman," Mrs. Han said apologetically. "I couldn't get a sitter, I was
called on such short notice."

Eddie, who had a crew haircut, looked at everybody with joy ram-
pant on his round-cheeked face and continued chattering in Chinese.

"Eddie doesn't know any English," Mrs. Han said.

Ho handed over his papers. "Wait till Eddie starts school. He
won't speak a word of Chinese," he said. "He'll understand it, but
he'll refuse to speak anything but English."

"Goodness gracious!" Mrs. Han exclaimed, taking the papers
from Ho, and said something softly to her son in Chinese.

"That gets mimeographed," Ho told her, and turned to a young
man who was handing him a typewritten sheet of paper. "Wow!" he
said, and read aloud: " 'S.-G.'s. appointments today [Sunday] so far
[as of 1 P.M.]: 10 A.M., Foreign Minister Wigny, of Belgium; 11
A.M., Deputy Foreign Minister Kuznetsov [U.S.S.R.]; in the course
of the afternoon, the S.-G. plans to see the representatives of
France, the U.K., the U.S., Poland. S.-G.'s appointments Saturday
night [that was yesterday]: 9 P.M., reps. of Ceylon, Tunisia, Argentina and Ecuador; 10 P.M., reps. of African countries—Ethiopia,
Ghana, Guinea, Liberia, Morocco, Sudan, Tunisia, U.A.R., Mali; 12
midnight, Egidio Ortona [Italy].' Wow!"

We left him shaking his head, and, proceeding to one of the three
subbasements of the building, came across a good-natured, very polite, yellow-haired, handsome Swiss named Paul Haag, who told us
he was assistant manager of Internal Reproduction of U.N. Documents, a Division situated practically inches away from the Franklin
D. Roosevelt Drive traffic and the river. Mimeograph machines,
folding machines, gathering machines, photo-offset equipment, and
presses were slapping out documents right and left. "We are not

dealing only with the emergency upstairs," Mr. Haag told us, and handed us the nearest document, a beefy booklet entitled *Information from Non-Self-Governing Territories: Summary and Analysis of Information Transmitted under Article 73e of the Charter. Report of the Secretary-General. Pacific Territories Netherlands New Guinea.* Mr. Haag said that his division had been working steadily since Saturday morning, when the S.-G. had announced that he was flying back for the Security Council meeting. "To work around the clock is not a new experience for me," Mr. Haag said. "I am just arriving from Geneva in the month of April. In Geneva we worked very hard. It was in Geneva that I had to learn English in a few months in order to speak with our English and American colleagues."

We said goodbye and, in the company of a U.N. information official, a young man from Peru named Oscar Faura, headed for the S.-G.'s floor, the thirty-eighth. "The S.-G. arrived from the Congo last night at 6:20 P.M., and at 7:15 P.M. he was here, sitting down for a conference with his assistants," Mr. Faura told us in the elevator. "The S.-G. has been called an apostle of quiet diplomacy. You can be quite sure he covered everything with Andrew W. Cordier, his Executive Assistant, and with Henry R. Labouisse, Special Adviser to the S.-G. The S.-G.'s Special Adviser on Civilian Operations in the Congo, Sir Alexander MacFarquhar, is here today, too. The S.-G.'s Military Adviser for the Congo, Brigadier Inder Jit Rikhye, is in Léopoldville, making a tour of the military installations that are being set up for the U.N. forces. The S.-G. has an apartment, with a bedroom, on this floor, but he doesn't use it. No matter how late he works, he always prefers to go home. Cordier often sleeps here, though. Ah, Arne!" he said, greeting a guard as we stepped out of the elevator. "We're just going back to the offices for a moment."

"O.K., Oscar," said Arne, with a Scandinavian accent.

"Heavy traffic?" asked Faura.

"Ambassador Lodge is with the S.-G. at the moment," said Arne. "The Polish Ambassador, I think, is due next."

We followed Mr. Faura into Room 3858, Dr. Bunche's conference room. The walls were decorated with charts headed "Air Unit" ("North Star, C-119—5, C-47—10") and "Military Personnel

(Ethiopia, Ghana, Guinea, Ireland, Liberia, Mali, Morocco, Sweden, Tunisia), and with a map ("Congo Belge") that had colored pins stuck here and there in it.

"Ah, Sherwood Moe!" Mr. Faura said, introducing us to a mild-mannered American in a wrinkled gray suit.

"Forgive our appearance. We've tried to turn this into an operations room, but we haven't had time," Mr. Moe said. "We had eleven thousand one hundred and fifty-five troops as of last week. The Malis sent five hundred and seventy-three troops today. Requests for contingents go out from the S.-G. The problem of the particular area in question, naturally, determines the composition of the force. This problem demands primarily African forces. There's Sir Alexander. All you get of him these days is a glimpse."

We got a glimpse of a tall man in shirtsleeves shooting by.

"The things he has to worry about for the Congo!" Moe said. "Food, health, transportation, postal operations—everything."

"Let's see if we can get a glimpse of the S.-G.," said Faura. "I hear he looks marvellous."

"He does, he does," said Moe proudly.

We walked down a corridor and looked in on the S.-G.'s outer office. "There's Loretta Cowan, on the job," Faura said, indicating a pleasant-faced woman in a glassed-in switchboard booth in the outer office. "All the S.-G. has to say is 'Get me Moscow' and Loretta has the call in in two minutes flat. Terrific girl!"

At that point, Ambassador Henry Cabot Lodge came out of the S.-G.'s inner office, waving back and calling, "Well, take care of yourself!"

"They keeping you busy, Mr. Ambassador?" one of the secretaries asked.

"Well, I've got a little election coming up on the eighth of November," Mr. Lodge said. "Got a little campaigning to do. Well, hello, Oscar!" He shook hands with Faura.

"Cómo está usted, Señor Embajador?" asked Faura.

"Muy bien, gracias. Y usted? Bien?" Lodge replied.

"Me permite felicitarle su designación como candidato a la vicepresidencia," said Faura.

"Muchas gracias por su felicitación, amigo," said Lodge. He nodded graciously to us and left.

Mr. Hammarskjöld popped out of his office just then, wearing a cream-colored linen suit and a maroon tie, and looking healthy indeed. Smiling, in remarkably good humor, he waved confidently to all before retiring to wait for the Polish Ambassador.

GELBER

JACK GELBER, the twenty-eight-year-old author of *The Connection*, which has been running at the Living Theatre for the past year, which recently won an Obie (Best Off Broadway Play), and which has made him famous on and around Broadway as well as off, lives with his wife and year-old son in a Yorkville railroad flat, where we had the pleasure, the other evening, of talking with him. Gelber is unbeat and unbeaten, with sandy hair, a soft voice, a relaxed manner, a round nose, a round and open face, and a nice expression of confidence in his eyes. At the time of our visit, supper was over, the baby was asleep in his crib, Mrs. Gelber was in the kitchen transcribing some of her husband's scribbled notes on the typewriter, and a gentle breeze was blowing through the windows in the living room, overlooking First Avenue. Against a contrapuntal background of automobile horns, shouts of hopscotch players, and other summer street noises, Gelber offered us some coffee, insisted that we take the most comfortable seat in the room—an old-fashioned wicker rocking chair with a flowered cushion—and told us that he's been making a good enough living, an average of a hundred dollars a week from *The Connection*, and has been free to work on exactly what he wants to. Gelber, who looked pretty free to us, was wearing, from bottom to top, desert boots, white woollen socks, chino pants, and a sports shirt open at the collar. At the moment, he is working on the script for a film version of *The Connection*, to be shot in New York. He has finished another play, called *The Apple*, which he hopes to have produced by the Living Theatre in the fall.

Explaining what the new play is about (*The Connection* is about a group of heroin addicts waiting in a flat for their connection to arrive with the drug) is very tricky, Gelber told us. "At first, I went around telling the people who asked me that the play is about New

York," he said. "Then I told them it was a political satire. Now I just say it's a satire on death. I really don't know how to go about reducing things to simplicities. The new play is written in the same free style as my first. I tried the more conventional forms, but it didn't come out right and I threw it away. I don't put down the other way. It's just that it always comes out, for me, like some kind of puppet show. Maybe I can't do the more conventional thing because I don't know anything about it. I am very little involved in the history of the theatre. As a kid, I was never taken to the theatre. I went off to the movies. I didn't even know the theatre existed until I got to college. If I know anything about what I do now, it's intuitive. I love some of the old hokum plays and movies. I admire it. It's marvellous. But I don't want to do it myself. I don't think I chose the form of The Connection. I think it chose me. The Connection came out of what it was. It didn't occur to me that anything else would work.

"When the play opened, it was summer, and we got lambasted by all the second-string critics. The first-string ones have just got around to seeing it recently, and they have liked it. At first, we thought the play would close. Two weeks after the opening, I drove my wife, Carol, and our little baby, Jed Randall—he's older than the play by one month—to Chicago, to see my family, and then to California, to see Carol's family. We drove in a 1949 Ford, which I still have. It's a two-door maroon sedan that I bought in 1957 for a hundred dollars. We did eighty miles per hour going across the desert. My kingpins and bushings are beginning to go, but driving out to the Coast was easy. We stayed with Carol's parents for a month, then took another ten days driving back. By the time we got back, word of the play had got around and people were starting to come to see it. I wasn't exactly surprised; I had thought the play would be popular, because it had jazz in it. During the early months of the run, many people who came were Negroes, because they had heard there were Negroes in it. I thought the Negroes would like the play. I knew I'd written a play where white and Negro characters were interchangeable without making any difference in the play. Whatever else happens, the race issue doesn't come up. I didn't have to score any points. I wanted to say some things in the play, and the most important things were said in humor. The play is funny when it's most serious.

"Now all the doors are open to me. Most people know who I am. And a lot of people have been very good to me. But I don't want to do anything different. I don't want a whole bunch of aggravation. I'm selfish. I don't need anything except to eat and pay rent. It takes a good deal of pushing to get me to buy a pair of socks, and then Carol usually buys them for me. I don't have any television set now. I have a portable phonograph and about eight records—a Monk, some Parker, and some old boogie-woogie. If I make some money, I must buy some new records. I hear all the music I need on the radio, which is in the kitchen, where I also listen to the ball games. And I don't need big audiences. Shelley Winters started negotiations with me about buying The Connection for a movie. But I dropped them when I realized the talk was all business and neglecting what the play was about. The question I put to myself was 'Do I want money or do I want a way of life?' It's no big problem for me to know my answer. That little baby asleep in there doesn't need a lot of money. One way or another, he'll get to go to college. Even if you asked him now, he'd say he'd choose to have the way of life. I'm doing exactly what I want. I've found a place to work—New York— which I love. I don't see myself climbing. About fifteen thousand people have come to see my play. That's fine. I just plan to keep on going."

Gelber's parents—his father, a sheet-metal worker, is Chicago-born, the son of an ironworker who emigrated from Rumania—live in Chicago, with his two younger brothers, Mike, twenty-four, a sheet-metal worker, and David, seventeen, who plays tennis on his high-school team. "I was born in Chicago, on the eighth floor of Mt. Sinai Hospital, at exactly the moment on the clock that my little son was born—eight minutes after eight—but my date is April 12, 1932," Gelber said, autobiographically. "On my thirteenth birthday, Franklin Delano Roosevelt made it out. I'm a jazz baby, without a doubt. I played tuba in the high-school band. With my gang, I'd hang out in strip-tease houses, tell them we were twenty-one. I was a smart kid. I played basketball in high school, graduated from the John Marshall High School, then went to the University of Illinois, in Champaign. I left home then and never went back. I was a chemistry major at first, thinking I'd be a chemist or chemical engineer. Then I wound up studying journalism, which dealt mainly with how to get a job in radio and television. Which I didn't want. Within two weeks after graduation, I got a lift in a friend's car to San Franciso. I had a hundred dollars saved up from working summers as a sheet-metal worker, and when that ran out I got a job as a shipfitter's helper. I lived in North Beach from 1953 to 1955, working and then drawing unemployment insurance. The beatniks appeared in San Francisco after I left for New York. I met Kerouac there once, but I didn't know he was a writer.

"I always wanted to come to New York. It seemed to be the center of everything. I felt I belonged in New York. When I got here, I never felt, as some people do, that I was an outsider. I felt I would be at home here, and I have been. My first nine months here I spent just going to movies and walking the streets. I had a three-year-old beard that everyone seemed to consider a fire hazard. But I got a job at the United Nations—seventy dollars a week, as a mimeograph operator, working the night shift, midnight to eight in the morning. I shaved off the beard one day when I suddenly realized that people were looking at me, when I wanted to be looking at them. I wanted my anonymity. Carol and I were married three days before Christmas, 1957. The following summer, I started writing *The Connection*.

"The whole experience had a kind of magic quality to it. After I'd written the play, I said to Carol, 'I don't know anybody on Broadway or Off Broadway. Whom am I going to take the play to?' I bought the *Times* to get a list of producers out of it, and then I ran into an old friend on the street who suggested that I take the play to Julian Beck. I called him up, and he said to put it in the mail. I took the subway up to his house to give it to him, feeling terrified, and a week later he called me up and said he and his wife, Judith Malina, loved the play and wanted to do it. After that, I was in on most of the casting. I was at every rehearsal. I was at every reading. Anything I wanted I told Judith, the director, and she would get it done. And I can tell you I wanted a lot. In my innocence, I gobbled everything up, every aspect of the production, including the box-office, the tickets, the financial. I wanted to know everything."

We asked him about literary influences.

"I haven't read too much," he said. "But at the University of Illinois I had a job in the library, where I came across a lot of things that interested me. The Books of the Dead, Egyptian and Tibetan, that give advice to people who die. Early Greek philosophy. I've been attracted to Turgenev, Gorki, Gogol. I never really read Proust, but I read Rilke and the German Expressionists of the twenties. *Alexanderplatz, Berlin* and *The Sleepwalkers* had a great effect on me. In the library, I first got interested in Buddhism. I've always had a great interest in religious states of being. That little baby in there knows everything right now that he's ever going to know, but someday it will all be revealed to him. That's the way I was in the library. I was in a conducive state. I wanted to know."

THE VINYL SANTA

OUR LIGHTED fireproof plastic Christmas bells are strung all through the house, not a creature is stirring, and our mail-order catalogues—now piled high on the back porch—have been under surveillance since August, when they started coming in from Atlantic City, New Jersey; Oshkosh, Wisconsin; Evanston, Illinois; Chicago, Illinois; Falls Church, Virginia; Omaha, Nebraska; Vineland, New Jersey; Northport, New York; New York, New York; and elsewhere, including points across the seas. We did our shopping during Indian summer, without leaving our chair. Our house is full. Our task is completed. We are ready.

On our front door is a "Deck the Door Knob of red-and-green felt with touches of glittering gold that has three jingly bells to say 'Hi! and Merry Christmas!' to all comers." On our windows are "Press-On Window Scenes" of snowmen and reindeer, and the windows are further ornamented with "Giant, 29-inch by 20-inch Personal Balls Artistically Hand-Lettered with the Family Name." Mounted outside on the wall of the house are "The Three Wise Men in Full Color in a Procession of Heavy Weatherproof Methyl-methacrylate Plastic." Each Wise Man is three feet tall and illuminated. A "Life-Size Climbing Vinyl Santa" is on the rooftop, and on the front lawn we have "3-D Thirty-Inch High Full Color Carollers of Strong Vinylite Carolling 'Oh, Come All Ye Faithful!' " In place of our regular doorbell we have a "glowing, jingling Santa stamped with the family name with a cord that visitors pull that raises Santa's arms in welcome, jingling bright brass bells." The garage door is covered with a "Giant Door Greeter Five Feet High and Six Feet Wide, Reading 'Merry Christmas.' " Indoors, all our rooms have been sprayed either with "Bayberry Mist, the forest-fresh scent-of-Christmas" or with the "pungent, spicy, exotic, sweet and rare frankincense-and-myrrh spray—gift of the Magi to the newborn Babe." Each light switch is covered with a "Switchplate-Santa made of white felt with red bell-bedecked cap—the switch comes through his open mouth, the sight of which will make you feel jolly." The towels on the bathroom racks are hand-printed with designs of sleighs and candy canes. The rug next to the tub has "Jolly Old Santa centered in deep, soft, plushy, white pile, and he's wreathed in smiles and in cherries, too, for 'round his head is a gay, cherry wreath." All the mirrors in the house are plastered with red, green, and white pleated tissue cutouts of angels with self-adhesive backs. In the dining room, "Full Size Santa Mugs of Bright Red-and-White Glazed Ceramic are 'Ready' for a 'Spot' of Holiday Cheer." In the living room, we have a "giant holiday chandelier of metallic foil discs reflecting a rainbow of colors," and "giant four-foot electric candles in festive red-and-white candy stripes are glowing cheerfully from their rock-steady base to their dripping wax 'flame.' " On the hall table stands our "Electric Musical Church, five inches high, with inspirational strains of 'Silent Night' pealing reverently from behind lighted, colorfully stained windows."

The tree is trimmed, all the way from a "Perforated Golden Star Making the Sun Envious of Its Brilliance, as though the Blazing Star of Bethlehem Were Pausing in Its Orbit at Your Home," down to the "Christmas Tree Bib Covered with a Profusion of Christmas Designs and Colors" on the floor. Reflecting the light of the Perforated Golden Star, which is made of anodized aluminum with "Hundreds of Holes through which the Light Twinkles just like a Real Star," hang dozens of "Personalized Tree Balls with Names of the Family Nicely Applied in Shimmering, Non-Tarnishing Glitter." Bare spots on the tree are filled in with "Luminous Tree Icicles of Plastic," "Luminous, Plastic, Heavenly Angel Babes Who Have Left the Milky Way," "Handcarved Wooden Angels Holding Hymnals on Gilded Hanging Strings," "Frosty White Pine Cones Lit with Colored Bulbs," "Miniature Felt Money Bags Gayly Trimmed in Assorted Designs of Yuletide," and "Yummy-Yum-Yum Santa Sweetest Holiday Lollipops."

On Christmas morning, there will be plenty of laughs when everybody gets dressed. Dad will be wearing his "Personalized Holiday Ringing Bell Shorts of White Sanforized Cotton with Santa Claus

Handpainted in All His Glory on One Side with a Tinkling Bell on the Tassel of His Cap and Dad's name embroidered in Contrasting Red on the Other." Big Sister will have on "Bright Red Holiday Stretch Socks of Bright Red Nylon Embossed with Contrasting White Holiday Motif." Little Sister and Mom will have on matching "Candy Striped Flannelette Housecoats." Brother will have on a "Clip-On Bow Tie of Red Felt in a Holly Pattern" and also "The Host with the Most Bright Red Felt Vest with Colorful Christmas Accent." Auntie will have on "Ringing Bell Panties Boasting a Ribbon Bedecked Candy Cane Handpainted in Brilliant Yuletide Colors with a Real Tinkling Bell for Extra Cheer." And Shep will have on his own "Personalized Dog Galoshes Embossed with Dog Claus on the Toes." Odds and ends under the tree will include a "Jingle Bell Apron that Plays a Merry Tune with Every Movement," "Donner and Blitzen Salt and Pepper Shakers," a set of "Holly Jewelry for the Holly-Days," a "Ten Commandments Bookmark of Ten Radiant Gold-Plated Squares that Look Like Ancient Scrolled Pages of the Old Testament with the Commandments Etched Upon Them," and "Hi-Fi Bible Stories on a Personalized Record." And our Christmas dinner will be prepared with the help of the "No Cooking Cookbook, with a Collection of Easy-To-Fix Recipes for Busy Mothers that Turns Canned and Frozen Foods into a Banquet of Gourmet Dishes."

✿✿✿ LIFE LINE

ONE EVENING last week, the uproar about coffeehouses in Greenwich Village having died down, we headed for the Figaro, on the corner of Bleecker and Macdougal, to get the latest on *caffè espresso*. The streets were teeming when we arrived—motorcycles, sports cars, Cadillacs, Larks, bicycles, tricycles, little kids, bigger kids, boy gangs, man gangs, girl gangs, young couples, old couples, middle-aged couples, loners, black-garbed Italian ladies in their seventies, panhandlers, book carriers, and Beats of various shapes, sizes, and natures. Paperback books, handwrought jewelry, antiques, sandals, pottery, straw objects, paintings, simmering Italian sausages, onions, and pizzas, and freshly boiled sweet corn were being marketed in neighboring stalls and shops, with enough customers, apparently, for everybody. Out of this festival, like a ghost, there suddenly loomed a distinguished and formerly subdued artist we know, who was now wearing boots and a T shirt (a fancy kind, with an inlaid panel at the throat). "Greetings," he said coolly. "I have just moved down here from the upper East Side. If you want to see something peculiar, go to the Cedar Street Tavern, on University Place. It's full of painters."

"You Beat?" we asked.

"It's a legitimate thing to be a Beatnik, even though most of the time it's the provincial thing," he said. "It draws me. It's the power of innocence."

Inside the Figaro, the power of innocence was going full blast—a jukebox playing Bach's Toccata and Fugue in D Minor, two *espresso* machines hissing, a white-aproned, blond-bearded dishwasher playing chess with a customer, an old Chaplin film flickering on a movie screen in a corner, abstract paintings hanging on the walls, a collection of Tiffany lamps hanging from the ceiling, a grand piano (quiet) to one side, the customers brooding, reading, or buzzing with discussions, polemics, and harangues on faith and life. It drew us. We cornered Tom Ziegler, the owner, a clean-cut man of thirty-one, whose hair was slicked back on his head with water, and whose T shirt showed faintly under a conventional white one, open at the collar.

"We're sometimes called the square coffeehouse, but we don't mind, because we know we're not square," Ziegler told us. "It's simply that when you come here you have to behave. We don't permit the weekend tourist Beatniks—a lot of them come down from the Bronx sporting day-old beards—or any would-be Beatniks who read about press-created-image Beatniks and try to be like them, to work out their psychic difficulties here. Look around. You'll see plenty of Beatniks, but they're nothing like the exhibitionists exploited in stories in the News. Our Beatniks are the real, true, old-fashioned wonderful bohemians. There's been some harassment of coffeehouses that didn't meet fire-law standards, despite the fact that hundreds of eating places in town with the same conditions weren't bothered. But I maintain that the market for coffeehouses is unlimited. This is just the beginning of the boom. It's going on all over. In London two years ago there were two hundred coffeehouses; now there are twice the number. In 1956, when my wife and I started the Figaro, there were a few coffeehouses around, and I wondered whether the Village could stand another coffee place. Last month, there were more than two dozen new ones since we'd started, and I've stopped counting. The coffeehouse fills a real need; people have to congregate. There are two possibilities for a young girl, say, who comes to New York and doesn't know anybody—Y.W.C.A. dances and coffeehouses. She doesn't want to make the bar scene. For a young man, a coffeehouse is a place for him to sit down and talk to people without being jostled by drunks. One of the things we enjoy is Europeans who find their way here. Americans they've met in Europe tell them the best place for a stranger to go is to the Figaro. Here they have a place they feel they belong in, where they can exchange ideas, talk, carry on a social life. In a way, it follows the high-school corner drugstore for a lot of kids. Where did I go when I was eighteen? I went up to Hell's Kitchen and hung out on street corners and eventually got into trouble. Here we keep an eye on the teen-agers. They play chess or checkers, or just talk, and we get them to drink milk. And we don't let them hang around too long. Some of them I ration to three visits a night. Look around. See them? Nice kids."

Mr. Ziegler drew a deep breath and did some looking around himself. "Coffeehouses have been under attack down through history," he said, turning back to us. "I recently came across an article that reported there was hostility to coffeehouses at Oxford in the seventeenth century. They were criticized as being gathering places of students and teachers, who consequently lost respect for each other and frittered away their study time. I don't agree. I'm sure there were people then who benefited tremendously from coffeehouse life, as there are now."

We asked Mr. Ziegler for his coffeehouse background.

"I didn't know a thing about it, and neither did my wife, when we started," he replied. "It was probably a good thing that we didn't have any restaurant experience, because to run a coffeehouse as a restaurant is impossible. We got into the business to make some money to pay my way at N.Y.U.; I started college when I was twenty-five. I've lived in the Village all my life—except for two years in Hell's Kitchen—and I went to school here. My father is a painter. One thing I know—in the Village, you can find somebody who knows about anything. Originally, the Figaro was in a former barbershop across the street. That's how it got named. I bought it from a friend for three thousand dollars that I borrowed. He'd had it a couple of months and was tired of it, or so he told me. We put another two thousand dollars into it across the street, and then we took this corner, the site of two former stores—drygoods and instrument repairs. I practically built the place with my own broken hands—put up the walls with a friend who is a writer, who also helped me put in this floor. Marble scraps. My own idea. Cost me twenty dollars, and the marble man I bought the scraps from thought I was crazy. I bought the furniture at auction. I dropped out of college when I discovered that the coffeehouse was more complicated and more enjoyable than I had expected. We filled the place up with chess players during the week and made our money on weekends. My wife and I worked a sixty-hour, seven-day week. We invested an additional twelve thousand dollars here. We had trouble finding an old espresso machine, because these machines haven't been made since the nineteen-forties. The Italians don't like them, and now make those hydro-compression ones, which I think are ugly. I got a beautiful old one through a bookie who had a brother-in-law in the old-style Italian coffeehouse business. Now there are about a dozen wholesale places that import newfangled pushbutton machines from Italy. We have twelve waitresses and two waiters, from all parts of the world. Our dishwasher is from Texas. He's a writer. One of my managers is a high-school English teacher who likes working here better. We have other people who should be out building their careers but can't stand doing that. I make it a point to avoid hiring any girl who just left home to get away from her parents or her husband. I don't mind boasting that each of our waitresses is an adult woman, even though she might be only twenty-two years of age. By that I mean they all have plenty of understanding of themselves and of other people. On Sundays, we have afternoon chamber-music concerts that cost a hundred dollars and that I lose money on, but I don't care."

The conversation was interrupted by a mime in whiteface, selling flowers. "He's a pretty good mime, but there's a better one at the Café Wha?, on Macdougal," Ziegler said. "There are all kinds of coffeehouses, with all kinds of attitudes. The venerable ones, the Rienzi and the Manzini, cater to tourists. The Phase 2 and Limelight don't cater to tourists, but if you're a tourist you're acceptable, anyway. The upper West Side has the First Born, at Amsterdam and a Hundred and Eleventh; the East Side has the Right Bank, at Madison and Sixty-ninth. In between, at Orsini's, you have to wear a necktie."

We were joined by Ziegler's wife, a pretty girl with bangs, whom he introduced as Royce, and by one of his part-time assistants, a wide-eyed young man named Alan Eisenberg. "Royce and Alan can testify to the fact that we're known as the only *swinging* coffeehouse," Ziegler said.

"This place is what Beatism is all about," Royce said. "It's an authentic old-fashioned bohemian place, the kind of place Edna St. Vincent Millay would have liked."

"A truer bohemia than the Montparnasse of the late twenties," a chess player next to us threw in.

"I hate to use the word *rapport*," Eisenberg said, "but that's what we have here. After all, what is true Beatism but an awareness of life? It sounds corny, but that's what the basic meaning is. Trying to feel things. Instead of getting all tied up with things that distort the meaning of life. People come here to look at us and laugh, but we're laughing right back. There's a Beatism that's destructive, but that should have a different name. The coffeehouse is a life line against compromise, which some people think is a great thing. Compromise to me is a synonym for defeat. Admittedly an anti-conformist, adolescent attitude, but a good one."

"Alan is a lawyer," Royce said, "but he can't stay away from the Figaro."

"Look around," Ziegler said. "What you see is a young society reacting."

✿ DAME EDITH

WE HAD a great lunch last week with a great actress, perhaps the greatest of all, in the opinion of many actors and actresses—Dame Edith Evans, who is here for the first time in over a decade and is rehearsing for her first American television play, "Time Remembered," an N.B.C. *Hallmark Hall of Fame* production scheduled for February 7th, the day before Dame Edith's seventy-third birthday. We called for Dame Edith at her rehearsal hall, the Central Plaza, at Second Avenue and Seventh Street, just as she was finishing a run-through of a scene. She detached herself, quietly and respectfully, from her producer-director, George Schaefer, and from a fellow-actor, Christopher Plummer, for one more walk over the floor markings that had just been worked out for stage positions in the play. The walk took no more than fifteen seconds, and it did our heart good every second of the fifteen to watch her—looking at least twenty years younger than her age, with her gray hair bobbed short and her shoes low-heeled and Britishly sensible, and wearing a gray tweed skirt, a dark-gray sweater with a gold pin at the neckline, heavy Indian silver bracelets on her wrists, rings on her fingers, and bells, we'd swear, on her toes. As she finished her quick walk over the floor markings, she gave a nod of assent to herself and to her director, who freed her for lunch and suggested that we try Ratner's, the celebrated Jewish restaurant, which was right downstairs, so she wouldn't have to bother putting on her coat.

"Sounds wonderful," Dame Edith said. "Yesterday, I had a great big delicious Italian lunch, and it was too much. An enormous, delicious veal cutlet, and it was absolutely delicious. Today, I'd like to eat pancakes. I've been looking for pancakes or waffles ever since I arrived. All the old waffle places are gone. I looked for a place I used to know—Childs—and when I found it, I discovered that it had been torn down. I walked about with a friend, and we couldn't find any of the old waffle places, but then, luckily, we found some waffles at a Howard & Johnson."

Dame Edith put on a chic black stove-pipey hat, and we went down to Ratner's, where she asked our waiter for pancakes.

"Blintzes," the waiter said. "What kind?"

"What kind do you have?" Dame Edith asked.

"If I told you, would you remember?" the waiter asked.

"Yes," Dame Edith said.

"All right," the waiter said, and recited, "Potato blintzes, kashe blintzes, cheese blintzes, lekwar or jelly blintzes, and huckleberry, pineapple, cherry, and strawberry blintzes. All right?"

"Sounds wonderful," Dame Edith said. "I shall be very pleased to try cherry blintzes."

"In the meantime, eat a pumpernickel bagel," the waiter said, indicating a basket of rolls on the table.

Dame Edith peered longingly at the basket. "It would be too much," she said. "Last night, I couldn't eat more than porridge and a glass of milk after that delicious veal cutlet. I'm staying at a small hotel near here. I couldn't face coming all the way down every day. I have no luxuries, like hot milk at night, and no night services, but I have a nice little bed and a nice little bath, and I love to find my way about. I love walking. I walk to rehearsal from the hotel through streets that are a quiet part of the world. I love old city. Last time, I stayed at a hotel on Fiftieth Street, and I loved walking about, looking for gardens and little houses. I think new city should be new, but leave the old alone. I've been here for several days, and I can't say I was at all tired when I arrived. I am very fortunate that way. I travel by plane, and the minute I leave England, I start thinking American time. On arrival, I just get a bath and go out to dinner. I need only six or seven hours' sleep a night, but I seldom get them in one whack. I get them in three or four goes. I am very, very lucky that way."

The blintzes arrived, and Dame Edith tasted one. "Delicious!" she said.

The waiter looked pleased. "Fifty years ago, people would come in here and for ten cents they would get a blintz that big." He measured off a foot with his hands. "Now it costs three times as much, and look at the size!" He shook his head.

"I don't know how working people can afford to eat," Dame Edith said. "You have to pay so much for everything."

"You said it!" the waiter exclaimed. "Now eat."

Dame Edith ate. Between bites, she told us that although this play was her first try at television here, she had made several television appearances in England, and that she liked acting in any medium. "Good acting is good acting all over the world," she said. "And bad acting is bad acting anywhere. I'm satisfied as long as I have a sensitive director, and not someone who wants to be tricky. Tricky is always bad. In rehearsing for television, you have two or three weeks to make up your mind about how you're going to play a part, and you don't have much more than that for a play. I like to find a way to do things that gets the biggest result with the least amount of effort—that is, effort that can be seen. I'm a great believer in the process of deletion. I don't do more as I go along in rehearsal. I do less."

After a pause for a few more bites of cherry blintz, Dame Edith went on, "I was very lucky, very lucky. I didn't have to fight to get on the stage. I was put there. And I started late. I didn't go onstage until I was twenty-four. Before that, I was a milliner for ten years. I made hats. I always worked for someone else, and I did like it, but when I went on the stage I knew I was home. I felt comfortable. I don't make my own hats any more, but I do watch them. When we made hats, we used to stretch the velvet onto canvas. I think they stick everything on now. When I buy a hat, I know what to do to it if it's not quite right. I was never interested in the stage before I went on it. I never acted as a child. My father was a civil servant. I was an only child, and very, very active. I had a brother, who died when he was four years old and I was two. I had a great deal of physical energy. As a child, I was considered naughty. At church, I would kneel on the seat and look round and sing very loudly. My poor mother! I read a lot and played rough games. I was always overactive. The energy is all right now. We've got it harnessed. But it's taken a long time. Because I was put on the stage—a friend put on Shakespeare, and I went into it and was seen by a famous old producer, and he gave me a contract—I've always been aware that things came easily to me, and I've always felt I must not take advantage of it.

"In the old days, you made your way up by steps. It was lovely, because you learned to speak, to be heard. Nowadays, a good many actors are too busy talking with microphones. I learned with good people—all good actors. The older actors would teach me how to make the best of myself. You were told the way you moved, the way you looked, the way you spoke. The older ones were professional. On the dot. The word *amateur* may come from the word *love*, but the professional makes the final sacrifices. Ellen Terry was a lovely person and a great professional, too. In 1918, a few years before I was married—my husband died twenty-six years ago; he was an oil mining engineer—I toured with her, when she was a very old lady, in variety theatres. She was gracious, kind, charming, thoughtful. She was someone you loved. And you could hear what *she* said. There was no television then and no cinema—just theatre and concerts. She'd say to me, 'Smile, child. *Smile*, child. You have a lovely smile.' I was shy and nervous and young and just beginning and gauche, and the older ones knew how to say things to make you feel good and to make you happy. All the older ones were like that.

"It's not as easy to help some of the young ones today. I've heard over here that so many of the young ones go to psychiatrists to find, as they say, their 'real selves.' Rubbish! I don't know any actors myself who go to a psychiatrist, and I'd think they were potty if they did. They're skipping *life*. They're shirking. You find your real self by getting around, battling life, keeping your end up. When I was young, I was always looking about. I wasn't a very conventional anything. The good actors, I believe, don't go about thinking about themselves all the time. You go about with your eyes open. You are open to all experience that comes your way. Character counts tremendously. It's the vase in which you hold the talent. I used to watch a young friend who had great talent, and I'd wonder if his character would someday equal his talent, as it would have to if he were to develop into a fine actor, and it did eventually. Today, it's difficult for the young person of talent, because of all the temptations to do things for money. Or, as soon as a young actor shows talent, he's immediately booked for films."

Our waiter returned and said to Dame Edith, "You left one blintz. You should eat it."

"I can't," Dame Edith said.

"You should have ordered one for two," the waiter said.

"I didn't know any better," Dame Edith said. "Would it be awful if I broke a piece off this—just a piece?" She pointed a finger at a pumpernickel bagel.

"You should eat the whole thing," the waiter said.

"Just a little piece," Dame Edith said firmly, and broke it off. "And I'll have a little bit of butter." She put the bit of butter on the bit of bagel and sighed. "I've been fortunate," she said. "I've had the most wonderful opportunities, and they're still coming."

❧❧ SYMBOL

IN CASE you haven't noticed, the old six-story Grand Central Terminal office building has been demolished, and in its place, on three and a half acres behind the Terminal, a New York investment builder named Erwin S. Wolfson, in partnership with a London investment builder named Jack Cotton, is putting up a fifty-nine-story octagonal building (address: 200 Park Avenue) that will have the world's largest number of enclosed square feet of commercial office space—two million two hundred and seventy thousand. More than a quarter of these square feet—six hundred and thirteen thousand, on sixteen floors—have been rented by Pan American World Airways, and the skyscraper will, as a consequence, be named the Pan Am Building. And because Mr. Wolfson, a thoughtful, modest, athletic, alert, fresh-air-loving man of fifty-nine who majored in philosophy at college and has since plunged into a variety of educational pursuits, has a keenly wistful eye on the arts, he has, while adroitly arranging with his right, or practical, hand for the financing of the building (banks' construction loans of sixty-five million dollars and a mortgage of seventy million dollars, just to give you an idea), with his left hand knowledgeably engaged the celebrated talents—in addition to those of the building's architects, Emery Roth & Sons—of Walter Gropius and Pietro Belluschi, to work on the building as design consultants. That's just the beginning, because Wolfson, now that his business hand has so efficiently freed the other, plans to go to work and join his business monument to the arts. To this heroic end, Wolfson last week invited us to march with him as he marched Drs. Gropius and Belluschi, and a young sculptor named Richard Lippold—creator of the golden radiating structure called "The Sun" at the Metropolitan Museum of Art, of the silvery brass-and-steel structure called "The Moon" at the Museum of Modern Art, and of the cloudlike cluster of polished-bronze rods suspended on stainless-steel wires above the bar at The Four Seasons restaurant, among other wire-sculpture works—over to the office of Pan Am President Juan Trippe, in the Chrysler Building, for a conference on the possible purchase of a Lippold creation expressive of Pan Am to be placed in the building's Vanderbilt Avenue entrance lobby, which is to be thirty feet high, forty-four feet deep, a hundred and three feet wide, and set back seventy-eight feet from the Vanderbilt Avenue curb. If things worked out, Lippold's sculpture—thirty feet high and eighty feet across—would be in the center of this large hall.

"I have no idea how Trippe will react," Mr. Wolfson said to us as we set out, "but this means a lot to me, and he's such a nice guy I think he'll listen." The architectural members of the delegation seemed faintly uneasy: Dr. Gropius, founder of the Bauhaus in prewar Germany, former chairman of the Department of Architecture of Harvard's Graduate School of Design, and now member of an architectural firm called the Architects Collaborative, wearing a beret and looking, at seventy-seven, energetic, literally highbrow, noble, suntanned, bow-tied, and as powerfully definite as a face on Mount Rushmore; Dr. Belluschi, born in Ancona and raised in Rome, dean of the School of Architecture and Planning at M.I.T., devotee of quality and humanism in architecture, and a gray-haired, gray-brush-mustached, gentle-voiced, patient man. Mr. Lippold, a pale-faced young man with wavy gray hair and got up in a chocolate-colored suit with cuffs, a tan shirt, and a golden necktie, looked confident, and ready, if necessary, to fight.

Up we went, via express elevator, to a high Pan Am floor, where everyone took a seat at a long, massive conference table with Mr. Trippe and a Pan Am vice-president named Willis Lipscomb, who were, like Wolfson, neatly dressed in business grays and blues. The table was filled out by additional comers—René d'Harnoncourt, director of the Museum of Modern Art; Alex Cvijanovic, an architectural colleague of Gropius; Ivan Chermayeff, a young expert on the lettering on buildings; Edward Larrabee Barnes, design consultant to Pan Am; and a few others—who lent a solemn, Cabinet-like air to the gathering. Dr. Gropius removed his beret.

The first note was struck by Lippold. "Positively baronial!" he said, giving the table a cavalier slap and looking for a response from Mr. Trippe, who returned a small, reluctant smile.

Wolfson cleared his throat and politely and briskly got the meeting down to business. "There's no point in my saying anything now," he said. "I think Dr. Gropius should tell us what he thinks of Lippold's idea for the sculpture." All heads turned toward Mount Rushmore.

Dr. Gropius took a deep breath and said, "It is a way of making sculpture many of us think is beautiful." He held up a drawing of the planned sculpture—very abstract. "It symbolizes the globe of the world."

"Yes," Trippe said, cordially but not batting an eye. "I wish we had some way of seeing how it would look."

"I want to tell you," Dr. Gropius said. "All my life, I have tried to coöperate with painters and sculptors to create work for buildings that would be at one with the buildings, and this is the first time it has happened. Lippold's sculpture comes to one with our building."

"Yes," Trippe said again, cordially, and gave a nod to Vice-President Lipscomb. "We have a twofold problem here," Trippe went on. "I have a board of directors to reckon with, and when I showed them this flat picture they didn't go for it. We have several directors interested in art, but we've got a lot of doubting Thomases who just don't go for it. And then we've got a large number of directors in need of education in modern art. I don't know if I include myself with them or not." He smiled apologetically at Dr. Gropius. "Couldn't we get something better than just this flat picture?"

"It would cost almost as much to make a scale model as it would to make the sculpture," Dr. Gropius said. "But I think Lippold should talk now."

Lippold stood up, giving the baronial table another slap—much gentler this time. "I'd like to read my own description of the sculpture, because it explains my thinking," he said. "But first I want to tell you, a few weeks ago I got my father and mother, who are in their late seventies, to fly for the first time. I got them to take a *jet*, from Chicago to New York. At six hundred and eighty miles per hour. And they had never flown before."

Trippe gave the sculptor a heartfelt smile.

"And when I got them home," Lippold continued, "I showed

them this drawing of the sculpture, and they said, 'Why, it looks like our *flight.*' "

A parent-loving murmur went around the table, and Lippold took a sheet of paper from an inner coat pocket and read:

> The forms in this work are derived from the performances and shapes of modern aircraft except for a sphere of the world in the center. From this sphere, a seven-pointed star radiates symbolically toward the seven continents (and seven seas), its long conical arms originating in Great Circles of the globe, like the routes followed in intercontinental travel. The central sphere is further developed by fragments of Great Circle areas suspended in the arms of the star, like parts of the world transported by means of swift air travel. The entire globe is thus made very spatial in character and less material, as one experiences it in an air age. Surrounding this world-sphere with its radiating elements are silver forms whose general character suggests the direct ascents and descents and flight patterns of jet aircraft, as well as wing and tail sections of modern planes.

Lippold was holding the drawing up with one hand, and, as he continued to read, Trippe and Lipscomb leaned forward to look at it, as though trying to make out a wing or tail section.

> Two materials are used [Lippold read on]: a high-carat gold over bronze for the globe and star, and stainless steel for the silver-colored elements. These relate to the gray Travertine marble of the interior. The shapes have been chosen and placed with regard to the space of the lobby, in an effort to continue the unity of form of the architecture, and also to echo the unique angularity of the exterior of the building.

Lippold stopped reading.

Dr. Gropius said, "It goes up like a flower," and threw his arms open to indicate a flower.

"Perhaps this is a dumb question," Trippe said, "but where is the light?"

"Inconspicuously built in," Dr. Gropius said.

"One of the beauties of this is that it has size without weight," Dr. Belluschi added.

"Will this symbolic globe be held by wires?" Trippe asked.

"The whole thing is in a state of tension," Lippold said.

"Well, it's hard to tell," Trippe said, and again nodded to Vice-President Lipscomb, who threw Lippold a friendly smile and said, somewhat apologetically, "We've been doing considerable thinking about this versus a more literal approach. We ran a survey internally on the question to determine which would linger longer in the minds of the people who see it. The majority felt that a more literal approach to a globe might capture the interest of the public on a more continuing basis."

"To be expected," Lippold said quickly. "It's people dealing with the unfamiliar. It's like asking somebody if he likes his own mother better than somebody else's mother."

Another parent-loving murmur warmed the table sitters.

"There are two ways of approaching it," Dr. Gropius said. "One is the realistic way—to show a great globe. The other is the *artistic* way. Art always tries to symbolize the image of what is behind the scene. This design will really make a hit with the people." He sighed deeply. "In the ticket room or someplace back somewhere, you could put the realistic globe, with the lines showing people where they fly from one place to another."

Wolfson began to look pleased. "Perhaps we ought to hear some other opinions now," he said.

"Mine?" d'Harnoncourt said. "I'm very happy to give mine. We were the first people lucky enough to have one of Lippold's space designs in our lobby. I would say that this one would be one of the most important pieces of indoor sculpture of the twentieth century. If you want the impact of a great symbol, giving the feeling of speed through space, of expansion and lightness, you have it in this sculpture. No one who sees it is ever going to forget it."

Trippe and Lipscomb looked reflective.

"You feel as though you're in this sculpture," Dr. Gropius said. "You stand in the lobby and you're right in the sculpture."

"But are you sure people will remember it?" Vice-President Lipscomb asked.

"Let me ask you," Trippe said. "On modern art, I know the

Rockefellers are for it. As a matter of fact, they took me on a tour of their museum when it was finished. But I wonder—about modern art, won't many people be offended by it?"

"I'll tell you a very amusing story," d'Harnoncourt said in answer, smiling paternally at Trippe. "I saw David the other day. You know the very, very modern paintings he put into the new branch of the Chase National Bank? And he told me his people at first made nasty remarks about the paintings, and now none of them wants to have the things taken away."

Trippe gave a mild laugh at the story.

"People who do not ordinarily like abstract art like *this*," Wolfson said.

"Where would you put your signature?" Trippe asked Lippold.

"This needs no signature," Lippold said.

"Tremendously interesting," Trippe said. "I've been partly educated. Now I've got to put it up to our doubting Thomases."

AMBASSADOR STEVENSON

ONE OF the quietest places in town just before the inauguration was the headquarters of the United States Mission to the United Nations, at 2 Park Avenue, and there, last week, we came upon Adlai Stevenson. He was en route from Libertyville, Illinois, to Washington, for the Senate Foreign Relations Committee hearing on his appointment as Ambassador to the U.N., and he was temporarily using an office on the nineteenth floor. The floor was watched over by a sleepy-looking guard, and rows of unoccupied, slightly dusty desks, each bearing a rectangular green desk blotter and a telephone, led to a small corner office whose door was tabbed "MR. STEVENSON." The office was gray and impersonal, its only decoration a dark painting of Abraham Lincoln. The new Ambassador looked bright indeed—his face sunburned, his bald head freckled, his back hair freshly clipped, his eyes Palm Beach blue and clear—behind a desk stacked with letters and notes, printed, typewritten, and scribbled. An outsize caramel-colored briefcase with a gaping top was at Stevenson's feet. These were encased in badly scuffed but nicely polished brown shoes, and, for the rest, he was outfitted in a dark-blue pin-striped suit that looked tight on him; a light-blue shirt with French cuffs, gold cufflinks, and a straight silver pin at the collar; and a dark-blue necktie. As he pulled up an armchair for us to the desk, he pushed the briefcase to one side, giving it a somewhat tolerant look.

"I have an enormous collection of briefcases, and this one is one of my mistakes," he said. "It's divided into compartments, which at first I thought would be efficient. Now I find that when you try to stuff things in, you run into compartments. What I would like is some time to work on a large accumulation of undisposed-of mail. Every time I try to get at it, I have to make telephone calls to people about appointments and personnel. I have just now come from a long-deferred engagement with Mrs. Roosevelt. I wanted to see her about various problems of the United Nations and some other things she wished to talk about. I haven't had an opportunity to get to know the staff here. As soon as I take over officially, I'll go around and call on them in their offices."

The phone rang. The Ambassador spoke to somebody about making arrangements for a car in New York, and hung up. "My goodness!" he said, turning back to us. "The things you have to do in order to live here! Our government puts the Ambassador up in an apartment at the top of the Waldorf Towers. It's a handsome apartment. Very handsome. And equipped like an embassy abroad, with a living room, a dining room that will accommodate forty people, and —let's see—one, two, three, four, five bedrooms and five baths, and a full pantry and bar, and cabinets with beautiful china and all that. But the kitchen is empty. I'm going to need pots and pans to cook with, and there's not a pot or a pan in the place. I'm bringing my housekeeper, Viola Reardy, from the farm at Libertyville. I like to cook when she will let me and there is time, which isn't often. Mostly, what I do is mix up what's left over. In any case, we shall need things to cook with. I may have a kitchen shower. I have a birthday coming up February 5th. My friends always give parties for my birthday, and I think this time I'll ask them to give me a kitchen shower." He threw us a grin. "I'm going to be sixty-one," he said. "As Holmes did not say, oh, to be fifty again!"

We asked the Ambassador whether he thought he'd like living at the Waldorf. "I'm sure I'll love the view," he said diplomatically. "I've never really enjoyed living in big cities. I'm a country boy. I love the feeling of the country. I love being on my farm, and I hope to be able to get back there occasionally for weekends. My children and grandchildren spend holidays with me at the farm. I have three grandchildren. Of my sons, Adlai III is the only one who's married so far, and they're his children—Adlai Stevenson IV, Lucy Wallace Stevenson, and Katherine Randolph Stevenson. They're four years, two and a half years, and nine months old, in that order, and the two older ones are at that rough and roly-poly stage where they're beginning to talk and seem virtually indestructible. Lucy Wallace is a little tougher than the boy, at this stage. She's named for her Great-Great-Great-Aunt Lucy, who is Mrs. A. Kingsley Porter—the widow of A. Kingsley Porter, who was a distinguished archeologist at Harvard. Aunt Lucy lives in the James Russell Lowell house, Elmwood, in Cambridge. She's now very frail, very delicate, and very old. How old we're not sure. Aunt Lucy is a favorite of all my boys. All three of them went to Harvard, and while they were there, all three had the great pleasure of Sunday dinner with Aunt Lucy—the best dinner of the week. I love to read to the two older grandchildren. They always ask me to read to them. I'm impressed with their power of concentration. I can't say I have any special favorites among their books at this stage. They're not old enough for me to read favorites like *The Wind in the Willows*."

The phone rang again. Mr. Stevenson listened attentively for a few minutes, and then said, "Oh, no, please, I wouldn't want her to go to all that trouble. My goodness! Making two telephone calls, and all that." After he had hung up, we asked him how he liked his new headquarters. "I believe I'll be in an office upstairs somewhere," he said. "As I remember, I lived in these very offices in 1946 and 1947, right along this corridor—in this very one, or one or two down. We were all strung out along here. I started with this business in San Francisco in 1945, at the conference at which the United Nations Charter was written and adopted. Before that, I'd spent a good deal of time abroad. I've always loved to travel. In 1926, as a newspaperman, I had gone all across the Soviet Union and the Balkans, and as early as 1932 I was president of the Chicago Council on Foreign Relations. I'd had considerable grounding in foreign affairs, and all through the Second World War I'd been assistant to Secretary of the Navy Frank Knox. I'd been at the front in most of the war theatres. I'd travelled a great deal with Frank Knox, and also on missions for President Roosevelt, including a survey mission to relieve the suffering and restore the economy of Italy. I'd seen the misery, waste, destruction, and savagery of war, so, as time went on, I'd become more and more concerned with the problems of maintaining peace. After Secretary Knox died, I resigned and returned to my law practice in Chicago. But I was then asked to come back to Washington by Archibald MacLeish, my long-time friend in the

State Department, to work on plans for the United Nations. I'd intended to go only to the San Francisco conference and after that go back to my law practice in Illinois. When the conference was over, I went to Washington and helped with preparations for Senate ratification of the Charter, and after the Senate voted for the Charter, I went back home. But then Jimmy Byrnes, our new Secretary of State, asked me to come back to the Department and go with the United Nations to London. So, after V-J Day, I went to London with him by ship, the *Queen Mary*—a troop transport she was then. I became deputy to former Secretary of State Stettinius as our government's representative on the Executive Committee to set up the machinery for the first United Nations Assembly. Stettinius soon fell ill, and I replaced him as chairman of the United States delegation to the Preparation Commission, which put the flesh on the bare bones of the United Nations Charter. I stayed in London for six months, through the first meeting of the first General Assembly of the United Nations, in January and February of 1946. I inherited General Eisenhower's office at 20 Grosvenor Square, which he had occupied before D Day. Our delegation to that first Assembly, in war-torn London, included Secretary Byrnes, Senator Vandenberg, Senator Connolly, Mrs. Roosevelt, John Foster Dulles, and Congressmen Bloom, of New York, and Eaton, of New Jersey. Because I had worked with the U.N. from birth to adolescence, the delegation looked to me for advice on almost everything, and I felt more competent then, I confess, than I do now.

"After that General Assembly meeting in London, I again went back to my law practice in Illinois, but then I was appointed to our government's delegation for the next General Assembly, and I spent the autumn of 1946 working at U.N. headquarters, which was then at Lake Success. Again, I felt very much in touch with things, and deeply involved, emotionally and intellectually, with the U.N. I represented our government on various issues in the committees. After the third General Assembly, in 1947, I left again to go back to Illinois. I was almost at once asked to run for governor. And thus began my meteoric career, which"—Stevenson gave us the grin again—"went up and down with some rapidity."

"Anything different in your approach to the U.N. now?" we asked.

"I was much younger then, and I think I'm more realistic about some things now," he said. "But the intervening years haven't destroyed my hope and confidence in the U.N. Certainly I've been disillusioned about how soon we can achieve what we're working for, and about some of the infinite difficulties—the Russian expansion, the stubborn trouble in the Middle East, the consolidation of Communist power in China, the difficulty of maintaining solidarity among the Western countries, the effect of thirty new countries on the old prewar balance, the growth of atomic weapons, the speed with which the old empires have dissolved to create new independence and instability, the African tumult, the new societies that have arisen, and all the changes and torments of the period in which we live. We originally worked to create an organization to keep the peace, after seeing the ultimate failure of the League of Nations and after living through the war. The League of Nations had worked hard to reduce the threat of war, and then there was a war. With the new machinery, our hearts were full of hope that the everlasting curse of war might be controlled, if not extinguished, by the organization of international society for collective security. The U.N. was a step in that direction. Up to the Kennedy administration, the United States Mission has been treated as an embassy, to execute orders from the State Department. Now I hope to spend more time in Washington participating in the formulation of policy and shall have something to say about the orders I must execute. I have not lost any of my faith in the United Nations. It will be difficult. The United States has been on the defensive too much of late, and the Afro-Asian nations now have a majority. Many are neutralist and want no part of the Cold War. No longer can we take majority votes for granted. I wonder sometimes what will happen to public opinion in our country when we begin to lose votes, and decisions go against us now and then. But I still have confidence, and I still have hope. One thing has remained constant: the fact that the United States, in spite of its frustrations, has had no recurrence of isolation or clamor to withdraw from the world scene. We can't withdraw. We dare not withdraw."

❧❧ FIRST REHEARSAL

It MAY still be summertime for some people, but around, and off, Broadway last week actors and actresses from far and wide were gathering on bare stages to start rehearsals for the 1960-61 season. From London came Margaret Rutherford, to co-star with Mildred Dunnock and Leueen MacGrath in a comedy, about two spinster sisters who earn their living designing greeting cards, called *Farewell, Farewell Eugene*—Miss Rutherford's first appearance in this country since 1947 (when she played Lady Bracknell in John Gielgud's production of *The Importance of Being Earnest*), although she has been around for several months, to our delight, in a movie called *I'm All Right, Jack*. And to Miss Rutherford we went the other morning, a few days after her arrival, to accompany her to her first rehearsal. We found her, white-haired, gracious, observant, and charming—looking very much the way she did when she played the hearty, bicycle-riding medium in the movie version of *Blithe Spirit*—in an upper West Side hotel called, of course, the Oliver Cromwell. She was in a three-room, twenty-first-floor, Central Park-view suite that she shares with her husband, Stringer Davis, who is also in the play, and who was also present. White-haired and pink-faced, he was wearing a Harry Truman-type short-sleeved sports shirt that hung loose over the top of his trousers, in the solid American way. Miss Rutherford had on black strap shoes with sensible heels, a blue-green cotton frock, a man's wristwatch on a leather strap, a necklace of Chinese stones, and four rings, two on each hand.

"We've been to your Jones Beach and we did get colored up a bit, but we loved it," Miss Rutherford told us.

"My wife is the open-air type," said Mr. Davis. "We took a taxi to the Penn Station, and after a brisk exchange with the information gentlemen there we got on the ten-nine and did the change to the bus. At the beach, we hired private rooms, and then went out and landed in those enormous rollers. My wife was bounced about."

"My husband breasted the waves and got beyond them," said Miss Rutherford. "I'm quite a good swimmer, but it was a man-size sea."

"We found the wild hamburger in its lair," Mr. Davis said dreamily.

"Jones Beach is all so beautifully *organized*," said Miss Rutherford. "Have a filter-tip?" She held out a box of cigarettes.

We said we weren't smoking.

"So many here don't smoke," she said. "I feel quite licentious. Both of us have been feeling quite licentious since we arrived. This is quite an adventure for us. The first thing we did the night we arrived was to stock up the fridge. My husband went out and had a look, and came back in a very short time loaded with lovely things, including a saucepan and a frying pan."

"This is a village here," said Mr. Davis. "All sorts of shops. I got a pressure cooker at a wonderful place down the street called Mat's."

"We do want a broiler," Miss Rutherford said. "The gentlemen at the hotel are quite coöperative. We plan to have a discussion with them to see if they'll meet us. We hope to discuss the matter of the broiler."

"The pressure cooker is lovely," her husband told us. "And your fish is so lovely. At any rate, fish you can grill is so lovely."

"We want to grill very badly," said Miss Rutherford. "We've also patronized Gartner, the nicest ironmonger on Columbus Avenue. He sold us the loveliest coffeepot, mats, and trays. It's been such fun getting our house in order, getting all our kitchen equipment. I do wish the hotel gentlemen would give us an oven."

"The oven *is* going to be an awfully bad miss," said her husband.

We noticed a soup plate, with the tops of white flowers floating in it, on a table, and another soup plate, with peaches and pears, on a window sill. Near the second soup plate sat a brown stuffed rabbit wearing a two-piece blue velvet dress. "That's Minnie," Miss Rutherford told us. "We take her everywhere with us."

"Minnie was greeted as a kangaroo in Australia," Mr. Davis said. "She took it on the chin, however. Minnie has learned to accept."

Miss Rutherford moved Minnie from the window sill to the sofa.

"She'll get a draft on her back at the window," she told us. "I know her. I've had Minnie for sixteen years."

"She was established when I came into your life," said Mr. Davis.

A few minutes later, as we were riding down to the Helen Hayes Theatre with Miss Rutherford and Mr. Davis, they told us that they had given up their North London flat and put their things, including a broiler, a pressure cooker, and a coffeepot, in storage. "We have no idea how long we'll be in New York," Miss Rutherford said. "We take it as it comes. Though we do hope to have a little house of our own outside of London, with a bit of land, someday. Have our own garden."

"It's always best to start where you stand," Mr. Davis remarked.

"Oh dear!" Miss Rutherford said, looking out at Broadway as we headed south. "New York is so little different since 1947! I'm so glad!"

"Oh, Margaret, it has changed a lot," her husband said, in a tone of soft reproach. "I couldn't find the Rockefeller Center yesterday. And that one little skyscraper we were so fond of near the New Weston Hotel—now it's surrounded. It was quite an unimportant little commercial one, but we did like it so much."

"I was afraid the skyline was going to look different," Miss Rutherford said. "I'm still in love with the skyline. And there are so many adventures to be had here! It all seems to have come together so beautifully! Eight months with this same play in the West End and seven weeks touring, and now New York! I don't, as a rule, like to go back on my tracks at all. I'd much rather go forward. Doing the play here will be like the start of a new production. I do so love a first rehearsal. I always find it thrilling."

"Margaret is such a dynamo!" said Mr. Davis. "She has such electricity in her body! I gave her a watch last Christmas, and it went all askew when she first wore it." Then, as we approached the Helen Hayes Theatre, he exclaimed, "Oh, Margaret dear! We have our dear friends from *Five Finger Exercise* just around the corner!"

"How lovely!" said Miss Rutherford.

Onstage at the theatre—the boards taped with white to show the actors where stairs and walls would be; the ropes for the scenery hanging above; the stage braces and jacks used to support sets lying against the back wall; the classic single, unshaded thousand-watt work light over a long wooden table surrounded by straight-backed chairs; the auditorium dark, musty, and hot—Miss Rutherford and Mr. Davis were greeted warmly by Ron Rawson, the producer; John Vari, one of the authors; Ronald Winston, the director; and Frederic De Wilde (father of Brandon), the production manager. There were handshakes all around, and a good deal of nervousness, expectation, excitement, and enthusiasm in the air.

Then Miss Rutherford was escorted by Mr. Rawson to her dressing room, a freshly painted pinkly pink oasis, with a pinkly pink closet, empty except for several loosely swinging wire coat hangers, visible through an open door. Mr. Rawson turned on an air conditioner.

"Oh, how sweet! How cool!" exclaimed Miss Rutherford. "I shan't be running to the window, as I do in London!"

There was a knock at the door, and Mildred Dunnock entered, sighing with joy. Her face was agleam with admiration as she shook hands with her co-star. "I'm so happy to meet you!" she said. "I'm so happy to be working with you! I'm looking forward to learning a great deal!"

Miss Rutherford graciously offered her a box of cigarettes. "Have a filter-tip?" she asked.

"I'm afraid I don't smoke," said Miss Dunnock.

"This is Bella," Mr. Rawson said, introducing another arrival, a small, wise-faced woman carrying a tape measure, who immediately got to work taking Miss Rutherford's measurements. ("Forty-three bust, thirty-nine waist . . .")

"I'm told I have an Edwardian back. I pay for it by sticking out in front," said Miss Rutherford. "What is your full name, my dear?"

"Bella Kelly," said Bella.

"What a lovely name," said Miss Rutherford.

After a while, everybody went back onstage, where Miss Rutherford and Miss MacGrath were introduced.

"So happy to see you!" said Miss Rutherford.

Miss MacGrath said, "Oh, ooh, oh!" and her face shone with admiration as much as Miss Dunnock's had.

Herbert Voland, the fourth principal, beamed around at all the ladies.

Robert Fletcher, the stage designer, held up a pasteboard model of the set and pointed out the various gates and sliding doors of a basement apartment.

"Steampipes!" said Miss Rutherford. "A brilliant touch!"

Mr. Fletcher looked happy.

John Vari put his arm around Miss Rutherford. "I was able to buy a motel with the profits from the London production of this play," he said.

"Oh, how lovely!" said Miss Rutherford. "I had no idea that sort of thing happened."

"Would you all gather around, please?" Mr. De Wilde called out.

Everybody picked up a script and sat down at the table, and then they all started to read the play.

❧❧ SIMON

THE HOTTEST weather news these cold nights has been television's Simon McQueen, the newest of girl weather reporters, who appears every week night on Channel 7. We met her in person the other day, in the company of a couple of Channel 7 executives named Al Hollander and Les Dinoff. Miss McQueen ("This is Simon McQueen, your WABC-TV weather girl") is small, trim, pert, and constantly cheerful—as cheerful as she is on the program—and when we saw her, in a smoke-filled Channel 7 conference room just vacated by a pile of executives, she had on a bright look and a chic double-breasted purple suit.

"This suit is absolutely delicious," Miss McQueen told us in energetic, confident English accents as the Messrs. Hollander and Dinoff gleamed and chortled with reflected cheerfulness.

"Simon chooses all her own clothes for the program," Dinoff said. "A wholly different costume every night."

"Simon has a clothes sense," Hollander said. "Before Simon, we had a very lovely gal-next-door type, but we decided to look for a gal who in her own natural way was fresh. Simon has a natural unspoiled freshness. Simon is very much herself."

"Simon is both the producer and the star of the show," Dinoff said. "Simon gets all her own weather information from our central news agency, does her own makeup and goes to the beauty parlor twice a week, and combs the Seventh Avenue wholesale garment houses for model clothes to wear on the show."

"I give the clothes back right after I show them," Simon said. "I wore this suit on the program two months ago. It fit, so I bought it."

"As soon as Simon came on Seven, she was sold out to Snow Crop orange juice and Procter & Gamble," Dinoff said. "It's the first time in the history of television that Procter & Gamble bought a weather show."

"It's the first time in the history of television that weather, with Snow Crop and Procter & Gamble, is back to back with news, sponsored by Bromo-Seltzer and Sun Oil," Hollander said. "It gives the impression of one show, and yet we have different sponsors."

"Terrific!" Dinoff said, as though he were hearing the tremendous news for the first time.

"I made it in weather, and someday I'll make it as an actress on Broadway—in a comedy," Simon said, with determination. "I really think of myself as an actress now, but I'm stuck in weather."

"Nobody ever approached the weather from an entertainment point of view before," Hollander said. "Simon is the other side from Carol Reed. Jean Parr is more the tweedy type, and a gal like Beverly Bentley is comely and commercial. The gal on radio's *Monitor* used to whisper the weather. Simon is a gal with something of her own."

"I try to make it as relaxed as possible," Simon said. "I like to ad-lib."

"We don't let Simon get too mannered," Hollander said firmly. "She was pointing to P. & G.'s Dash in a too pointy way, the same way every night. We don't want our gal to get too mannered. Simon isn't supposed to do that any more."

"Sometimes people associate you with certain mannerisms, and that builds you as a personality," Simon said, and gave a very small sigh.

"Too theatrical," Hollander said.

"I love my theme song," Simon said. "It has bounce."

"We wanted a gal with bounce," Hollander said.

"I have a wonderful time," Simon said.

"How did you get here?" we asked.

"I came to America in 1956, and landed with six dollars," Simon said. "I wanted to see America very much. My parents have a country pub, in Kenilworth, near Stratford on Avon. My father, Douglas Leslie McQueen, went to sea when I was a child, and then, when I was grown, he got the pub. My mother's name is Edna, but I call her Robin, because she's very gay and very happy and very small. My brother, Roy, is sixteen. He doesn't want to go to school or do anything much except ride horses. I always wanted to be an actress. I've been dancing since I was five. Tap and ballet. Simon is not my real name, but I don't want anyone to know my real name, because it doesn't sound like an actress. I took the name Simon when I was fourteen and planned what I would be called as an actress. My father and Robin and Roy all call me Simon now. At seventeen, I went to the London Academy of Music and Dramatic Art. Diana Dors is one of our most famous graduates. I went to Australia and New Zealand with the Folies-Bergère. In the line. Two years later, I went to work for the American Army Special Services in Stuttgart, in a revue called *Something for the Birds*, and it was. I didn't understand a word the Americans said for three weeks, but after two weeks I felt I wanted to go to America. Back in London, I was mistress of ceremonies in a television variety series called *Jerry's Inn*, and I was in a panel game called *Yakketty Yak*, in which four glamour girls—I was one—are asked questions and give answers. It was very humorous. I was determined to come to America. If you're a success in England, you're known only in England. But if you make it in America, you're known all over the world."

"Terrific!" Dinoff said. "Terrific, terrific! Simon is very British. She has one of those little books she writes in—'Things to Do Today.'"

"I have a wonderful time," Simon said.

"Get with it, gal," Hollander said.

"I asked my uncle, who is a stockbroker in Philadelphia, to sponsor me, and I came to America by way of Spain," Simon continued. "I wanted to see a bullfight. I wanted to see flamenco dancing." Simon snapped her fingers over her head in a gay manner. "When I arrived in America, on July 28, 1956, with my six dollars, I was very fat from eating all that heavy Spanish food. Now I weigh a hundred and four."

"Simon is five three," Hollander said. "Simon's audience consists of the younger element. We send Simon's picture on a postcard to people who write to our gal."

"I love to get letters," Simon said. "My first job in America was as a receptionist in the Bergdorf Goodman beauty salon, at forty-five dollars a week. My hotel room was thirty dollars a week. I love to eat, so that was a sad time for me. I then became mistress of ceremonies at the Latin Quarter, in New York and in Miami. Miami was boring. I like to do things. I decided to give up the clubs. I did *Idiot's Delight* in summer stock in Cincinnati. When I heard that Mr. Hollander was looking for a weather actress, I auditioned for the job. I prepared a speech about myself and what I'd done, and I talked about the weather, and I gave a commercial about Schiffli embroidery, pretending to wear a dress as if it had Schiffli embroidery on it."

"Schiffli isn't the commercial now," Hollander said darkly.

"I love Snow Crop orange juice," Simon said cheerfully. "I like to drink it on the program every night. It's pretty good."

"What about the weather?" we asked.

"Mr. Hollander sent me to the Weather Bureau to learn about high-pressure areas, ridges, and things like that," Simon replied. "I felt very stupid about the weather—I'd never carried an umbrella in my life—but I understand it now. What I like is when I don't just talk about the weather. If anything special is happening to me, I like to talk about it. I have a basset hound. I may talk about him."

"The show has a sense of humor about it," Mr. Hollander said.

"I'd like to go back to doing this." Simon made what to us has come to be the classic Dash-pointing gesture.

"Too theatrical," Hollander said grimly.

❦ RIPPLES

WE PAUSED last week in front of the United Nations staff bulletin board—on the fifth floor of the Secretariat Building, just outside the Periodical Reading Room, which is just outside the Health Service Clinic, both rooms affording a soothing view of tugs and barges on the East River—a few hours after the 4:21 A.M. adjournment of the Security Council meeting that passed the joint draft resolution of Ceylon, Liberia, and the United Arab Republic giving Secretary-General Hammarskjöld what purported to be a larger and stronger framework for U.N. action in the Congo. (In favor: Ceylon, Chile, China, Ecuador, Liberia, Turkey, United Arab Republic, United Kingdom of Great Britain and Northern Ireland, United States of America. Against: None. Abstaining: France, Union of Soviet Socialist Republics.) Listed under a "For Sale" heading on the bulletin board were, among other items:

Beautifully Set Emerald Cut Topaz Ring—Best offer over $60.

After Ski Boots Best Italian Quality—Retail price $35, Sale price $20.
The boots have never been used.

Maple furniture—1 sofa.
          1 easy chair.
          1 office table—$50.

Camera Exposure Meter Received as Gift Never Used—List $29.95.

Antique (Directoire) Head Board of Four Foot Bed—
Wood painted $65.

Five Rolls of Color Film for an 8mm. Camera—Reasonable!

A Folding Bed, Good Condition, Mattress Practically New—
$10.

For sale—Buick 1950 Sedan in very good condition—$120.

Under "Wanted" we read, "Portable typewriter used but still
good—EN 2-4920," and "To exchange Spanish conversation for
English—Please call Mr. Lopez, Extension 2253, Room 1745."
On another bulletin board, on another floor, we found the U.N.
staff clubs looking busier than ever—the U.N. Flying Club, the
U.N. Gym Club, the Club del Libro Español, the Cricket Club, the
Chess Club, the Tennis Club (Miss Hardy, Extension 560), and
the Jazz Society, whose president (Mr. Fitzwater, Room 2714, Extension 3167) announced that the program for the next meeting
would include the playing of records of the Art Farmer Septet, Charlie Parker with Miles Davis, and the Modern Jazz Quartet. From the
Staff Cafeteria, nearby, came the comforting aroma of steaming veg-
etable soup, combined with the standard cafeteria tray-and-silver-
ware clatter and the conversational hubbub of lunch-on-our-own-
premises Gemütlichkeit.

Things in the Periodical Reading Room were slow, the magazines
(we noticed Pakistan Horizon, The Economist, Canadian Journal of
Economics & Political Science, African Affairs, Novoe Vremya,
Harper's, Bulletin of the Atomic Scientists) done up in clear-plastic
covers and neatly stashed in racks on the walls, and the newspapers
(Le Figaro, Le Monde, La Nación, the Times of India, El-Mous-
taqbel, Politiken, El Diario de Nueva York, the London Times, Iz-
vestia, Pravda, Trud, Literaturnaya Gazeta, Journal of Commerce,
the Washington Post, the Christian Science Monitor, the New York
Times, the Manchester Guardian, Swiss Review of World Affairs)
hanging from sticks on a rack in the middle of the room. A tall,
heavily built Negro, the sleeves of his suit jacket a couple of inches
short for his arms, sat in a corner of a sofa, asleep. An imitation-
leather briefcase, bulging, was on the floor at his feet. We looked in
on the clinic; men in white, women in white, and patients were

buzzing around various examination rooms. The clinic has a bulletin board, too. Poster:

THE LARGER THE BELT LINE
THE SHORTER THE LIFE LINE.

From a pamphlet rack we picked up a publication of Metropolitan Life entitled *Stress and What It Means to You*, and read, at random, "The emotional stress that gets us down is the kind that makes it difficult or nearly impossible to relax," and then "Statistics show that women are outliving men." At the U.N. Coöperative (drugs and prescriptions, automobile service station, phonograph records, gift center), still another bulletin board announced various charter flights to Europe.

All the wheels seemed to be turning nicely, so we made our way to a quiet lounge just outside Conference Room 8, where the first meeting of Secretary-General Hammarskjöld's eighteen-member Advisory Committee on U.N. Operations in the Congo (Canada, Ethiopia, Ghana, Guinea, India, Indonesia, Ireland, Liberia, Federation of Malaya, Mali Federation, Morocco, Nigeria, Pakistan, Senegal, Sudan, Sweden, Tunisia, United Arab Republic) since the passing of the resolution was getting under way. Hammarskjöld arrived looking as fit, energetic, devoted, and determined as ever. His immediate staff of assistants—Undersecretary for Special Political Affairs Ralph Bunche, Personal Assistant Wilhelm Wachtmeister, Brigadier Indar J. Rikhye, and others—came and went, looking rumpled, oversmoked, underslept, persistent, and cheerful.

"The joint resolution was like the stone tossed into the pond," one of the men entering said. "The ripples are now going out."

"What are you doing in there?" we asked.

"Talking," he said. "We'll probably be talking all through this night, too, and the next, and the next. When we come out, we prefer to be invisible. Like the S.-G. You might say that the resolution put yeast into the whole thing, and now it's diplomatically brewing."

An invisible exiter said, "The S.-G. is absolutely fantastic. This morning, at four-forty, he went straight upstairs from the Security Council to his office, and he was working there until six-thirty, telephoning and sending out cables. I suppose he cabled his Special Representative in the Congo, Rajeshwar Dayal, in Léopoldville.

Dayal meets with his aides in the cable room of U.N.O.C.—United Nations Operations in the Congo—every morning. The meeting is called Morning Prayers. I was there last week, and was standing with Dayal when the S.-G. called him up from U.N. Headquarters. The nature of the communication is determined by the nature of the exchange."

"What happens now?" we asked another invisible aide, who had a highly visible head cold.

"The Advisory Committee gets to work on how we go about starting what will undoubtedly be a long process," he said. "First, one has to establish what the member states are really prepared to do about providing the resources for halting the military operations, determining who is who and what is what in the Congo, arranging for the withdrawal of Belgian personnel, improving the desperate economic and social conditions, and getting the Congolese to start running their own affairs. U.N. personnel have been in the Congo for six months, working on health matters, food supply, the fiscal system, the transportation system—things like that. Nobody hears about these people, but an awful lot rests on them. The S.-G. is directly in touch with them all the time, keeping it going. In here," he said, opening the door of the conference room and taking the deep breath of a cold-sufferer, "we may clarify what to do about the military operation, the external political situation, the internal political situation. The idea is to keep juggling, keep all the balls in the air at the same time. A Herculean task! The S.-G. is doing it. It's part of the brilliance of the man. Here, read this." He handed us a pamphlet, *Today's World and the United Nations*, containing four addresses by Dag Hammarskjöld, and went inside. In the first address, entitled "The Vital Role of the United Nations in a Diplomacy of Reconciliation" (London, April 2, 1958), we read, "We should recognize the United Nations for what it is—an admittedly imperfect but indispensable instrument of nations in working for a peaceful evolution toward a more just and secure world order."

Pocketing the pamphlet, we left the lounge and fell in behind a visiting group of Cub Scouts (B.S.A.) in blue uniforms, with gold kerchiefs, blue caps with gold stripes, and gold patches that identified the troop as being from Eastchester. Led by a pretty, dark-haired U.N. girl guide, the troop paused at a window looking out on the flags of the ninety-nine member nations.

"Does anybody know the flag of the first alphabetically listed nation?" the guide asked.

"America!" a Cub answered.

"No. Afghanistan," she said. "And the last country is Yugoslavia, because it begins with the letter Y. You're nine years old. You should remember that."

We went along with the troop as they marched to the General Assembly Building, filed into the Security Council Chamber, which was empty, and took seats in the gallery.

"Have you been to the movies lately?" the guide began, and the Cubs nodded.

"And you have seen newsreels? Of this room? What is this room called?"

"The Security Council," a Cub answered.

"Very good. And what is this room for? Does anybody know?"

The Cubs were silent.

"It won't hurt you to open a newspaper now and then," the guide said. "Now I'll explain it to you. You have little brothers or sisters, and they fight with each other?"

The Cubs nodded.

"And your mother or father or your teacher will step in and stop them from fighting? That is what the Security Council is for. To settle problems, to make peace whenever anything is in dispute, to prevent war. Any little dispute that could lead to a bigger dispute. In the Security Council, there are eleven members. Six of them are elected from different countries for two years each, and the other five are the United States and the countries that were her allies in World War II. Now, who was the main ally of the United States in World War II?"

"Japan!" one Cub called out.

"No," the guide said. "England. And France, China, and the Soviet Union were the other allies. Together, they sit on the Se-cur-i-ty Council. Now, I want you to tell me what 'Se-cur-i-ty' means. To prevent war and keep . . ."

"Peace!" the whole Cub Scout troop shouted, looking proud.

❦ PLAYWRIGHT

WE HAD a talk recently with Lorraine Hansberry, the twenty-eight-year-old author of the hit play *A Raisin in the Sun*. Miss Hansberry is a relaxed, soft-voiced young lady with an intelligent and pretty face, a particularly vertical hairdo, and large brown eyes, so dark and so deep that you get lost in them. At her request, we met her in a midtown restaurant, so that she could get away from her telephone. "The telephone has become a little strange thing with a life of its own," she told us, calmly enough. "It's just incredible! I had the number changed, and gave it to, roughly, twelve people. Then I get a call from a stranger saying 'This is So-and-So, of the B.B.C.'! It's the flush of success. Thomas Wolfe wrote a detailed description of it in *You Can't Go Home Again*. I must say he told the truth. I enjoy it, actually, so much. I'm thrilled, and all of us associated with the play are thrilled. Meanwhile, it does keep you awfully *busy*. What sort of happens is you just hear from *everybody!*"

Miss Hansberry gave a soft, pleased laugh. "I'm going to have some scrambled eggs, medium, because, as far as I know, I haven't had my breakfast yet," she went on. "I live in the Village, and the way it's been, people sort of drop in on me and my husband. My husband is Robert Nemiroff, and he, too, is a writer. Yesterday, I got back to writing, and I wrote all day long. For the first time in weeks. It was wonderful. We have a ramshackle Village walkup apartment, *quite* ramshackle, with living room, bedroom, kitchen, bath, and a little back workroom, and I just stayed in that little old room all day and wrote. I may even get time now to do some of my housework. I don't want to have anyone else to do my housework. I've always done it myself. I believe you *should* do it yourself. I feel very strongly about that."

The medium scrambled eggs arrived, and Miss Hansberry sampled them vaguely and went on to tell us something of what life has been like since her play opened, a few weeks ago. "I now get twenty to thirty pieces of mail a day," she said. "Invitations to teas, invitations to lunches, invitations to dinners, invitations to write books, to adapt mystery stories for the movies, to adapt novels for Broadway musicals. I feel I have to answer them, because I owe the people who wrote them the courtesy of explaining that this is not my type of thing. Then, there are so many organizations that want you to come to their meetings. You don't feel silly or bothered, because, my God, they're all doing such important work, and you're just delighted to go. But you're awfully busy, because there are an awful lot of organizations. The other morning, I came downstairs to walk my dog—he's sort of a collie, and he'll be six in September—and there, downstairs, were the two most charming people, a middle-aged couple who wanted me to have dinner with the New Rochelle Urban League before it went to see the play. I just couldn't say no. Meanwhile, I'd been getting telegrams from Roosevelt University, in Chicago, which is a very wonderful institution back home, asking me to come and speak. I kept sending telegrams back saying I couldn't come, and then they got me on the phone, and they had me. Once I'm on the phone, I just can't say no. I sometimes find myself doing things for three or four organizations in one day. The other morning, I started the day by taping a television program. Then I went to the National Association of Negro Business and Professional Women's Clubs Founders' Day Tea, at the Waldorf, where they were giving out Sojourner Truth Awards—awards named for Sojourner Truth, who was a very colorful orator who went up and down New England and the South speaking against slavery. Then I went home and went to the Square with my dog. When I got back home, I fed the dog and put on a cocktail dress, and my husband and I had dinner in a new Village steak house. Then we went to a reception for a young Negro actor named Harold Scott, who had just made a record album of readings from the works of James Weldon Johnson. A very beautiful album. Then we went home and had banana cream pie and milk and watched television— a program with me on it, as a matter of fact. It was terrifying to see. I had no idea I used my face so much when I talked, and I decided that that was the end of my going on television. The next day was quiet. I had only one visitor—a young Negro writer who wanted to drop off a manuscript for me to read. We had a drink and a quick conversation, and he was off. I actually got to cook dinner—a pretty good one, with fried pork chops, broccoli *au gratin*, salad, and banana cream pie. I'm mad for banana cream pie. Fortunately, there's a place in the neighborhood that makes marvellous ones."

Miss Hansberry told us that she had written her play between her twenty-sixth and twenty-seventh birthdays, and that it had taken her eight months. "I'd been writing an awful lot of plays—about three, I guess—and this happened to be one of them," she told us. "We all know now that people like the play, including the critics. Most of what was written about the play was reasonable and fine, but I don't agree that this play, as some people have assumed, has turned out the way it has because just about everybody associated with it was a Negro. I'm pleased to say that we went to great pains to get the best director and the best actors for this particular play. And I like to think I wrote the play out of a specific intellectual point of view. I'm aware of the existence of Anouilh, Beckett, Dürrenmatt, and Brecht, but I believe, with O'Casey, that real drama has to do with audience involvement and achieving the emotional transformation of people on the stage. I believe that ideas *can* be transmitted emotionally."

"Agreed," we said, and asked Miss Hansberry for some autobiography.

"I was born May 19, 1930, in Chicago," she told us. "I have two brothers and one sister. I'm the baby of the family. My sister, Mamie, is thirty-five and has a three-year-old daughter, Nantille, who is divine and a character. She was named for my mother, whose name is Nannie, and her other grandmother, Tillie. My older brother, Carl Junior, is forty, and my other brother, Perry Senior, is thirty-eight and has an eighteen-year-old daughter, who is starting college and is very beautiful. Carl, Perry, and Mamie run my father's real-estate business, Hansberry Enterprises, in Chicago. My father, who is dead now, was born in Gloster, Mississippi, which you can't find on the map, it's so small. My mother comes from Columbia, Tennessee, which *is* on the map, but just about. My father left the South as a young man, and then he went back there and got himself an education. He was a wonderful and very special kind of man. He died in

1945, at the age of fifty-one—of a cerebral hemorrhage, supposedly, but American racism helped kill him. He died in Mexico, where he was making preparations to move all of us out of the United States. My brother Carl had just come back from Europe, where he fought with Patton's army. My father wanted to leave this country because, although he had tried to do everything in his power to make it otherwise, he felt he still didn't have his freedom. He was a very successful and very wealthy businessman. He had been a U.S. marshal. He had founded one of the first Negro banks in Chicago. He had fought a very famous civil-rights case on restrictive covenants, which he fought all the way up to the Supreme Court, and which he won after the expenditure of a great deal of money and emotional strength. The case is studied today in the law schools. Anyway, Daddy felt that this country was hopeless in its treatment of Negroes. So he became a refugee from America. He bought a house in Polanco, a suburb of Mexico City, and we were planning to move there when he died. I was fourteen at the time. I'm afraid I have to agree with Daddy's assessment of this country. But I don't agree with the leaving part. I don't feel defensive. Daddy really belonged to a different age, a different period. He didn't feel free. One of the reasons I feel so free is that I feel I belong to a world majority, and a very assertive one. I'm not really writing about my own family in the play. We were more typical of the bourgeois Negro exemplified by the Murchison family that is referred to in the play. I'm too close to my own family to be able to write about them.

"I mostly went to Jim Crow schools, on the South Side of Chicago, which meant half-day schools, and to this day I can't count. My parents were some peculiar kind of democrats. They could afford to send us to private schools, but they didn't believe in it. I went to three grade schools—Felsenthal, Betsy Ross, and A. O. Sexton—the last of them in a white neighborhood, where Daddy bought a house when I was eight. My mother is a remarkable woman, with great courage. She sat in that house for eight months with us—while Daddy spent most of his time in Washington fighting his case—in what was, to put it mildly, a very hostile neighborhood. I was on the porch one day with my sister, swinging my legs, when a mob gathered. We went inside, and while we were in our living room, a brick came crashing through the window with such force it embedded itself in the opposite wall. I was the one the brick almost hit. I went to Englewood High School and then to the University of Wisconsin for two years. Then I just got tired of going to school and quit and came to New York, in the summer of 1950. The theatre came into my life like *k-pow!*" Miss Hansberry knocked a fist into the palm of her other hand. "In Chicago, on my early dates, I was taken to see shows like *The Tempest, Othello,* and *Dark of the Moon,* which absolutely flipped me, with all that witch-doctor stuff, which I still adore. In college, I saw plays by Strindberg and Ibsen for the first time, and they were important to me. I was intrigued by the theatre. Mine was the same old story—sort of hanging around little acting groups, and developing the feeling that the theatre embraces everything I like all at one time. I've always assumed I had something to tell people. Now I think of myself as a playwright."

✿ HENNY

WHEN, last week, we received an austerely engraved invitation to the Plaza's Persian Room to see Henny Youngman, the first stand-up comedian to be engaged there since the place opened, in 1934, we determined to nab Mr. Youngman a couple of days before his historic appearance. We found him in his favorite hangout, the Stage Delicatessen, at Seventh Avenue and Fifty-fourth Street, wearing a black mohair suit, a white voile shirt, and a black-and-maroon striped necktie. He was drinking coffee, eating a macaroon, smoking a cigarette, and haranguing his table companion, who was the Stage's owner, Max Asnas. Mr. Asnas, as everybody in show biz knows, is small and round, and has the voice of a frog. Youngman, as everybody in show biz also knows, is a big, awkward, good-natured, warmhearted, mannish-looking boy of fifty-five and the favorite comedian of most old-school, pre-intellectual comedians.

"Max, where you going to eat?" Youngman was saying. "Go to the Colony, Max."

Max stayed put, and we sat down.

"Henny, did you hear the story of the wife who says to her husband—" Max began.

"Probably," Youngman interrupted. To us he said, "I've got the biggest collection of wife jokes. One-liners. Short jokes. I believe in making them short. Short and plain, so people don't have to figure out too much. Like 'You take my wife. Please.' "

We laughed.

Youngman looked happy. " 'My wife has an even disposition. Miserable all the time,' " he said.

We laughed.

Youngman looked happier. " 'My wife is on a diet of coconuts

and bananas. She hasn't lost any weight, but can she climb a tree!' I
make them short and plain. I go after the masses."

"Why?" we asked.

"The masses deserve it," he said. "Besides, I discovered thirty
years ago, when I started in this business, that if I told long jokes
and they flopped, I used up all the time I was on, so I made everything brief. Like 'Look at my mohair suit. It used to take three years
to get a suit shiny, and now you buy it ready-made shiny.' If it flops,
I'm in the middle of telling another one anyway. It's my style. I
started it on my first job in the mountains, at the Swan Lake Inn,
which was owned by my cousin Herman Davis."

"You think he started with strangers?" Max said to us. "He
started with *relatives!*"

"It's much harder with relatives," Youngman said. "You have to
be funny all day long. I've been very lucky, the way I've always been
able to break up the guys in our business. Red Skelton is wonderful.
When he meets me on the street, he kisses me. If a guy is funny, I
holler. Milton Berle always mentions my name for luck. Max," he
said to Asnas, who was smiling dreamily, "steal me a hunk of cake."

Max obligingly went off, and Youngman continued, "I know Max
over thirty years. He used to feed me when I was broke. My daughter lives right around the corner. We eat at the Stage. She's married
to Jack Kelly, the jazz pianist. I have a grandson, Larry. Four. The
love of my life. Every time I'm back from the road, I stop in to see
Max. I just came back from Milwaukee, where I appeared at a wed-
ding. A fabulous affair, at the Brynwood Country Club. Somebody
in the padlock business. His daughter. I was paid fifteen hundred
dollars, plus expenses. I gave them a good time. I talked about my
marriage. I said, 'Every man should be happily married whether he
likes it or not.' I talk that way naturally. It's my style. You have to
have a backlog of jokes that can be used any time."

"When did you start?" we asked.

"In London, March 16, 1906, my birthday."

Max placed a dish of glossy brown raisin-studded pastries, glisten-
ing like high varnish, before him, and went away.

"We moved to Brooklyn when I was six months old," Youngman
said. "My father was a display-card writer for Martin's Department
Store. My mother used to be a schoolteacher in Riga, Latvia. Mama

is the life-of-the-party type. She's in her eighties, lives in our old
house in Borough Park, not too far from my home, on Ocean Avenue, and often travels around the country with me and Sadie, my
wife, when I'm on the road. We drive to Vegas. For twenty-five
years I wouldn't fly. On account of my religion. I'm a devout coward. Mama is quite a clown. She's always on. She's got jokes like
'Two elderly women meet, and the first says, "What did you do to
your hair? It looks like a wig." The second old lady says, "It is a
wig." So the first says, "You know, you could never tell!" ' I was
brought up in Bay Ridge. I took up the fiddle at twelve and studied
for nine years, with Mr. Di Trinis, who had a big, elegant Italian
mustache and wore tails for my lessons. I went to P.S. 2 and then to
Manual Training High School. I was always breaking up the class
saying funny things, and was supposed to go to the detention room
in the basement. Instead, I always went to the Prospect Theatre or
Loew's Metropolitan, for fifteen cents, and later to the Palace. I
memorized everybody's act—Eddie Cantor, Lou Holtz, Frank Tin-
ney, Al Jolson, George Jessel, Dave Vine, Pat Rooney. At parties, I
was always a riot, doing the acts, and I couldn't keep quiet in high
school. So I was thrown out and went to Brooklyn Vocational High
School and learned printing. I used to print cards for musicians and
sell them two hundred for a dollar. I played fiddle at weddings and
dances. Then I got a job on one of the smaller vaudeville circuits, Al
& Belle Dow—it hit places like Shamokin, P-a.—for forty dollars a
week. I played the Kentucky Club, was house m.c. at the Brooklyn
Fox, and in 1930 I worked in the Yacht Club. I was an overnight
sensation with all the material I had gathered for the past eight
years. Like 'I'll never forget the day I was born. I cried like a
baby.' "

He was interrupted by a pat on the cheek from a lean man, who
asked him what his act at the Persian Room was going to include.

"Same formula," Youngman said. "The fiddle, tell jokes, talk top-
ical. I'll tell some new Off Broadway jokes. Like 'I got in a cab and
said, "Take me to an Off Broadway theatre," and the driver said,
"You're in one." ' "

The well-wisher gave him another pat on the cheek.

"How did your engagement at the Plaza come about?" we asked
as the well-wisher took off.

"I was the first one who had the nerve to ask for the job," Youngman said. "I called up Neal Lang, the manager of the Plaza, and said, 'Why don't you put a comedian in?' He said, 'When you're in the neighborhood, drop in to see me and we'll talk about it.' I said, 'I'm in the neighborhood. I'm downstairs.' So we talked. Any one of the stand-up comedians could play there. All they have to do is put on tails in respect to the image of the fabulous chantootsies. Berle, Jessel, Jan Murray, Archie Robbins, Syd Gould, Harvey Stone, Morey Amsterdam, Jack E. Leonard, Jack Durant, Don Tannen, Jack Waldron. All great comedians."

We were joined by an apple-cheeked young man with thick, gleaming black hair in a modified Kookie Byrnes style, who wore an approximation of a black mohair suit, an approximation of a white voile shirt, and a dark necktie. Youngman drew him down to the table. "Dave Vine," he said, introducing us. "He wants to be a comedian. Billy Vine, Dave's father, who just passed away, was a great comedian." He turned to Vine and said, "I used to see your grandfather, the first Dave Vine, in vaudeville. I'll never forget the way he used to come out carrying his cap, his coat, his galoshes, and he'd say—"

" 'I don't trust those actors back there!' " Dave Vine said, in chorus with Youngman. "I never saw him, but I heard about it."

"Why do you want to be a comedian?" Youngman asked, and immediately gave his own answer. " 'It's better than working.' The only reason I won't discourage you is I know you were brought up in the business."

"It's something I love," Dave Vine said. "I'm getting up a routine to go out with to the hotels in the country this spring and summer."

"Remember, you've got to come out and do jokes reasonable for your age," Youngman said. "About college. About rock 'n' roll. You can't do wife jokes."

"I have a kid-brother joke," Dave Vine said politely.

"Speak right into the mike," Youngman said, offering him a round, varnished pastry on a fork.

"I come out and say, 'How do you like this outfit I'm wearing? It's my brother's. His hunting outfit. He's *hunting* for it.' "

Youngman laughed. "Add 'I got up *earlier* than my brother,' " he said. "Make it plain."

❧ BEFORE THE FÊTE

WE'VE HAD a longing these spring days to go to public school again —specifically, to P.S. 77, at the corner of First Avenue and Eighty-sixth Street. For there, one day last week, we had the privilege of watching several dozen honest-to-goodness sidewalks-of-New York sixth-graders rehearse folk dances for the Fifty-fourth Annual Park Fête, sponsored jointly by the Board of Education and the Girls' Branch of the Public Schools Athletic League. In the next three weeks, according to the 1961 Park Fête program, arranged by Mrs. Elizabeth P. Friedman, a saintly veteran of thirty-nine years in the public-school system, and a corps of devoted aides, there will be thirteen thousand children dancing around hundreds of Maypoles on green lawns in the five boroughs:

> The Bronx—Monday, May 8th (in case of rain, May 10th). The Lawn of Fordham University
> Queens—Tuesday, May 9th (in case of rain, May 12th). Cunningham Park—Athletic Field
> Richmond—Tuesday, May 16th (in case of rain, May 18th). Clove Lakes Park
> Manhattan—Wednesday, May 17th (in case of rain, May 19th). Central Park—The Sheep Meadow—66th Street & West Drive
> Brooklyn—Tuesday, May 23rd (in case of rain, May 25th). Prospect Park—The Long Meadow—Prospect Park West & Third Street

"The Park Fête is a great joy for all of us. We never stopped holding it, through two World Wars," Mrs. Friedman told us over the telephone from her office at the Board of Education. "We're all very excited about this year's. P.S. 77 is very enthusiastic. I'd like to visit them with you, but I'm going to a Park Fête band rehearsal on Staten Island. Ask for the principal, Mr. Efrem Feld."

At the ancient (1883) red brick schoolhouse, we went through the timeless portals, to be met by the classic school-hall aroma; found the principal's office deserted; and, outside it, found, sitting on a lonely bench under a bulletin board ("Class 6-1 Visits the New York *Times*. . . . Headlines—Why are headlines of a newspaper important? Read a headline and think about it . . ."), a nine-year-old boy in a Cub Scout uniform. We said hello, and he said, "By mistake, I fell off a chair in the library. So the teacher thought I was *throwing* the chair at her. So I'm here, waiting for the principal, He's in the play yard—that room over there at the end of the hall. I never *threw* that chair."

"Stick to your story," we said, and hurried over to the play yard, where Mr. Feld, a slightly built man with graying hair, a ragged, graying mustache, and a brown-and-orange polka-dot bow tie, stood in the center of a group of nine circles, eight children to a circle. He was just winding up an exhortation. "You've got to work *together!*" he said. "You rehearse like any chorus or any dance group! That does not mean . . ." Mr. Feld paused and looked into the eyes of a nearby skinny, serious, blond twelve-year-old girl, who was a good head taller than the two males at her sides—one colored, one white, and both impatient to get started. "That does not mean," Mr. Feld repeated, more slowly, "that you are going to be hired by the Metropolitan Opera House." He gave a good-natured ha-ha, and then soberly continued, "Mrs. Fleischer will now give you instructions. Follow instructions, boys and girls, and the result will be beautiful! Mrs. Fleischer!"

As Mrs. Fleischer, a cheerful-looking woman in a cotton print dress and spectacles, took over, Mr. Feld joined us and shook our hand. "Look at them," he said, pointing to the sixth-graders as they held hands and got ready to dance. "The pleasure of this work is that when administrative burdens become too onerous, we can always watch the children. Ah, here's our real spark, Al Matheson." He introduced us to a red-haired, freckle-faced young man who was wearing shell-rimmed glasses. "Al is health counsellor for the East Side school district. He's the one who gets the boys to dance."

Mr. Matheson beamed at the children in pretty much the same way Mr. Feld had. "I love it," he said. "I like to take my coat off and get out and dance with them. There's something about a man teacher, when the kids see him dance, it breaks down the idea it's sissyish to do it. I develop a lot of little jokes that I use to relax them. Like making references to my own two left feet. It gets them going."

Mrs. Fleischer started up a gay tune on a portable record-player.

" 'Captain Jinks,' " Mr. Matheson said. "Go to any one of twelve schools of the nineteen in the district from a Hundred and Sixth to Eleventh Street, on the East Side, and you'll see them rehearsing like this. This is one of the schools that were under-utilized two years ago, so they brought children in from the overcrowded schools in Harlem. At first it was rough. Now it's wonderful. They integrated beautifully. See all these kids dancing together?"

"Beautiful," Mr. Feld said as the children stamped their feet, held hands, clapped hands, and held hands again in "Captain Jinks."

"When you see this, it's a great thrill," Mr. Matheson said. "It's one of the great joys of working with children. Look at that little Negro boy in the coat."

"He won't take the coat off," Mr. Feld said. "The sleeves of his shirt are too long. The children in this school run the gamut from wealthy to poor. This is my first school as principal. The day I arrived, I heard rumors that the school was going to close. I hate to see it go. Where are the children going to go? They're tearing down the old buildings and putting up luxury apartment houses. Beautiful, but who can afford to live in them? The position of the parents is clear: Keep this school open until they get a new one. Just today, I met a man who went here in 1906. A grandfather now. When I told him P.S. 77 is going to close, he was very upset. Hello, Mrs. Eisenson."

In came a short, eager-faced woman, who told us she was the remedial-reading teacher in the school.

"We have ten classes of aphasic children here, from the School for the Deaf," Mr. Feld said. "They all dance."

"They're terrific," Mrs. Eisenson said.

" 'The Sicilian Tarantella,' " Mr. Matheson said as the children whooped it up with handclapping, finger snapping, and hand waving.

"I see some of the kids I work with," Mrs. Eisenson said. "I'm getting a different view of them. They're very graceful."

"This is the most valuable thing," Mr. Feld said. "Getting the children out there all together, dancing together."

"We're doing eight dances on this year's program," Mr. Matheson said, "in addition to the bugle call 'To the Colors,' the Pledge of Allegiance to the Flag, singing the fourth verse of 'America,' and, of course, the finale, with 'The Star-Spangled Banner.' Each school decorates its own Maypole."

"Last year we had green and lavender," Mr. Feld said. "This year, Mrs. Fleischer says, they want Shocking pink and red. The boys will wear red bow ties and green cummerbunds."

"Green with the *pink?*" Mr. Matheson said.

"Now, children," Mrs. Fleischer was saying, "carefully take your partner's hand and make a circle, girls on the outside."

"She's showing them a new dance," Mr. Matheson said. "The most difficult dance in the Park Fête—the 'Fado Blanquita.' A Spanish dance. Children tend to take big steps. They've got to take little bits of steps for this one. Very difficult."

The "Fado Blanquita" was mastered, winding up with an exuberantly shouted "*Olé!*" Mr. Feld then took his place in front of the dancers and said, "Now it's time for relaxation, but before you go, I want to tell you your dancing has filled us with a tremendous amount of admiration and given us a tremendous amount of enjoyment!" The dancers, smiling and with mustaches of perspiration on their upper lips, were dismissed.

Mrs. Fleischer came over to where Mr. Matheson was standing with us. "Mr. Matheson is our guiding star," she said.

"You're the one," Mr. Matheson said.

❧ ALBEE

WE HAD a talk last week with Edward Albee, the thirty-three-year-old playwright whose three one-act plays now on the boards Off Broadway have established him as the critics' current man-of-promise. The Zoo Story opened at the Provincetown Playhouse on January 14, 1960, and has been produced in London and in Berlin, among other places; The American Dream and The Death of Bessie Smith, which opened January 24, 1961, and March 1, 1961, respectively, are both at the York Playhouse. We found Mr. Albee at home, in a ground-floor, six-room apartment in a ninety-year-old, yellow-stucco-front house on West Twelfth Street—an apartment packed to the gills with modern paintings, a stereophonic record player, fresh white pompons, books on the drama, a roommate named William Flanagan (who composed the music for Bessie Smith and another Albee one-acter, called The Sandbox), and three orphaned cats rescued by Albee: Cunégonde, three and a half; Vanessa, two and a half; and a still nameless thirteen-week-old semi-Siamese kitten. Albee, who is a handsome, lean, dark-haired young man with a crew haircut and considerable charm, and who was wearing a gray tweed sports jacket, gray flannel slacks, a button-down-collar white shirt, and a black wool tie, directed us to avoid a collapsing modern sofa and to sit in a non-collapsing modern chair, out of which he shooed his cats with a few firm, authoritative, affectionate, non-sticky words.

"I get them from the Greenwich Village Humane League," Albee told us. "The League people go out and look for abandoned cats on the street, and save them from the awful things that happen to homeless kittens in New York, like being tossed into bonfires by mean kids. That sort of thing can happen in the Village, I'm sorry to say. Although I wouldn't live anywhere but in New York. I like to

be in the center of things. There are ten thousand things you can do
in half an hour in New York if you feel like it. I've lived in a lot of
places—a fifteen-dollar-a-month cold-water flat on the lower East
Side, a great big loft right in the middle of the garment district, for
seventy a month, and a couple of other places around the Village.
All the good places in the Village, all the lovely nineteenth-century
houses, are being torn down now and six-story tenements are being
put up instead. Do you want to see something amazing in my back
yard? A real one-story little cottage with somebody living in it." He
showed us the amazing view through a rear window. "Will probably
be torn down soon. But I'll try to stay in the Village. It's one of the
few areas where you can be in the center of things and still feel
removed."

Albee lit a cigarette and sat down carefully on the sofa, and we
asked him to give us an autobiographical outline. "Born in Washington, D.C., on March 12, 1928, and came to New York when I
was two weeks old," he said. "I have no idea who my natural parents
were, although I'm sure my father wasn't a President, or anything
like that. I was adopted by my father, Reed A. Albee, who worked
for his father, Edward Franklin Albee, who started a chain of theatres with B. F. Keith and then sold out to R.K.O. My father is
retired now. My mother is a remarkable woman. An excellent horse-
woman and saddle-horse judge. I was riding from the time I was able
to walk. My parents had a stable of horses in Larchmont or Scarsdale
or Rye, or one of those places. I don't ride any more. Just sort of lost
interest in it. My parents gave me a good home and a good education, none of which I appreciated. I attended Rye Country Day
School until I was eleven, and then Lawrenceville, where I got
thrown out after a year and a half for refusing to go to classes. It was
probably that I was too young to be away from home, but instead of
going home I was sent to Valley Forge Military Academy—Valley
Forge Concentration Camp—where parents send their children for
one of three reasons: discipline, or preparation for West Point, or in
the hope that they'll get an education. You do get an education
there, but it's not a purely scholastic education. You march practically all the time and wear a grayish-blue uniform like West Point's,
with the hat with the patent-leather brim. I had the usual routine of
discipline, institutional food, and dreary living quarters. When I

finally left, after a year, I decided not to get thrown out of another school. I went to Choate next, and it was marvellous, but by then I was a few years older. I appreciated Choate after the aridity of a military school. I was very happy there. I went on to Trinity College, in Hartford, for a year and a half. I didn't have enough interest in it to stick it out for four years. I wouldn't go to chapel, and I wouldn't go to one of the math courses. It was probably a basic discontent with myself that hadn't taken a specific form yet. After a year and a half, the college suggested that I not come back, which was fine with me."

Albee gave a quick laugh and, inhaling with all the abandon of the carefree pre-filter age, continued, through the smoke, "I got my first job at Station WNYC, where I spent a year and a half writing continuity for the music programs. After that, I had an *awful* lot of jobs: forty-dollar-a-week office boy for Warwick & Legler, the ad agency; salesman in the record department of Bloomingdale's; salesman in the book department of Schirmer's; luncheonette counterman at the Manhattan Towers Hotel. Then, starting in 1955, I was a Western Union messenger for three years, all over the city. I liked it. It wasn't a job that tired you out with mental work. I liked walking, and I met all sorts of interesting people. In 1949, I had come into a very small income, from a trust fund set up by my maternal grandmother, that was not quite enough to spoil me. In 1952, I went to Florence for four or five months and tried to write a novel. The novel was awful. I had written a lot of poetry, and had even managed to get one poem published, when I was seventeen, in a Texas magazine called *Kaleidoscope*. It had something to do with turning eighteen. Then, in the spring of 1958, when I hit thirty, a kind of explosion took place in my life. I'd been drifting, and I got fed up with myself. I decided to write a play. I was getting a little bit more money from the trust fund—thirty-five hundred dollars a year—and I quit work.

"I wrote *The Zoo Story* on a wobbly table in the kitchen of the apartment I was living in at the time—at 238 West Fourth Street. I did a draft, made pencil revisions, and typed a second script, and that's the way I've been doing my plays since. I finished *The Zoo Story* in three weeks and showed it to a few uptown producers, who

said it was nice but they wanted a full-length play. Then Bill Flanagan sent a copy of the play to David Diamond, the American composer, who was living in Florence, and Diamond sent it to a Swiss
actor, Pinkas Braun, in Zurich, who later did all the German translations of my plays. Braun made a tape recording of the play in English and sent it to Mrs. Stefani Hunzinger, in Frankfurt, who is head
of the drama department of S. Fischer, one of the biggest publishing
houses in Germany. From there it went on to a producer named
Barlog, in Berlin, and that's where I had my first audience—on September 28, 1959. *The Death of Bessie Smith* was produced in Berlin
about a year ago, before it was put on here. Aside from the interest
that German audiences take in the contemporary foreign theatre,
they seem to find some application to their own lives in my plays."

We asked how things were going financially.

"Strange," he said. "My income is growing. In 1959, I made about
a thousand dollars on my work. In 1960, it was ten thousand dollars.
In 1961, I've made five thousand dollars in two months. The New
York income is a small part of it. It means I don't have to take an
outside job, and I like that. Although my tastes are inexpensive, I
like to sit in good seats at the theatre, so I can see what's going on. I
don't think about clothes. I don't own a suit. I have a couple of
sports jackets, and what I like to wear is sweater, slacks, and
sneakers."

"Any plans?" we asked. "Any special thoughts on your last birthday?"

"I'm not looking forward to getting older, but I'm not horrified by
it, either," he said. "I've got about two—maybe three—years' work
planned out, considering how lazy I am about what I want to be
doing. I'm behind, but I'd rather be behind than be completely
caught up. I have three plays in mind and I'm trying to finish two
others—*Who's Afraid of Virginia Woolf?* and an adaptation of
Carson McCullers' *The Ballad of the Sad Café.* I'm doing the second because it's sort of a challenge. I've never seen an adaptation of
anything that was any good. I'm curious to find out if it's possible to
do one without running into what usually happens—the lessening
and coarsening of the material. The other play is about a two-in-the-
morning drunken party of two faculty members and their wives.

These will both be what they refer to as full-length plays, 'they' being people who think the theatre has got to start at eight-forty and end at eleven-ten."

"Any special influences in your writing?" we asked.

Albee gave us a cool laugh. "There are anywhere between five hundred and a thousand good plays, and I'd have to go back to the Greeks and work my way right up," he replied. "It's been an assimilative process. Of my contemporaries, after Brecht, I admire Beckett, Jean Genet, Tennessee Williams, and Harold Pinter. In fiction, I have a special preference for Salinger and Updike. I feel happy and comfortable in what I'm doing. I've become freer and less free. One develops obligations to oneself, having had one's productions reasonably well received. I more or less play it by ear. Unless you're a man like Bernard Shaw, who knew what he was doing at all times, you get yourself in trouble trying to talk about the way you write. It makes for self-consciousness. I'd like to preserve an innocence, so that what I do can surprise me. I've been forced lately to articulate what's been happening to me, and that makes you self-conscious about trying to remain unself-conscious. I go to more parties than I used to. I find I start talking and other people shut up. And that's terrible. I've met more people this past year than I ever met in the past thirty. It's interesting and valuable to meet accomplished people. It's instructive. You can always learn from your elders and betters. When I sit down to work, four or five hours at a time are all I can manage. Then I have to go out to the San Remo and have a couple of beers with friends. Summers, I go off to the beach at Riis Park by subway and bus. I stayed with all the plays throughout casting and rehearsals. It's a pleasant agony."

❧❧ THE SOUND

THE SPEEDY WAY we're singing along these days, old Johnny Ray is being pushed as hard as old Frank Sinatra by a crowd of rock-'n'-rolling sprinters, of whom the Big Five popularly recognized by both former teen-agers and current ones (placed these days, in the music trade, between the ages of nine and thirteen) are Fabian, Frankie Avalon, Paul Anka, Bobby Darin, and Elvis Presley, who still holds forth as Emperor. The present teen King, Bobby Rydell, is just breaking out among the adults, but close on his heels are a pack of ambitious singing, dancing, acting, record-selling babies called Bobby Vee, Chubby Checker, Jimmy Clanton, Buzz Clifford, Ben E. King, Gene Pitney, Neil Sedaka, Connie Francis (the present Queen), Annette (a nineteen-year-old would-be Queen), Brenda Lee (sixteen-year-old up-and-coming Queen), and Dion. It was Dion whom—at the invitation of his manager, Sal Bonafede—we went to meet last week, in a mirrored rehearsal hall, on Sixth Avenue, called Dance Players Studios, for Dion, twenty years old and a graduate, after five years, of a rock-'n'-roll singing group known as Dion and the Belmonts, was there embarking on a program previously set by the pacemaking five and the reigning King; namely, to invade the adult (otherwise known as the Vegas-Miami-Copacabana) territory of his elders while bringing along behind him, and holding, every one of his teen-age fans. Dion, who intends to go on using only his first name unless he can come up with a satisfactory replacement of his second name, which is Di Mucci, was qualified as a member of the pack pushing the young Kings and the elder statesmen by a hit record of his called "Lonely Teenager," which came out last year, as well as by a more recent album, "Alone with Dion." On the strength of his earnings, he has just purchased an eight-room house in White Plains for his parents and two teen-age sisters, to replace the Bronx brownstone apartment in which he grew up; an elegant gray-and-black Thunderbird hardtop; dental capping for two front teeth; an abstract painting by a Detroit artist named Lee Forrest; a gold wristwatch for Sal Bonafede; a large number of gifts for pals from his old neighborhood in the Bronx; three tuxedos, ten pairs of slacks, and seven custom-tailored suits combining what Dion calls an Ivy League and a Continental look; several pairs of custommade Italian shoes, with elastic on the sides; and, for ten thousand dollars, the services of a team of experts to help him work up a nightclub act with which he can invade the green fields of adultdom.

On hand to greet us when we turned up for the launching was Bonafede, a husky, sad-eyed, gentle twenty-eight-year-old former basketball player, who is sharing living quarters with Dion on East Fifty-second Street during the rehearsal period. He looked proud and fatherly as he pointed to his young charge standing at an upright at the far end of the room and working things over with the team of experts: Lou Spencer, a former dancer turned choreographer and night-club-act creator; Noel Sherman, song and special-material writer; and Joe Zito, song arranger and conductor. Dion was singing, in what we were informed was up-tempo, a Zito arrangement of the standard number "By Myself," and he kept trying one line over and over, with all the concentration of a nuclear physicist dedicated to solving a crucial problem. He sounded rather fetching—pleading, melodic, fervent, burning to be King. A wary young man with a delicate face, an uneven complexion, and twice as much hair as President Kennedy, he was wearing Italian shoes, pin-stripe blue trousers, and a moss-green sweater—double-breasted, with silver buttons —and he snapped his fingers in time with the singing.

Bonafede smiled at the sight and sound of Dion. "This is real growth for him," he said. "I love growth. I'm not negating rock 'n' roll, but we're aiming for other areas now. This boy has a chance of becoming a real balladeer. I wouldn't take films for him right now. We're not motivated by money. This boy is not hungry. He's a kid who's not grabbing right away. This kid isn't going to be mishandled or overplayed. This kid isn't going to be taken. Among other things, he has tremendous dramatic content. He takes drama lessons. He's serious about the stage. He's growing. He's a contender."

The music stopped, and there was an explosion from Spencer—a volatile man in shirtsleeves, with a bald spot on the top of his head and a long, thin cigar in his mouth—about some notes Dion was singing. Dion glanced at his manager, but Bonafede stayed put. "I'm not perturbed," Bonafede told us. "Lou knows his business. Lou played night clubs for thirty years. He was a fantastic hoofer. He knows how to reach people. Noel Sherman has written some marvellous special material for Dion. He is a terrifically talented composer. If I had a prognostication to make, I would say that Noel Sherman will write a big hit soon. His aspiration is to write a Broadway show. He's an educated man—Phi Beta Kappa. Lou gets right to the point, the way he assists this boy. We don't have too much time. One more week of rehearsing the act, then a week in Washington, D.C., trying out the act at the Casino Royal. After that, eleven days at the Three Rivers Inn, in Syracuse, and then a week at Sciolla's, in Philadelphia. Then we open in New York for a three-week run at Silverman's International, on Broadway."

There was another explosion around the piano. Bonafede remained unperturbed. "Dion is a deep prober," he said. "He always wants to know why. He has this knack of knowing what's good for himself, what's right for himself as an artist. An artist needs to have that egotistical way." Bonafede edged closer to the piano. "Living with Dion in the same apartment, the way I do, I try to help him like a father," he said. "Sometimes he gets me so upset I descend to his level. This girl I go out with says to me, 'Sal, you have to stay on your own level.' It's hard when I see some of these kids from his old neighborhood hanging around the apartment with him. They don't work. They take money from him, like leeches. And he feels he can't turn them down, because he's gone out and made it." He sighed. "I found out long ago you can't help people by trying to tell them things."

Bonafede stopped talking and nodded as Spencer pulled Dion a few feet away from the piano. "You're straining for that note. You're straining," Spencer was saying to the young singer. "If you're gonna have any fun with this act, it's got to be relaxed. You can't expect the audience to have any fun if you're not having fun. All right, you're on the floor singing. They see you twisting your neck to hit that note, they know you're not having fun. That one little note, that one thing, it's not so great we can't do without it. Besides, it's like hitting them with the big gun right away. We gotta save it for where you're going."

"Where am I going?" Dion asked angrily. The atmosphere was a little tense.

"You're going for forty minutes of entertainment, and you're going over the top," Spencer said. "Dion is gonna reach both teenagers and grownups. That's what you're going for. Right?"

"Right," Sherman, a tall, studious, well-mannered young man, said quietly behind him.

"If Noel says I'm right, then I'm right," Spencer said, laughing, and everybody began to laugh. "Do it again, and I'll show you exactly what I'm talking about."

At the piano, Zito started playing "By Myself" again, and Spencer, humming the tune and snapping his fingers, moved in front of Dion in a slow, cool, jazzy shuffle, demonstrating how he wanted Dion to move. "You're a singer, and a singer is supposed to move with the beat," he said, moving with the beat and raising his voice above the music. "First thing we want the audience to see is a nice-looking, clean-looking young guy. Next, we want them to hear Dion singing in a voice that's got the Dion sound. I want you to be you *within* you. The way you just sang it, you're trying to reach the guy in the last row up there. Let the microphone do that for you. All you gotta worry about is to reach the guy in the *first* row. I want you to sing relaxed. I want it to be you. The Dion sound is a great sound. Why distort it?"

"But that's my opening number," Dion said. "It should be a smash. I should sing it out." He looked over at Bonafede, who kept mum.

"No! No!" Spencer said. "You keep all that in your head. You know it's your opening number. Think it. Feel it. But what you sing, sing in a quiet way, and it will get over. It's not the loudness that gets over. It's what's in your mind. It's what you feel."

"Impossible," Dion said.

"Not impossible," Spencer said. "Here's what's happening. The lights are out. Watch." Again Zito started playing the song, and Spencer moved forward singing, " 'I'm all by myself,' " the way he wanted the line to be phrased.

"Who's singing?" Dion asked, with a cranky smile.

"It's still Dion!" Spencer cried triumphantly. "Deep down in here"—he hit himself in the solar plexus—"it's still Dion. It's all in your mind. It's in your attitude. Let me tell you something. The way you were starting this thing, you've got nowhere to go."

"Times have changed," Sherman said quietly. "You have to start soft now."

"If you're onstage, and it comes out naturally, it's the right thing," Spencer said.

"The man knows," Zito said.

The crankiness faded from Dion's face and he looked interested. "But I'll keep my sound," he said.

Spencer smashed a closed fist against the open palm of his other hand. "Pow!" he said. "Like that! Dion! You're having a ball. Right there!"

Dion glanced at Bonafede, who gave him a smile and a paternal nod.

"I know you're gonna get bugged, and you're entitled to get bugged, but we're the guys you should always get bugged at, and I want you to remember that," Spencer said. "Yell at us. Don't take it out on your manager, or anybody else."

Bonafede looked pleased.

"In order to bring in a great act, we've got to pull you apart," Spencer told Dion. "That's the way we get Dion to be Dion."

MR. KENNETH

"GO GET YOUR HAIR done by Mr. Kenneth and don't spare the expense," we said last week to Miss Rogers, the wild-haired typist who sits across the hall from our man Stanley and has picked up a trick or two from him. For the past couple of months, all Miss Rogers has been able to say is "Jackie Kennedy goes to Mr. Kenneth. Mrs. Joseph Kennedy, Sr., goes to Mr. Kenneth. Mrs. Peter Lawford goes to Mr. Kenneth. Mrs. Sargent Shriver goes to Mr. Kenneth. Mrs. Stephen Smith goes to Mr. Kenneth. Marilyn Monroe, Judy Garland, and Sheila MacRae go to Mr. Kenneth." Mr. Kenneth, Mr. Kenneth, Mr. Kenneth. Miss Rogers has her own special kind of charm, but her hair, lately, has been hanging over her eyes, slowing down her typing. "Get the works," we told her. "Put yourself completely in his hands. And get an interview while you're at it." Five hours later, Miss Rogers, looking like a dream, returned from the Lilly Daché Beauty Salon, where Mr. Kenneth presides. She was waving what must certainly be a fictional bill for $57.50 and babbling about the Actors Studio and not wasting yourself and how are we going to keep her down on the farm now that she's seen Lilly Daché. She handed us a sheaf of notes and went spinning off. What we read follows:

"Wahoo! Wahoo! Mr. Kenneth says I'm not perfect yet, because I've got a lot of hair lengths he doesn't understand yet. But Mr. Kenneth says I'm ninety per cent nearer perfect than I was before he did my hair. I *feel* perfect. Mr. Kenneth says that's all that matters. Before Mr. Kenneth started me, he said that what's most satisfying to him is making women feel prettier than they've ever felt before. Making them not look as though they'd just come from the hairdresser, all stiff and done. Giving them a natural, easy look. Like Jackie. Like Pat. Like Eunice. Like Judy. Like Marilyn. Like me.

Like me. Lady who took me to the dressing room, a Miss Gilbert, told me, 'Mr. Kenneth is the marvel of the century.' He is. Miss Gilbert told me that the Lilly Daché Beauty Salon has expanded in a matter of weeks. 'Do you want a facial?' she asked me. 'A massage?' 'First the hair,' I said. I didn't want to bring back a big bill. 'Mr. Kenneth is tall, slim, and attractive, and always perfectly tailored,' Miss Gilbert said. 'Put on this pink robe. Everything here is pink and white. Miss Daché is very feminine. She loves pale pink. You look better already. We'll put you in a booth next to Sheila MacRae—you know, of Sheila and Gordon MacRae, of the Empire Room.'

"Got put in pink booth with pink sink and pink chair. Mrs. Mac-Rae very tall, very blond, very beautiful, very chic. *Très élégante.* Wearing pink robe, too. 'Mr. Kenneth is studying Mrs. MacRae,' Miss Gilbert said. 'He'll be right over, after Burdie does your shampoo.' 'Egg shampoo?' Burdie asked me. 'Does Jackie Kennedy get egg shampoo?' I asked. 'All the Kennedys get egg shampoo,' Burdie said. Ordered egg shampoo. Mr. Kenneth, tall, slim, and attractive, wearing double-breasted vest and suit with cuffs, came over. I got to work right away and interviewed Mr. Kenneth about his vest. 'I copied the style from the one Cary Grant wore in the movie *Suspicion*,' Mr. Kenneth said. Interviewed him some more. 'I was born on April 19, 1927, in Syracuse, New York,' Mr. Kenneth said. 'My full name is Kenneth Everette Battelle. Have you ever heard of anything like all those e's? I have four younger sisters, all married, all with children. My father was in the shoe business. I went to Nottingham High School, and after graduation I was in the Navy for two years. When I got out of the Navy, I didn't know what else to do, so I decided to learn hairdressing. I went to the Wanamaker Beauty School, here in New York, for a thousand hours, which takes six months. Then I went back to Syracuse and worked in a hotel beauty salon for four years. Then to Miami for eight months. I watched the fashion magazines and decided that Michel, then at Helena Rubinstein's in New York, was the greatest hairdresser. I worked with him for five years. Then I became restless and left. Life must go on. Lilly Daché's was right for me. I was left alone by Miss Daché. I could do things. I could think out loud. If I wanted to, I could work twenty-four hours a day. About forty per cent of my clients are in the world of glamour. We get a rush in here every time there's a big ball; everybody wants to come at once. For the Embassy Ball, I did thirty-eight settings and combings in an eleven-hour day. When I have time, I go out to people's homes and do their hair there. I have a portable case with brushes, combs, lotion, pins, rollers, hair spray, scissors, and hair nets. I carry a portable dryer in one hand and the case in the other. Everybody gets the same case and the same dryer. Even Mrs. John Kennedy. Her hair is lovely. She has beautiful hair. Who cuts yours? Did you cut it yourself? All women are secret haircutters. They all want to be Eve in the Garden, or something. This hair is too curly. I can't stand it this way. Let us straighten it.' 'Go ahead,' I said. 'I'm completely in your hands.' 'Rosemary!' Mr. Kenneth called. 'Straighten this hair, while I start Mrs. MacRae.' Rosemary got to work straightening. 'I'll call you Princess Yellow Hair,' Mr. Kenneth said to Mrs. MacRae. 'I hear that Carol Channing is upstairs,' Mrs. MacRae said. 'We're supposed to be at a cocktail party together at six, and I'll bet she doesn't make it.' 'Sure she will,' Mr. Kenneth said. 'Everybody makes everything from here.'

"Hair straightening cost twenty-five dollars. Was worth it. Mr. Kenneth looked so pleased when he returned. 'Now you have the easier look,' he said, rubbing newly straight hair with pink towels. 'You remind me of Judy Garland. I was out till two this morning in Newark with Judy Garland on her concert, doing her hair. Before her concert and between acts. She gets very wet. I dry her hair and comb it differently between acts.' Mr. Kenneth combed straight hair back off my forehead. 'I may call you Princess Brown Hair,' he said. Wahoo! Mr. Kenneth snipped away at hair with scissors. Very delicate touch. Artistic. Mr. Kenneth takes his time. None of this clip-clip-clip, razzle-dazzle rush stuff with Mr. Kenneth. After haircut, he started putting hair up in rollers. 'Spray a little pink lotion on Mrs. MacRae, Gregory,' Mr. Kenneth called over his shoulder. 'Put the net on gently and put her in the oven.'

" 'Do you enjoy the hairdressing life?' I asked Mr. Kenneth, still interviewing but keeping a careful eye on those rollers and beginning to feel like Princess Brown Hair. 'At night, I go home and sit in a coma,' Mr. Kenneth said. 'I have no friends, no life, no time to myself. I have a low tolerance for noise. I can't stand noise. This place gets very noisy, everybody talking at once, all calling for Mr. Kenneth. But I like cutting and designing. I crusade for hair not to look studied, as it has in the past. I work for a look of easiness. Easy and young and pretty and natural—that's the way women say they feel after I do their hair. I've always been allowed to attempt what I want to do—my thoughts, my ideas. My job here is called artistic director. I like to go to clients' homes. I enjoy seeing those fantastic apartments, those houses with solidly eighteenth-century French furniture and paintings. It sinks in. But my major concern always is, How is the hair? Your hair color is pretty. Show it off, I say. What are these *things* in back here?' Mr. Kenneth pulled at back wisps of my hair. 'They're cut like *kindling* wood,' Mr. Kenneth said. A little more gentle, artistic snipping, and I felt kindling wood disappear. Just before going under pink dryer—which comes to client, client does not have to go to it—I caught a glimpse of Miss Daché. *Très élégante.* 'The fabulous Miss Daché,' Miss Gilbert said, in whisper. 'Fiery, active, fabulous Miss Daché. She's beautiful.' 'I am off to Paris,' Miss Daché called out, in Parisian. 'Au revoir, Meestaire Kenneth. I renew myself in Paris.'

"Four hours gone by, almost. Was halfway through manicure with Helena. Half hour later, saw Carol Channing come in and start jawing away with Princess Yellow Hair. Took dryer off head so could hear. 'Jack Paar has definite ideas about hair,' Miss Channing was saying. 'That time Geneviève appeared with curly hair—remember Jack told her she *ruined* herself?' Mr. Kenneth came over and put dryer back on me. Later, after pedicure with Camille, emerged from dryer. Saw Mr. Kenneth put finishing combing touch on Princess Yellow Hair. *Très élégante.* 'I feel prettier, easier, younger, more natural,' Princess Yellow Hair said. Then my turn. Me, too. Me, too."

❧❧ 1650 BROADWAY

WITH the Decoration Day weekend on the horizon, at least one unchanging promise of the summer season gets close; for hundreds of comedians, harmonica players, accordion players, jugglers, magicians, ballroom dancers, tap-dancers, novelty dancers, blues singers, and sopranos the lean, irregular-eating days are petering out as they begin to get booked into the entertainment programs of summer resorts, hotels, and country clubs along the Eastern seaboard, with a heavy concentration, of course, in the Catskill Mountain area that is known professionally to bookers as Sullivan County. The biggest and busiest of some fifteen bookers in the trade is Charles Rapp, a fifty-two-year-old, bald, freckle-faced lover of show business, and it was to his offices, at 1650 Broadway, that we sped last Thursday morning. We found Mr. Rapp in a small room that had a fine Great White Way view and was equipped with four cigarette-burn-scarred wooden desks and eight telephones. With Mr. Rapp were two assistants, Mrs. Chickie Nathans and Mr. Shelly Rothman, both of whom, like him, were talking on the telephone. Pasted on the wall over Rapp's head were typewritten lists of hotels (Ambassador Hotel, Atlantic City, N.J.; Banner Lodge, Moodus, Conn.; Brookside Swim Club, Union, N.J. . . .), lists of performers' agents (Adair, Rose, CI 7-3900; Adler, Harry, PL 7-2535 . . .), and lists of entertainers, grouped according to their specialties. On the desk before Rapp was still another list, handwritten on lined yellow tablet paper and headed "Decoration Day Availabilities." Mr. Rapp, who looked healthy and sunburned, and was wearing heavy black-rimmed eyeglasses, a black silk suit, a white silk shirt, and a white knit necktie, spoke into the telephone with great patience. "Let me tell you something, doll," he said. "If you hear a guy singing 'Ol' Man River,' you don't need to hear him sing 'Otchi Tchornyia.' . . . All right. I'll get you a swell harmonica player." He hung up and waited until Mrs. Nathans, a buxom young lady wearing a white-and-red striped sweater, had also hung up.

"Chickie, make a note of this," Rapp said. "The dance team of Margo and Chiverto go out of the Laurels Country Club, and Stan Harper, the harmonica player, goes in."

"How come?" Chickie asked.

"Not a big crowd there yet," Rapp said. "A harmonica player is more intimate for a small group." He answered his telephone again.

"The season isn't here in full force yet," Shelly Rothman said to us. "Wait till next month—we start working fifteen, eighteen hours a day. And, starting July 1st, a seven-day week. Wait till we start with the business of going to bed at six in the morning, and we're back in the office by ten. Keeping track of all those doubles! Two-shows-a-night performers. Getting replacements for ones who get flat tires or something." Shelly actually rubbed his hands in anticipation. "The shortest ten weeks of your life!" he said. He is dark, earnest, devoted, and on the threshold of forty.

"It gets in your blood," Chickie said. "This is my tenth year with Charlie. My husband has a good business, thank God, in garden furniture. My daughter, Abbey Lynn, was three years old yesterday. Do I have to do this? No! But it's in my blood."

"Charlie deceives people by keeping the outdoor, country, summer-resort look on himself all year round," Shelly said. "Thanks to the Lone Star Boat Club, on top of the Y.W.C.A. at Fifty-first and Eighth Avenue."

"You want a girl singer?" Rapp was saying over the telephone. "How about Linda Hopkins? She stops the show cold." As he listened to the reply, he turned his outdoor, country, summer-resort look toward us, cradled the telephone against a raised shoulder, and lit a cigarette. "Comics?" he went on. "Larry Alpert, Gary Morton, Mark Robbins, Rip Taylor. Rip Taylor. Good-looking guy. Terrific jokes. This kid works like Red Skelton. A very clever kid. He stops the show cold. . . . O.K., Linda and Gary." He hung up and yawned, and his telephone immediately rang again. "We're still very slow here," he said to us before answering it. "This is very mild."

After listening for a while, Rapp said, "You'll need a comedian. A comedian is the backbone of the show. I've got the perfect guy. Rip

Taylor. We used him all winter, and he's great. If he's got a hip crowd, he's great. He's like Red Skelton. He's not the average mountain type. His price is going up in June. This kid played Laurel in the Pines about ten times. He played Fallsview. You're at liberty to check all the hotels I mentioned." Calmly, he hung up.

"This is the most intangible business there is in the world," Shelly said.

"There's a bigger need for entertainers than ever before," Rapp said. "Vaudeville is dead, but in those days how many places could you work? About sixteen houses. Now there's over a hundred places we book alone. And the entertainers are better today. In the old days, all a singer needed was a strong voice. If you couldn't belt, you were dead. Today, everything gets enlarged over a mike."

"Every new act today is a new challenge," Chickie said.

"I've been in the business twenty-seven years, and I still keep on the go with it," Rapp said. "I started in at the age of fourteen, at P. S. 45, when I entered some kids from the school in a Fox Crotona amateur contest. We had a five-piece band, two dancers, and a singer, and we won first prize. Fifty dollars. I took fifty per cent. Now I take fifteen or twenty. We pay the acts, and the hotel pays us. When I was seventeen, I was booking acts for all the Knights of Pythias lodges. I'm always geared for action. One minute I'm booking a monkey act, the next I'm worrying about a magician. Each one is important. To entertain nice people. Comes Saturday night in a resort, and they can do one of two things after they eat. Constantly dance the whole night, or be entertained. They're good family people. They like to sit and listen."

Rapp's telephone rang again as Shelly and Chickie took calls of their own.

"What type of act do you want?" Rapp said into the phone. "Sort of a fine-looking type that can introduce the acts, without telling funny stories or with telling funny stories? You want a name strong enough to draw people? Have you any idea of the budget? Let me ask you a question. Are you acquainted with any names? For example, you know Larry Storch? Morey Amsterdam? Harvey Stone?"

"A group of dancers," Shelly was saying. "Israeli dancers. Who can sing, dance, play instruments—you know?"

"We just started to fill up the booking sheet now," Chickie was saying. "Charlie will be here every day, morning to midnight."

"You can't get Joey Bishop," Rapp said, still on the same call. "I'll reel off the names of some others to you. Jackie Mason. He opens at the Copacabana June 1st. He was on the Perry Como Show. How about Henny Youngman, who just played the Persian Room at the Plaza? I may be able to get Ricky Layne and Velvel, the ventrilo-quist, that Ed Sullivan uses all the time on his show. Gene Baylos— you know *him?* . . . You want somebody that comes from the *South?* Andy Griffith would want a load of money. . . ."

Into the room came a tanned, relaxed, silk-suited man smoking a cigar. He shook hands with Shelly, sat down, talked for several min-utes about the merits of group insurance for entertainers, and left, smiling cheerfully.

"He used to be a singer; now he sells insurance," Shelly said to us. "Now he's extremely secure."

"I fail to see how he can leave show business," Chickie said. "Once it got into his blood."

"Let me tell you something, doll," said Rapp, who was still on the phone. "This may be a little out of my line. Like I wouldn't know how to go in for the kind of people booked in the Blue Angel, for example. What you may need is one of those offices that go in for picture people, which is slightly off the beam for myself. Unless you want to change your mind about a big name, in which case I have a terrific young comic on the order of Red Skelton. . . ." He finally hung up. "Some nut," he said to us. "He's got a big golf exposition in a sunny climate and he wants the exposition big-name type. For twenty-five hundred dollars. So he starts off with Gene Barry, who probably wants ten thousand dollars."

"Stan Irwin!" Shelly yelled as another visitor entered the room—a sleek-looking, good-natured fellow with old-fashioned matinée-idol graying hair, a smooth suntan, black silk slacks, highly polished black loafers, a gray-and-red plaid jacket, a gray silk shirt, a black knit tie, and mother-of-pearl cufflinks the size of half dollars. The others also gave Stan Irwin a big hello.

"We used to book Stan, a great comic, and then he went on to become a very big man in Las Vegas," Shelly said, introducing us to the visitor. "The last place we booked him was the Brickman Hotel, in South Fallsburg. Eight years ago. Remember, Stan? You look great, Stan." Big clapping on the back for Stan from Shelly and Rapp.

"Doesn't Stan look good, Charlie?" Chickie said.

"I'm in town checking out the Broadway shows, to see if any of them lend themselves for Las Vegas presentation," Stan said.

"Hey, I'm going to get George, the agent for the Brickman, on the phone and put you on with him for a surprise!" Shelly said. Everybody laughed as he dialled the call.

"The Brickman. The last place I worked as a comic before I went out to the Club Bingo in Las Vegas, where I came in for eleven days and stayed eight months," Stan told us. "I became their booker. You name it, I did it. Then they rebuilt the club as the Sahara. Now I create shows for various Vegas clubs from allied fields of entertainment. Eleanor Powell at the Sahara, after eleven years out of the business. Marlene Dietrich. Lauritz Melchior. That's my bit. And whole musicals. *Tenderloin* opens at the Dunes this week. *Gypsy* is coming to the Riviera. Not bad? When I come to New York, I like to keep up old friendships." He threw Rapp a laugh.

Shelly waved a hand in the air and then beckoned the visitor to the telephone. "George, here's a comic, he needs a job, he wants to say hello," Shelly said with great joy into the phone, and handed it to Stan Irwin. Rapp and Chickie looked on proudly.

"Hi! Can you use a great comic at the Brickman?" Stan Irwin said, going along with the gag. "I worked there eight years ago, the best basketball player ever worked the hotel. . . . What do you mean, 'Who is this?' This is Stan Irwin. . . . Yeah, *Stan*." He burst into laughter, and Rapp, Chickie, and Shelly were convulsed.

THE
ATTORNEY GENERAL

ROBERT KENNEDY came to town one hot morning last week to look things over in the offices of the local United States District Attorneys and to make a speech at a State Attorneys General meeting, and, thanks to a long-distance chat the day before with his public-information aide, Edwin Guthman (a 1950 Pulitzer Prize reporter on leave from the Seattle *Times*), we were on hand to greet the Attorney General at LaGuardia. He arrived at 8:30 A.M., at which time, he told us, he already had behind him his usual tennis-before-breakfast with his wife at their home, Hickory Hill, in McLean, Virginia; a glass of orange juice with his seven children (ages one to nine); blueberry pancakes and a glass of milk on the plane; work on a written speech that he might discard in favor of talking impromptu to the Attorneys General; and the reading, up to page 164, of George F. Kennan's new book, *Russia and the West Under Lenin and Stalin*. Taking long, fast strides away from the plane, and followed by Guthman and two other travelling companions from Washington—an administrative assistant named John Reilly and an assistant director of the F.B.I. named Courtney Evans—the Attorney General was joined by a couple of equally fast-striding local F.B.I. men, who informed him of their pleasure at being assigned to accompany him, as a break in their regular work as bank-robbery agents. The Attorney General looked pleased and serious at the same time. His face was freshly sunburned, and he had on a navy-blue worsted suit, a white shirt with a button-down collar, and a blue-and-silver striped necktie held by a brass pin, in the shape of a PT boat, that was inscribed "Kennedy 60." In addition to the Kennan book, he carried, in a transparent plastic wrapping, a white Sulka shirt, 15½-33 (no button-down collar), with a blue paper laundry band around it. As he walked along, he passed both book and shirt back to Guthman for safekeeping.

"My wife handed me that shirt as I was leaving," the Attorney General said. "I'll change into it just before the speech, I guess. My wife hates to fly, but she would have come with me anyway, only she had to go to the White House with Mrs. Johnson for a reception there, pinch-hitting for my brother's wife. My wife gave me this tie to wear. I had another one on, but she said it didn't look good. I don't have any other tiepins. I bought this one during the campaign. We were selling them for fifteen cents. One thing I hope to do here before leaving on a six-thirty plane tonight is visit a toy store and find something for my son David. He's six tomorrow, and he's been talking about his birthday since the day after Christmas. He wants a billy goat, and my wife got him one, unfortunately. My second son, Bobby, collects animals. He's also a junior botanist. Bobby picks up bees with his fingers. I caught two turtles for him while riding last Sunday, to fill out the collection we've got at home—chicks, geese, horses, ponies, tadpoles, frogs, lizards, birds, cats, puppies, and dogs. I got a seal for the children for Christmas two years ago. He escaped once and was found by the milkman in the middle of town and had to be captured by the local police. This seal got to be real friendly, but when he found out food came from the kitchen he was always trying to get into the kitchen, so we had to give him to the zoo. We had a deodorized skunk once, but it escaped while being transported from Hyannis Port to Washington and is still missing. A friend brought Bobby a toad the other day for his collection, half of which is kept in the house, the other half out. Bobby is really terrific with animals—has a wonderful way with them. I get to see more of my children now than I did during the campaign. At least, I see them Saturday night and part of Sunday and at breakfast. They're lucky in being aware of what is going on in the country and in the world, which I think is a great advantage. We do a lot of talking about what I do and what my brother does. We talk in the context of the history of the country—Lexington and Bunker Hill and the Boston Tea Party and the Civil War and so on. We talk about the kinds of things Jack does. The older children know all about Khrushchev and

de Gaulle and Harold Macmillan—who they are and why Jack went
to visit them. They're just regular children. The older ones wanted
to know who the Freedom Riders are. That was a difficult one. Trying to explain to an eight- or nine-year-old that some people don't
like Negroes. We have a Negro nurse who's been with us since my
first child was born, so this doesn't make any sense to them."

"General, here's the car," one of the F.B.I. men said, opening the
door of a Chevrolet sedan.

The Attorney General ushered us into the rear with him as
Guthman got in beside the driver and the rest of the party headed
for another car. A pink-faced and perspiring policeman in a short-
sleeved shirt put his head in at the rear window on Mr. Kennedy's
side.

"Well, well, glad to see you again, sir," the policeman said, and
the Attorney General shook hands with him through the window.
"Haven't seen you since the electioneering days. Remember those
days? It's a long time ago."

"I certainly do," Mr. Kennedy said. "Nice to see you again."

"You've got good color. Keep it up," the policeman said.

"So have you," Mr. Kennedy said.

"Mine is high blood pressure," the policeman said. "Sorry we've
got such terrible hot weather for you here. Hope it won't bother
you."

"It won't. Thanks. Good luck," Mr. Kennedy said.

As we started off, Mr. Kennedy told us, "I went to South-Central
Asia in 1955 with Justice Douglas, and the temperature there got
over a hundred and thirty degrees—very dry heat, but even that
didn't make me become accustomed to it. I don't like cities generally. The part of New York I like the best is Central Park—especially the zoo. If the election had turned out differently and if Mr.
Nixon hadn't made me Attorney General, I'd probably be making
short trips to New York only to visit the zoo."

"Is your present job more difficult than being a campaign manager?" we asked.

"The hours are equally long," Mr. Kennedy said. "There was
more real public pressure, actually, in the campaign, where one mistake could cost you a whole area. I was travelling continuously,
speaking fifteen or twenty times in an eighteen- or nineteen-hour

day. You're always open to pressure as a campaign manager. And when I worked with the Senate Rackets Investigating Committee, the public and the press were continuously interested. I think the decisions I make now have a more lasting effect and affect people more materially than anything I've done in any other job I've ever had."

We started down the Franklin D. Roosevelt Drive on our way to Foley Square. The East River was swarming with tugs, barges, and other boat traffic, but Mr. Kennedy paid little attention to it all. "I travelled this route from LaGuardia to the Federal Court House half a dozen times a year during the three years I worked for the Senate Rackets Committee," Mr. Kennedy said. "I used to come in from Washington to our office here. We did an awful lot of work in New York—investigating rackets in garbage disposal, jukeboxes, and the rest. We had a staff of fifteen or twenty people here working on the investigations of Johnny Dio and Tony (Ducks) Corallo. This was a very active area for us. I always interviewed the witnesses myself before they testified. I was looking into the unpleasant side of New York. I never had time to visit the zoo."

It was a few minutes before nine when we reached the Federal Court House, and a guard at a side entrance looked up in dreamlike surprise as the Attorney General walked briskly inside. After shaking hands with the guard, Mr. Kennedy looked in on a couple of offices and shook hands with a few ladies at typewriters. Then we followed him to Room 401, the office of United States Attorney Robert Morgenthau, who is in charge of the District here.

"You really had your hands full the last month or so," Morgenthau said as they shook hands.

"Yes," Mr. Kennedy said, admiring a Brady photograph of Lincoln that was lying on a table. "Is this with McClellan?" he asked.

"That's right," Mr. Morgenthau said. "We haven't had time to get our pictures up yet."

"I never saw this one before," Mr. Kennedy said.

We stepped outside, where Mr. Guthman and Mr. Reilly were waiting, and the latter, a heavyset young man with large hands, told us that he was in charge of the administrative office for all the United States Attorneys. "Have you ever seen anybody with his drive?" he asked us, nodding in the direction of the Attorney General. "And he's a lot tougher, and smarter, with a lot more experience, than in 1957. He's been to the well a lot of times since then. He's tough, he's fair, he's smart, and he's considerate. He has all the decent qualities."

"He doesn't want the people around him simply to say yes," Guthman said.

"When he makes a decision, you know some thought and consideration have gone into it," Reilly said.

Mr. Kennedy came out and told us he was going around to talk to some of the federal judges about eight new district judges and three new circuit judges who he hoped would be named soon by the President to take care of the tremendous backlog of cases piled up in the courts, but first he was going to greet the staff of assistants to the United States Attorney. A few minutes later, he stood, hands in pockets, below a photograph dated 1903 and showing the nine-man staff of the United States Attorney's office (we spotted a boyish-looking Felix Frankfurter and a young Henry Stimson), and greeted the thirty-odd members of Morgenthau's staff who are in the criminal division.

"I'm delighted to be here," Mr. Kennedy said. "There's no question but that the Southern District of New York is the showcase for the Justice Department. . . . I wanted to come up and tell you how grateful we are to you for all the time and effort you give to the work, which I know is not for financial satisfaction. . . . We are always available to you and at your service. . . ."

Then the staff members, short and tall, fat and thin, young and very young, shy and very shy, and all looking happy and impressed, lined up to introduce themselves and shake hands with the Attorney General. He asked several of the very young ones, who identified themselves as voluntary student assistants from law school, what their school was or how they liked the work, and one informed the Attorney General that his father ran the Melody Tent in Hyannis Port. Would the Kennedys please come? Mr. Kennedy said that the Kennedys always came to the Melody Tent.

"Sheldon Elsen, Criminal Division," one older young man, handsome, smiling, and wearing shell-rimmed glasses, said as he shook hands with the Attorney General. "I've worked here for a year. Left private practice to come here."

"Enjoy it?" Mr. Kennedy asked.

"Love it," Sheldon Elsen said.

"Where did you go to law school?"

"Harvard," Sheldon Elsen said, grinning.

"Good luck to you," the Attorney General said.

A beaming gray-haired lady wearing spectacles said, "Ethel Backenroth. I'm the librarian. I have thirty-nine years of service to the United States Attorney for the Southern District."

"You were here before I was born," Mr. Kennedy said.

"I'm proud of my service," Miss Backenroth said.

"Five years before I was born," Mr. Kennedy said, looking slightly stunned.

The greeting-and-handshaking routine was repeated later on with another group of attorneys, in the anti-trust division, and then, with pauses to shake hands with guards, a shoeshine man, and other well-wishers, and to give a few autographs, Mr. Kennedy started out of the building.

We asked him whether he remembered the people he met in such long lineups.

"I'm not too good at it," he said. "Jack is really good at it, and my wife is terrific."

❦ SUNNY HILL

ALMOST EVERYBODY is taking polio vaccine these days, but nine years ago this summer only fifty-one people, mostly children, were taking the first, later-to-be-proved-effective vaccine against the disease. Early one Saturday morning recently, we flew out to Pittsburgh, where, at an institution called the D. T. Watson Home for Crippled Children, in a suburb called Leetsdale, Dr. Jonas E. Salk was going to have his ninth annual—and possibly his last—reunion and tests with his very first voluntary human subjects. It would be the end of a chapter of medical history.

In the last six years, more than ninety-five million Americans have been inoculated against polio. The first fifty-one subjects, who were tested on June 12, 1952, first inoculated in July and August, and written about by Dr. Salk in the *Journal of the American Medical Association* of March 28, 1953, in a paper entitled "Studies in Human Subjects on Active Immunization Against Poliomyelitis" ("Investigations have been under way in this laboratory for more than a year, with the objective of establishing conditions for destroying the disease-producing property of the three types of poliomyelitis virus without destroying completely their capacity to induce antibody formation . . ."), received acknowledgment at the outset in a footnote: "Although one might take for granted the fact that these investigations were performed in human subjects, it should be evident that the work could not have been undertaken without the support and coöperation of a great many individuals. We cannot express adequately our admiration for the parents and the patients who have contributed so much."

Reunion day dawned bright and clear. Dr. Salk, now forty-six, met us, by prearrangement, at a hotel near the University of Pittsburgh, where he is Commonwealth Professor of Experimental Medicine.

He looked cheerful, expectant, and impressively neat and well organized. With him was the middle of his three sons, Darrell Salk, fourteen, neatly echoing his father, with the same kind of shell-rimmed
eyeglasses, curly dark hair, and unmatched jacket and trousers, and
the same sort of single-track scientific gleam in his eye.

"Darry's coming with us," Dr. Salk said as we started out in his
car over the small hills of Pittsburgh. "He's interested. We've followed the children long enough now to see that the good antibody
levels induced in them initially have persisted essentially the same,
remaining as they were one year after we gave them the last dose
of the vaccine. It's been astonishing to see this persistence, and it
looks as though the immunity provided by the 'killed-virus vaccine'
—which is the way this vaccine is distinguished from others—was
durable. This day is quite a significant one for us. The tiny group
we're going to see today helped us look into the future. They were
mostly polio patients at the Watson Home, and then we branched
out and included their families, all of whom were eager to coöperate, of course, because they knew from painful experience what it
meant to have polio. The first human inoculations are always given
to the experimenters themselves, and then usually to volunteers in
prisons and mental institutions. But it occurred to me that parents
of children who had already had polio would be most understanding, and, as it's turned out, they've been more than that. Eventually,
we enlarged our original group to include other people in this well-
to-do community and somewhat beyond it, until the nucleus grew to
more than a thousand people, most of whom had economic advan-
tages. They were perfect for giving us a high concentration of individuals with no previous exposure to polio. Blood tests showed that
sixty per cent of the younger people had no antibodies at all for any
of the three types of polio. To a poliovirologist, this was paradise.
And it did something wonderful for the community. It gave people
an opportunity to give and receive something you can't buy—an
opportunity to participate in a human experience that was at the
time secret and unique. There's no reason for any of the original
subjects to come back today for tests—no selfish reason. But this has
been a joint affair. They've all been collaborators of mine, and I
think they'll all be there.

"Pittsburgh is a working town, and I like it here," Dr. Salk went on as, driving along the Monongahela, we passed steel mills, smokestacks, pyramids of slag. "You get the feeling of being surrounded by life. Now I'm planning to move in a year or so to San Diego, where, with support from the National Foundation—the new March of Dimes organization—we're establishing an Institute for Biological Studies next to the new University of California campus. I entered medical school with the idea of doing research, and never changed my mind. It's a way of projecting yourself ahead of yourself, I suppose, and there was something appealing in the search for understanding that had some bearing on human problems. I guess I felt the unreasonableness of life in so many ways. Research was one way to get at reasonableness and logic."

In the midst of lush green farm country, we arrived at the Watson Home. "In the spring of 1952, we knew that the vaccines induced protective effects in monkeys, but we couldn't learn everything we needed to know without human subjects," Dr. Salk said as he parked the car. "We knew it would be completely safe to inject the children with a killed virus of the same type that had infected them in the first place. We got the permission of Dr. Jessie Wright, the medical director of the Home; of Miss Lucile Cochran, the administrator; of the board of trustees; and of the parents. Then, with the concurrence of all, we went ahead. I guess the facts are now common knowledge—the attack rate is way down, and all indications are that 1961 will be the lowest polio year in our history. In the late nineteen-forties and early nineteen-fifties, there were close to three thousand cases of polio per week during several consecutive weeks in most years, and in 1960 there were just over three thousand cases the entire year. If all children had been inoculated as soon as the vaccine became available, as was done in Denmark and Sweden, paralytic polio would have been suppressed, and might have all but disappeared by now."

The Watson Home, which is in the foothills of the Allegheny Mountains, had the appearance of a luxurious estate—spreading lawns and shady trees and arbors, with here and there groups of small children playing together. The auditorium of a red brick building near the original Home had been organized efficiently for the tests—lineups of chairs leading to several immaculate white tables, with Home nurses in attendance.

Dr. Salk immediately got to work with his staff and then began greeting his subjects. It was not yet 9 A.M., but about a dozen men, women, and children were waiting. Standing with them was Miss Cochran, a gray-haired, smiling woman wearing a pink linen dress, white pearls, and a pink cardigan sweater. Dr. Salk set to work with his blood-test tubes. Darrell, putting on a laboratory coat, took charge of the card files.

"Everybody's been telephoning since seven this morning," Miss Cochran said to Dr. Salk. "They all want to come. On the day of the Horse Show, too. Darrell, I hardly recognized you!"

"Well," Darrell said, blushing, "I'll be doing stuff like this some-day, I hope."

"You'll always be welcome at Sunny Hill," Miss Cochran said, and added, to us, "We never say 'Home for Crippled Children' here. We always say 'Sunny Hill,' because the D. T. Watsons, who founded the Home, always called it that."

We moved over to Dr. Salk's table, where he was being greeted by a lady with a cane, whom he introduced to us as Mrs. Walton Diven. With her were her husband, who had a crew cut, and three handsome, look-alike, crew-cut boys, aged nine to fifteen. "It's like Old Home Week for me," Mrs. Diven said to us. "I contracted polio when Johnny was five weeks old, and Johnny was eighteen months old when he got his first shot."

Johnny lifted his crew-cut head and looked pleased.

"Everybody around here has grown up so," Dr. Salk said.

"Is this really the end of the program?" Mrs. Diven asked.

"It may be," Dr. Salk said. "I probably won't need to take samples again for five years, anyway."

"You mean this may be the last time we'll all be reunited?" Mrs. Diven exclaimed.

Dr. Salk nodded.

"Well, you know we're all proud to have been part of the pro-gram," Mr. Diven said.

Dr. Salk smiled. Next in the lineup at his table was a ten-year-old girl with a brace on one leg. In the background, Miss Cochran started a record-player going with "Tip Toe through the Tulips with Me." Darrell Salk showed us the girl's record card, and we read,

"Barbara Bailey, paralyzed Sept. 18, 1951. First time blood taken— June 12, 1952."

There was quite a merry reunion with Barbara Bailey. "You were the cutest baby in the ward," Dr. Salk told her. "Only eighteen months old . . ."

We went outside into the sunshine, where Miss Cochran was welcoming another family of early subjects—Dr. Leslie Falk, medical administrator of the United Mine Workers Welfare Fund in the area, with his wife and four children.

"The whole community is so unhappy about Dr. Salk's leaving Pittsburgh," Mrs. Falk was saying.

"Well, the program is coming to an end," Miss Cochran said.

"Now he's interested in a number of things, and I think that one is suppressing viruses generally, as is happening with polio," Dr. Falk said. "There are over two hundred viruses that cause human disease, and he'd like *them* to disappear, too."

"He has the same dedication he had when he first came here, in 1952," Miss Cochran said. "As a matter of fact, he's the same man now as he was then, and you can't say that about many people."

"The real excitement for us was when he told us he thought he had the answer," Mrs. Falk said. "It was nearly a year before he included people from the community in his studies."

"Did you have any worries?" we asked.

"Most of us felt we were getting a big break," she said.

Dr. Salk joined our group as a pretty young woman started up the walk toward us, using two canes. With her was a young man carrying a chubby, dimpled baby boy.

"Why, it's Joan!" Miss Cochran exclaimed.

"She has no use of her legs at all," Dr. Salk said softly. "I heard she moved to Ohio."

Joan approached, smiling at everyone. "Dr. Salk, I want you to meet my son Lee," she said.

"Oh, Joan, how wonderful!" Miss Cochran said, waving to the baby.

"Sixteen months old," the young man holding the baby said.

"You're going to San Diego!" Joan said to Dr. Salk. She sat down and took the baby.

"Well, not for another year or so, anyway," he said, tickling Lee. "And I heard you moved to Ohio."

"I did, but I wasn't going to miss this for the world. What I want to know is, what about Lee? Does he automatically have my immunity now?"

"That goes away after six months," Dr. Salk said. "After that, he has to develop his own."

"Then I wish you would give him his first shot," Joan said. "He's a very good baby."

"It's so nice to have him visit Sunny Hill," Miss Cochran said.

"He'd like some of that Salk Special," Joan said.

Everybody beamed at the baby, and the baby beamed back and took some Salk Special.

✿ COFFEE
WITH COWARD

NOËL COWARD is in town these sultry days, directing *Sail Away*, his first musical show—book, music, and lyrics written by himself—since *Set to Music*, which was produced in 1939. As he prepared to start rehearsals last week, we heard a typist in our office named Miss Rogers, who has been sitting around here in her muu-muus and Mr. Kenneth hairdos, hinting hoarsely, "I'll *see* yoo-oo-oo *agayne*." Miss Rogers, who has learned a few things from our man Stanley, occasionally volunteers to leave her typewriter for a reporting assignment, so we told her all right, go to the Coward flat, in the East Fifties, and see what Mr. Coward is doing. A couple of hours later, she strolled back, languorously humming a new song, which she said was called "Something Very Strange," and, before wandering away, dropped the following notes, scribbled on music paper, on our desk:

"Who wants vacation? Who needs Saint-Jean-de-Luz? Who cares about Cape, Adirondacks, Las Vegas, Locarno, Grossinger's, Lake Tahoe, anyplace? Everybody who matters in everything that matters stays in good old N.Y.C. in July-Aug., getting ready for big season. Big productions. Big themes. Big money. Second-act-curtain crises. Terrif. Costume conferences. Billing crises. Script run-throughs. Song run-throughs. Reprise run-throughs. Dance routines down at Central Plaza. Onion rolls at Ratner's. Terrif. Everybody nervous, pale, sticky, worried, living on credit, dreaming of first full pay check. Hits. *Big* hits. No bombs. Lots of sweating. Losing weight. Stomach aches. Worse. No time to watch *Open End* repeats. *Live* theatre. Everybody alive. Fingers crossed. No time to read *Times* obits. Everybody gathered around piano. Everybody getting smacked in back with iced blasts from air conditioner. Black coffee—hot, bitter, boiled—on tap around clock. Everybody awake. Everybody on Cape asleep. Saint-Jean-de-Luz, asleep. Grossinger's, asleep. In N.Y.C., everybody awake around clock. In Adirondacks, everybody fat. In N.Y.C., everybody drinking black coffee, thin.

"Arrived Noël Coward's digs at 11 A.M. First get-together before rehearsals. Smoky. Iced. Everything according to blueprint. Two pianos—back to back. One producer. Eighteen cups black coffee. One star. Two featured players. Two photographers, one with cute avant-garde beard. *Bitter Sweet* man himself presiding, with lordly calm, eyes narrowed, Jamaica-Bermuda tan fading by minute. Madras jacket. Crisp beige slacks. Brown suède shoes. Hair wet. 'Press on! Press on!' he saying smoothly to photographers. Terrif.

"Sidled up to Coward humming 'I'll see yoo-oo-oo agayne.' He gave Noël Coward wink and showed beautiful teeth in Noël Coward laugh. 'What is *that?*' he asked. 'Have a cup of coffee? Charles will get you a cup of coffee.' Charles offered coffee. Charles one of three producers. Very thin. 'At the age of sixty-one, Noël could be spending the summer in one of his three cool houses,' Charles said. 'But he loves doing this. It's his first musical conceived, cast, and produced in America. He writes fiction and poetry, too.' 'Man! All that bread!' avant-garde photographer said.

"Coward introduced me to co-star—Jean Fenn, attractive blonde who plays lady-taking-cruise-away-from-her-husband in *Sail Away*. 'I knew there was going to be a mob, but I didn't know it would be such a mob,' Coward said, throwing another wink. Coward wink winks sort of whole side of face, down to chin. Terrif. 'The photographers arrived while I was in the shower. Ow!' Coward said as telephone rang sharply. 'That's supposed to be unplugged. I suppose I shall have to answer it.' Answered it. Said into telephone, 'Hello, Stritchie, dear. . . . Absolutely wonderful. . . . Au revoir, ma chérie.' Authentic Coward lines. Terrif. Hung up, said to me, 'I'll see what's going on about the photographers. I must get them out of the way. I've been up since seven-thirty. What I did was bash my brain to find a sort of recitative lead-in for the finale of the second act. Now the thing's ready. All that's left really is deciding about the reprise of this number or that.' 'He's a man of thorough preparation,' Charles said to Miss Fenn. 'He's checked on every costume, every color and every material of every costume. He's listened to the orchestrations. He's polished off conferences to get the billing just right. He's designed the show's poster himself. He's travelled all the way down to Central Plaza to inspect the dancers.' 'Press on!' Coward said merrily. 'Must get the photographers out of the way. I have to concentrate. One doesn't want to have to drag one's mind away once we start. Press on!'

"Non-avant-garde photographer urged Coward and Miss Fenn to sit at piano with James Hurst—very tall, very thin young man; plays Miss Fenn's romantic interest on cruise—and with Margalo Gillmore, who plays young man's mother. All on cruise. Elaine Stritch, co-star, plays cruise hostess—runs amusements, shuffleboard; learning Italian phrases, reading up on ruins. Was still on Cape. Non-avant-garde photographer said he wanted romantic head-and-shoulders photo of Coward with Miss Fenn. 'We shall simulate a duet,' Coward said. 'Press on!' Avant-garde photographer looked cranky. 'Can't you play the piano?' he asked Coward. Played a few bars of 'Something Very Strange.' Terrif. Avant-garde photographer looked crankier. 'Got a waltz?' he asked Coward. 'Like in *Bitter Sweet*?' 'Only one waltz,' Coward said. 'I used to use a lot of waltzes, but now it's the good old four-four. One or two of the twenty-two numbers in the show are nostalgic. The rest are modern.' Other photographer asked Coward to keep hands on piano, smiling face turned to other smiling faces, everybody singing. Avant-garde gave awful scowl. 'You look sad,' Coward said to him. 'Is the light wrong?' Started playing waltz, 'This Is a Changing World.' Light, gay. Avant-garde unfurled brow.

"Charles handed me second cup coffee. 'We open in the air-conditioned Colonial Theatre in Boston on Wednesday, August 9th,' Charles said. Coward came over, said, 'Clear the props away, chaps. Jimmy and Jean and I might have a read-through.' 'He started writing this show last Christmas,' Charles said. 'Jean Fenn flew here from the West Coast last February, sang four bars of "Vissi d'arte," that great aria from *Tosca*, for him, and that settled it. She was in.' 'Once I knew that I had two beautiful voices to work for, I pressed on and simply wrote music for their range,' Coward said.

"Took third cup coffee. Coward told me he was glad to be doing musical here, instead of in England. 'There's more expertise here, in choreography, orchestration, and so on,' he said. 'The show is rather nice. It's free, romantic, very gay.' Then he turned to Charles. 'Press on!' he said to Charles, ushering photographers out. 'Press on!' Winked. Terrif."

❧❧ LEARNING
❧

THAT SEVENTY-EIGHT-YEAR-OLD beatnik Stanley Isaacs, Councilman and Civic Father, wasn't going on his recent evening tour of Greenwich Village coffeehouses without us. When we heard that Mr. Isaacs had accepted an invitation from some coffeehouse owners, who were being plagued with summonses for not having cabaret licenses, to come down and see the places for himself, we telephoned him. "You're most welcome to join me," he told us. "All I'm going to do is bum around down there a little. The idea of requiring cabaret licenses for these places sounds wrong to me, but I want to see what they're like anyway. Meet me at the entrance to the Central Park Zoo cafeteria, where the city officials are getting together for an annual supper and barbershop-quartet contest. I am going to miss the contest. I'm giving up the good old songs for Greenwich Village."

We arrived in front of the zoo cafeteria just as Mr. Isaacs, natty in a light-gray suit, a red-white-and-blue striped bow tie, a white shirt with blue stripes, and a panama hat with a blue band, was taking his leave of the city budget director, Abraham Beame. "So long, Abe, I'm going down to Greenwich Village," Mr. Isaacs practically sang out, as if he were breaking into one of the good old songs after all. A minute later, he was whistling up a taxi for us with as clear and powerful a tone as we have ever heard produced by two fingers between the teeth.

"I don't go down to Greenwich Village very much," Mr. Isaacs said as we headed there at a wild clip with a young Puerto Rican driver. "Mrs. Isaacs and I have a wonderful cook, so we usually dine at home. My only previous experience in a coffeehouse was at a place called The Premise. They had a show that my son, who celebrated his fiftieth birthday yesterday, told me I ought to see."

We remarked on the speed at which we were travelling.

"I'm a fatalist," Mr. Isaacs told us calmly, and went on, "I think these things about licenses are idiotic. The big question is: Should you have any licensing of coffeehouses that have entertainment— which means that everybody working there must have an identification card and get fingerprinted by the police, who are supposed to decide who is a 'fit and proper person' to have a card? What's the sense? Especially since there's no good test for 'fit and proper.' It doesn't mean anything. But I want to see whether these places are run decently, and the kind of people who frequent them—how they operate and what they sell. Things like that. I have no preconceptions about them. People say that the identification cards help control the dope peddlers by keeping out people with jail records. I'm in favor of keeping these places free of dope and of people with records, but I don't believe they should be barred for life, either. Young man," he said to the taxi driver, "where do you live?"

"Madison Avenue and a Hundredth Street," the driver said.

"Then you don't know much about Greenwich Village," Mr. Isaacs said. "That's all right. You haven't got much on me, but I haven't got much on you. Here we are—the Phase 2, at 302 Bleecker Street. Can you find your way back?"

The driver said yes, and Mr. Isaacs, looking reassured, got out of the taxi.

We entered the Phase 2, which, according to a sign at the entrance, features "American and Armenian Food—Shishkebab—Large Portions of Skewered Marinated Lamb Grilled with Fresh Slices of Tomatoes and Onions, $1.90," and were greeted just inside by the proprietor, a young man named David Gordon, who was wearing a rectangular mustache, shell-rimmed eyeglasses, and a conservative business suit. Mr. Gordon, representing the Village Coffee House Trade Association, was going to serve as Mr. Isaacs' guide for the evening.

"Why, you have air conditioning!" Mr. Isaacs said.

"We're more sophisticated than the next place, the Café Bizarre, which doesn't have air conditioning," Mr. Gordon said. "The Bizarre is more informal, more commercial, and caters to a younger crowd."

"Younger?" Mr. Isaacs asked, looking with glinting green eyes at the customers, most of whom had rather downy cheeks and at least six of whom were drinking milk.

"Your secretaries have arrived," Mr. Gordon said.

"I'm the luckiest guy in the world to have them," Mr. Isaacs remarked as we followed Mr. Gordon to a table, where we were introduced to Mr. Isaacs' "uptown" secretary, Miss Millicent Sturm, and his "downtown" one, Miss Joan Hamlin. "I can't make a move without one or the other of these ladies, and they know as little as I do about coffeehouses," Mr. Isaacs told Mr. Gordon as we all sat down.

"I've lived in the Village for seven years, but I've never been in anything," Miss Hamlin said.

"She's only interested in politics," Mr. Isaacs said, looking around. He seemed to miss nothing about the place: artistic photographs on one wall; a small stage opposite, with drawn curtain; an upright piano, with Tiffany lamp overhead; a pretty open-air garden in the rear.

"I've done a good deal of work inside, but the garden is where I feel I've been really creative," Mr. Gordon said, and Mr. Isaacs smiled paternally at him. "You'll find that coffeehouse owners and their friends have built their places practically with their own hands. As a matter of fact, coffeehouse owners give each other ideas to help each other out. That's why we have the Coffee House Trade Association."

"Excellent photographs," Mr. Isaacs said, looking around again. "Exceptionally nice crowd of youngsters."

With a small sigh, Mr. Gordon passed out menus.

"We don't want 'compliments of the house,' " Mr. Isaacs said. "That's against the rules."

"But you'll have something?" Mr. Gordon said anxiously.

"I may wait till we hit the next place," Mr. Isaacs said. "I had a big supper at the zoo cafeteria. I'm just feeling my way, trying to find out the advantage, if any, of a license. I can't figure out where the license itself fits in."

"It would cost me a hundred and fifty dollars for a cabaret license," Mr. Gordon said. "So far, we've successfully resisted efforts of the Police Department to make us get one. They say we're a cabaret because we serve 'beverages.' Well, coffee is a beverage, because you drink it, but it's not an alcoholic beverage. We believe that what makes a cabaret is alcohol. And we don't think that just because we have entertainment we ought to carry identification cards and have to get fingerprinted."

"On the financial side, do you do good business without liquor?" Mr. Isaacs asked.

"I make a living," Mr. Gordon said. "My interest is to make the Phase 2 a showcase for new talent. We change our show every six weeks, and we're beginning to package shows for Off Broadway and for other café theatres around the country. The one you're going to see tonight is called *Lighthearted*. It's a lyrical revue. Resident director, resident producer, resident musical director, original music and skits, four talented performers. The whole thing costs two hundred and sixty-five dollars a week."

"Whew!" Mr. Isaacs said, looking impressed.

After we had all watched *Lighthearted* (a quartet singing "New York is the perfect place to be lighthearted," a skit satirizing motivational research, a skit satirizing television commercials, and a parody of a Village folk singer, all included for a seventy-five-cent cover), Mr. Gordon led the expedition on foot through crowded Village byways to the next stop, the Café Bizarre.

"We're learning," Mr. Isaacs said gaily, beaming at the Villagers. "I never saw such life and energy as they have down here. This is the kind of thing we're losing in New York. I like to see people in the streets of New York. I don't want to see big housing developments down here. I like the whole advantage of the little streets, winding in all directions, that don't attract trucks and heavy traffic, so the kids can play in them. In that respect, I agree with Jane Jacobs, of *Architectural Forum*; she's an extremist, but I respect her highly. You get a neighborly feeling down here, and I think it should be preserved. Where I lived as a child, in an East Seventy-third Street brownstone, we used to sit outside on the stoop on hot nights with the neighbors and talk to each other. That's the kind of thing they seem to have held on to down here."

"Step right in and see the bohemians in their natural habitat," a bearded, blue-jeaned barker in front of the Bizarre called out with a laugh to Mr. Isaacs, who smiled and gave him a gracious nod.

"Anything goes down here," Mr. Isaacs said, and marched into the room—a converted stable hung with metal saws, chains, and anchors, plastic figures of spiders and insects, and Surrealistic combinations of oversized eyes and other anatomical parts. We were greeted by recited words, via loudspeaker (". . . the wind blows on me and feels like lemonade"), which turned out to be coming from a young lady poet, dressed in white slacks and a black blouse, who was standing onstage.

"This place isn't air-conditioned, but it's the most successful coffeehouse in the Village," Mr. Gordon said, and introduced a young man, Bernie Teichman, who, he explained, was acting as host in place of the owner, who couldn't be there that night. Mr. Teichman was in his shirtsleeves.

Mr. Isaacs nodded graciously to him. "That's a good idea, taking off your coat on this hot night," Mr. Isaacs said, and immediately took off his own coat.

Mr. Teichman produced menus featuring such delicacies as Mish-Mash, Voo-Doo, Scorpion, Baby Scorpion, Clam Dip-Potato Chip, Calypso Flip, Italian Ices, Bizarre Pâté (chopped liver), and The Cannibal (raw-chopped-steak-and-raw-egg canapés).

Mr. Isaacs ordered a dish of coffee ice cream. "This is different from anything I've ever seen," he said as the lady poet was succeeded onstage by a folk singer who accompanied himself on an Autoharp.

"We have aspiring young artists coming in here," Mr. Teichman said seriously. "Mr. Isaacs, this is probably the only area in America where new talent has an opportunity to perfect its talent in front of a real live audience. It's our view that we don't belong in the same category with the old girlie houses on Fifty-second Street. These young artists come in here, and we let them pass the hat around."

The lady poet went by, looking very chic in her white pants.

"I don't like tight, skinny trousers on older people," Mr. Isaacs told us, "but I think they're all right on the young people down here."

"Definitely," Mr. Teichman said.

"This place is so jammed, and all with these nice young people, who look as though they're having a good time," Mr. Isaacs said, digging into his coffee ice cream. "There's *life* down here. That's what counts, isn't it?"

✿✿ DAG HAMMARSKJÖLD

LATE last Friday night, we made our way to the United Nations Secretariat's thirty-eighth floor, where Dag Hammarskjöld had his office, and where he worked at all hours of the day and night. The floor looked as busy as ever, with Hammarskjöld's immediate staff much in evidence—undersecretaries, special assistants and advisers, stenographers and typists, and a security guard who had been given the extra duty of watching over a set of memorial books in which U.N. staff members had been writing tributes to the sixteen people killed five days earlier in the African plane crash that took the life of Hammarskjöld. The staff were at work, as vigorously as though it were the first, rather than the tenth, or eleventh, or fifteenth, hour of their day. One assistant who worked closely with Hammarskjöld for the eight and a half years the late Secretary-General occupied his post invited us to take a chair in his own office. There, he lit a cigarette, and, without letting go of a sheaf of papers he held in one hand, he half sat on the edge of his window sill, his back to a picture window showing the city's buildings alive with light, and talked to us for a while about Dag Hammarskjöld.

"It's very hard to realize he isn't here, particularly when you know you'll never see anyone like that again," he said. "He was the most extraordinary man any of us here have ever seen. He had fantastic spirit, discipline, energy, and intellect, and you very rarely find all these qualities in one person. He was a diffident, unpretentious, slim figure, but you always felt his grandeur. You couldn't touch it. He couldn't be made to look cheap. However, he had no false humility. He was the epitome of common sense and decency and calm, and I'm sure he wouldn't like it if he knew he was being subjected to superlatives after his death. He was dedicated to the common-sense notion that it was possible to do something about the ridiculous way in which civilized man was stuck in his predicaments, and he had the strength of mind and body and spirit to do it. He was often criticized for possessing the very characteristics that so superbly qualified him for his job. But he was never put off by criticism. He knew that there were only a certain number of hours in the day and that there was not much time to do what he had to do, so there was no point in descending to the common level.

"There's been considerable serious misunderstanding about him, and some people have tried to judge him by public-success standards, which he disliked. It's been said so often that he was a cold man. He wasn't like that at all. He was a very unsentimental man, because he thought that sentimentality got in the way of truth. He felt that to be liked was beside the point. He had no need to set up a popular image of himself. He knew that the idea of a popular image was absolutely irrelevant and a thundering waste of time. He wouldn't do personal-publicity things. Dag was extremely shy. He had strong ideas about propriety, about how people should behave, and about the value of restraint and dignity. Many people said that his job was impossible, but in eight years he proved that the job could be done, and he built the U.N. into a working instrument for peace. It's depressing to realize you've seen the last of someone absolutely splendid. There's quite a bit of dismay around here, of course. But there's a lot of work to do, and everyone wants to go ahead with it for Dag's sake, quite apart from other considerations. He was dedicated to the notion that it was possible to avoid disaster and that you just had to make every conceivable effort to do something about it, and that you could always do something about it without being tied to a political ideology. It was true, and he proved it was true. Now the only thing to do is to go on. He's made the U.N. an indispensable machine, and here it is.

"One finds oneself discussing Dag in superlatives, and yet it's difficult not to; one can't tone them down. Anything less doesn't meet the case. There are some terribly important things to remember about the uniqueness of the man. It starts with what he tried to do—to establish machinery for peace and common sense. Secondly, he had very high standards of objectivity. His basic notion was that a man could be objective and act for the common good. The Soviet Union maintains that no one man in that office can be objective, and that's why they think there should be a three-man staff for the office. Dag demonstrated, in action, that a man in the job can be objective. The Congo operation is a good example. He was attacked by every side and every faction, according to whom he wasn't pleasing at the moment. It was the same in every crisis. It was utterly clear to him exactly what the United Nations was trying to do in the Congo, and he went ahead with his basic idea of what was for the ultimate good—that the Congo was going to decide for itself the form of its state, with all its political parties reconciled in a democratic government that would not be disturbed by civil wars or tribal wars. If you set yourself a task as difficult and complex as that, you need the combination of qualities he had in order to go at it. He would think of all the history, all the problems, all the long-term probabilities, all the practical possibilities for action by the U.N., and then of how to get the support to do something about it. He would turn this large mass of data over in his mind and decide what we could do, what we should do, what the objective was, what the operating principle would be, and then he would devote himself to getting it done. It was a solitary effort. In solitude, he would bring all his intellectual and moral faculties to bear on the problem, until he had worked out a complete, constructive view, and then he would decide what to do about it. He had enormous powers of concentration. He had this vision of things, and the driving urge—and the ability—to turn a vision into a reality.

"I never heard him say he was tired. His powers of work were beyond what one thinks of as human. He'd go for months and months with a very few hours of sleep a night, and look as fresh as a daisy. I always wondered how he did it. I think he husbanded his energies. He would never fidget or be doing two things at once. At the General Assembly, he'd sit completely still. He ruled out social time-wasting. Instead, he did things that refreshed him. Like walking in the woods at his country place, near Brewster, New York, or along Jones Beach in the winter. He loved walking about by himself. He had great gusto and a sense of the life going on about him. He was always interested in everything. He wasn't a social man at all, but he had true *joie de vivre*. He adored good food and company and seeing new things. He was a complete man—a universal man, really. He lived in a coördinated way. He was not at all ascetic or puritanical. He knew an incredible amount, had an incredible memory. He had a strong aesthetic sense, and was always walking through the building here thinking about where a new piece of sculpture should go or whether a painting was in the best possible place. He loved sightseeing and taking photographs. It absorbed him and refreshed him.

"Dag used great intellectual powers in tackling problems, and great strength of will. He would select a target and go at it, developing principles from which all his actions would proceed. But to be effective, to maintain the course of reason and justice, on this rarefied level requires powers seldom found together in one man. Highminded declarations of principle are one thing, but political reality is something else. Dag was disciplined and inspired at the same time, he had a sense of purpose, and all his intellectual faculties were brought into the service of his convictions in the most precise, orderly way. I've never seen anyone who had such effortless mastery of a fluid situation. But he would always think out the principle first. Once the principle was fixed, he could act with speed and confidence. One became used to the idea that he was ahead of the game, that he was ready and waiting for it. He had this feeling of wanting to make it easy for people to accept his suggestions. With him, there was never any question of personal triumph. He was the servant of an idea—an idea passionately and ingeniously executed. He was enormously clever in appreciating the interaction of forces in any situation, in understanding the preoccupations, the fears, the emotions of people, and he had a remarkable knowledge of history, economics, and law. And all this was harnessed to his common sense. He was a force, a force of a very unusual kind. It was a force for justice, common sense, and decency. It was an influence outside the sphere of normal influences. He sailed right into the middle of crises and got everything on the rails again. There was never any nonsense about doing something tomorrow. As soon as he made a decision, he'd send out the cables to governments, the instructions to people in the field, and all the rest of it.

"On top of all that, he was an extremely interesting and complex person. He was a deliberately impersonal man. He had a contempt for smallness, pettiness, double-dealing. He'd really boil over about injustice or crookery. He very much disliked the notion of special privilege. He disliked pompous ceremonies and display. At the same time, he had an impeccable sense of form that was ingrained, even to such matters as seating arrangements at a dinner table. It was important, he felt, to avoid hurting people's feelings. Although he detested sentimentality, in cases of real disaster his immense compassion would appear, and he'd do something about it. He was supposed to be distant with his staff, which was true, but the moment anyone on duty was placed in an exposed position, he would lend his personal support to him. If he thought someone was saddled with too much of a load in some distant place, he'd take over the responsibility himself. Dag had an astonishing sense of duty, a feeling of ultimate responsibility. If hell broke loose somewhere, he'd always go there. He did it in such an unpretentious way that people didn't know the kind of personal courage it took. At the same time, he despised bravado, or unnecessary risk. He thought it was vulgar.

"We were all here till midnight the day of the crash. There'd been a lot of anxiety about Katanga for two weeks. Dag had been planning to go to the Congo to meet with the new Congolese government. When he heard that people were being killed in Katanga, he felt he had to go there. Whenever he heard of unnecessary death or destruction, he was always revolted and always felt he must try to stop it. And there it was. A lot of people felt uneasy about his going. He had absolute physical courage, and he went. The morning his plane was reported missing, we all got back here in the small hours. The news got worse and worse—what there was of it—and that was that."

It was past 1 A.M. As we stood up to leave, our U.N. friend said, "I've spoken emotionally, but I'm afraid it's like that." He paused, and then added, "One mustn't mourn too long. On your way out, you might want to look in on the U.N. Meditation Room, which Dag designed. You'll see an inscription on black marble at the entrance. Dag wrote it himself." We went downstairs and over to the ground floor of the General Assembly Building. On the black marble plaque at the entrance to the U.N. Meditation Room we read:

THIS IS A ROOM DEVOTED
TO PEACE
AND THOSE WHO ARE
GIVING THEIR LIVES
FOR PEACE

IT IS A ROOM OF
QUIET WHERE ONLY
THOUGHTS SHOULD SPEAK

🌿 THE FIRST ONE

LAST WEEK, we went to the new Children's Zoo, in Central Park, with a four-and-a-half-year-old from Brooklyn Heights named Victor, who showed up for the occasion in a tan windbreaker (with six pockets), blue corduroy overalls, red sandals, and a Davy Crockett coonskin cap. Under one arm he carried a plastic giraffe. The new zoo, which was donated by Governor and Mrs. Herbert H. Lehman to the children of the city, instantly had a soothing effect on us—ten-cent admission (the only ten-cent admission to anything we know of in town), highly comforting yellow ducklings to greet us at the entrance, fairy-tale structures, and occupants that were, like most of the visitors, very small and very easy to look at. So we looked, dreaming, mouth shut; followed Victor; and let him do the talking. He said:

"Hold the giraffe. I go to Prospect Park. I feed peanuts to the squirrels in Prospect Park. I never went to Central Park before. This is the first time I've been this close, in fact. Where are the squirrels? Look at that white swan! I want a drink of water, in fact. Look at the mouse! Look at the other mouse! Look at that goat! That's a mountain goat. Be careful of the puddle. You get crackers for the animals out of the machine. Let's look at the rooster. Boo! Maybe I could scare the duck. Nothing is in this house. A monkey used to live here. We have coyotes up in the country, in fact. Let's get some crackers. Llamas won't eat. Hey, look! A pony! Ponies won't eat. Could I go in here? Down the Rabbit Hole. Let's get some ice cream. Let's get some peanuts. Where are the squirrels? Look! Ducks! Swimming! If I was a grownup, I could dive in that water if it was a lake. Now let's go in here. Smell the hay! Is that a real cow? Moo. Is that a real calf? Could we touch the calf? Pigs! Pigs won't eat. Let's touch the rabbit. I touched him! Look at the waterfall!

We have coyotes up in the country. Hänsel and Gretel's house! It's made of gingerbread. They were safe. I like other stories better. We've got to go out this way. This is where the witch burned. I want a drink of water, in fact. The pigs are sleeping. The llama doesn't eat. That's not a swan. They're geese. Coo, coo. I'm the first one here to feed them. Don't fall in this water. The whale isn't spouting. Let's get some crackers. I fed the rabbit from my palm. He ate a little bit. Hey, look! Penguins! One penguin blinked. Let's get some candy. Let's get some ice cream. Let's get some peanuts. Can we get some later? The pigs woke up. I fed the pig. He ate a little bit. Let's go up here. It's a boat. Will this really move? Ducks! I'll throw a piece of cracker down. I'm the first one here to feed them. I want to hold the rabbit.

"They don't sell candy here. They have things here. Turtle. You wind it up. I don't want it. Spouting whale. I don't want it. Alligator. It creeps. Ducks. Bear. Piano. I like these two guns. Do they shoot real bullets? I don't want guns with real bullets. I want that other gun. Junior burp gun. It shoots missiles. I like this gun. I want that horse. The black one. I can ride on the stick. I want the gun and the horse. Maybe I could scare the animals with this burp gun. Hold this. Let's go down here. Look at the reindeer! Maybe I could scare the girl. I hate girls, so I scare them. I might scare some fish. I see some clams. I shot a clam. I scared some rabbits. These are missiles. Could I shoot the cow? Where are the squirrels? Where are the peanuts? These are missiles, in fact. Maybe I could scare the duck. Maybe I could scare the mountain goat. He moved. I shot him. Where are the squirrels? Where are the peanuts? Did you bring the peanuts? Did you bring the Tootsie Rolls? I want chocolate ice cream, in fact. I'll take these Tootsie Rolls. I'll take these peanuts. You want some Tootsie Rolls? These Tootsie Rolls are cute. I'll put them in my pockets. There's a squirrel. The squirrel is on the grass. Hold this. Hold this. And hold this. I want to feed the peanuts to the squirrel."

❦ ON BRECHT
ON BRECHT

THE CHARACTERS: George Tabori—A reedy, thoughtful writer with an untidy mustache who arranged and translated most of the material for the Off Broadway show Brecht on Brecht, which has a five-month run behind it and unlimited possibilities ahead.

Bob Currie—The production stage manager. A young man from Peoria, Illinois, who is paid $112.50 a week, which is the Off Broadway minimum pay for actors. He came to New York from Peoria one year ago.

The cast of Brecht on Brecht—Dane Clark, a handsome movie star; Anne Jackson, who is red-haired, lively, and the wife of the actor Eli Wallach; Lotte Lenya, widow of Kurt Weill, who was a close collaborator of Bertolt Brecht's; Viveca Lindfors, Tabori's wife, a beautiful and moody woman; George Voskovec, a hard-working actor who talks little offstage; Michael Wager, a boyish-looking actor who talks a lot offstage.

THE TIME: Late spring, 1962. A very warm evening.

THE PLACE: The Theatre de Lys, on Christopher Street.

SCENE 1: The Alleyway.
(The alleyway leading backstage is cluttered with garbage cans, ladders, planks, and assorted machinery. Currie stands at an open door, the side exit of the two-hundred-and-ninety-nine-seat theatre. Tabori enters through another door, leading backstage and to the dressing room above.)

TABORI: I've got to run across the street to get the actors some candy.

CURRIE: Fruit slices? From the Lilac Candy Shoppe?

TABORI: Life Savers. From Ethel's Delicatessen. And some coffee.

CURRIE: You know, that Ethel is a curious combination. Very nice and motherly, but efficient. Did you ever notice how she worries about all of us? She worries about the way Dane eats chocolate-covered jelly rolls. She says they're bad for his diet, but she can't resist selling them to him.

TABORI: Candy helps calm the actors. With no separate dressing rooms up there, it's a tremendous strain. One big, long room with a curtain separating the ladies from the gentlemen. It's like a Brechtian bordello. (*He runs across Christopher Street, returns on the double, and goes upstairs. Lotte Lenya walks in from the street.*)

LENYA: I usually am not so late. (*She hurries upstairs, passing Tabori on his way down.*)

CURRIE: She's a good sport about the democratic billing for the show. Everything about this show is done democratically.

TABORI: There's something very *jeune fille* about Lotte. She runs like a sixteen-year-old girl.

CURRIE: She's the main Brechtian artist in the country.

TABORI: As an artist, she's tremendous. Extraordinary. There is a discipline in Brechtian tone, in Brechtian style. Lotte knows exactly how to do it. Theories are fine, but the proof of the pudding is in the eating. Lotte knows Brecht's kind of controlled emotion. She knows how to project a statement he makes in a song. Lotte knows how to sing in direct address to the audience. There is a cult about Brecht. Eric Bentley is the Pope—the first man to write extensively in this country about Brecht and his work—and there are Martin Esslin and various other cardinals. They are all very scholarly, but I wouldn't want to write an essay on Brecht myself. The point is that Brecht wrote more about the theatre than any other dramatist. If he wanted to say something about props, he would write a poem about them. He was never pompous or solemn. He always gave the theatre superb and gracious treatment. He deserves the same.

CURRIE: They're taking places, Mr. Tabori, if you want to look through the peephole.

TABORI (*moving over to a peephole in the back curtain*): All this has been quite an education for the actors, of course. They all get a percentage of the receipts, in addition to the minimum pay; that brings them each about three hundred dollars a week, which is unusually high for Off Broadway. I try to keep a kind of coöperative thing going here. Everything we decide we decide by democratic vote. Difficult, but worth it. Brecht always used to look through a hole at the audience. He wanted to know why people in the audience should always look so miserable. (*He watches the show through the peephole for a while, then wanders back to the alleyway.*) The essential method by which Brecht worked was to dig up contradictions within each of his characters, many of whom are simultaneously rogues and heroes. In his work, Brecht always enjoys what he's doing. He has very little despair. His major works were written after he left Hitler's Germany. He never seemed to stop functioning. It's interesting how differently people react to exile. I was lucky. Some people were famous and middle-aged when they ran from Hitler. I was only eighteen.

CURRIE: Where were you born, Mr. Tabori?

TABORI: Budapest. In 1914. I am exposing you to a mumbling torrent of unconsidered trifles. But, as Brecht says in *The Caucasian Chalk Circle*, "There you stand, asking me a question, and there is nothing more seductive than a question." When people ask me how I am, I tell them. I have been infected by Brecht's celebrated greed for life and work. This is the Age of the Twaddle. The art of conversation is not dead, unfortunately; only it has lost the quality of dialogue. The best way of discussing Brecht is making neat, Chinese-type statements in a cool, neat room. Brecht's grave in Berlin, close to Hegel's, is apparently unmarked. But he once wished for the following epitaph: "Here lies B.B. He was angry, clean, and matter-of-fact."

CURRIE: I've been trying to get a vacation schedule worked out for the actors, Mr. Tabori. They keep talking about it, democratically. But I still don't know who's going away or when. Or who will be the replacements.

TABORI: So many good actors are eager to play in the show. I'd never make moral judgments about people in the theatre; they are all victims. Our theatre is like a jungle. Brecht said that the function of the playmaker is "to entertain the children of the Age of Science, in a gay, bright, and sensuous fashion," and that "true scientists do not have to protest their love of inquiry, the true rebels do not have to spout their rage at injustice."

CURRIE: Intermission, Mr. Tabori.

SCENE 2: *The Dressing Room.*
(*A long, narrow room, one side of which has a mirrored wall over a continuous stretch of white-formica-covered table, cluttered with individual heaps of makeup equipment, personal effects, newspapers, magazines, books, Life Savers, and fruit slices, and a gigantic bottle of aspirin tablets. Along the opposite wall are a coin-box telephone, in the ladies' section, and two cots, one for each sex. Michael Wager lies on the cot in the men's section, Viveca Lindfors on the other cot. The others sit ranged along the dressing table. Tabori is pacing back and forth.*)

DANE CLARK: There is a dearth of air in this dressing room.

LOTTE LENYA: This is theatre to me. On Broadway, the actors have individual dressing rooms. So what happens? Each dressing room becomes a little suburban home, and the maid comes and puts up curtains and the pictures of the children. Here I like it.

MICHAEL WAGER: This is the most luxurious dressing room Off Broadway.

GEORGE VOSKOVEC: We are a little bit like wild animals confined in one cage. We are on top of each other.

VIVECA LINDFORS: We are all dispensable here. Brecht is the personality, and we are dispensable. When are we taking our vacations?

MICHAEL WAGER: How is the audience tonight?

VOSKOVEC: Good.

ANNE JACKSON: Terrible.

CLARK: The late Saturday-night show—the ten-thirty one—is the toughest show of the week. That's when they've all had dinner, and it's sleepy time down South.

WAGER: Last night, I had a visitor from the audience. My nature counsellor from camp thirty years ago. Camp Keeyumah, on Lake Champlain. Imagine! Being visited by your nature counsellor after thirty years!

LINDFORS: This show gets a high type of audience.

CLARK: In the beginning, we got aficionados. Now we get very young people.

LENYA: Half the audience understands us, the other half comes because Brecht is this year's playwright to know.

CLARK: There's a tremendous lost audience in this city.

LENYA: Don't think the Berlin audience wasn't made by snobs, too, in 1928. Brecht now is like a new toy. *Threepenny Opera* was done here in 1933, *Mother* in 1935, and *Galileo* in 1947, and nobody came.

WAGER: I am so hungry. I would like to eat a Pepeburger, with hamburger, cheese, onion, lettuce, tomato, pickle, and potato chips.

CLARK: You and Lotte, the way you two eat! You've got the constitution of a horse.

LENYA: You have a nervous stomach from too many chocolate-covered jelly rolls.

JACKSON: What every actor needs is a moment of silence.

WAGER: Annie, you didn't bring me anything to eat tonight.

JACKSON: Last night, I brought you a huge veal-and-sliced-onion-and-tomato sandwich from my friend Vivian Nathan's house. I am a well-known actress, and for you I marched through the streets carrying this veal sandwich wrapped in tinfoil. Now, will you please show your gratitude by switching your vacation time, so that I can take my month with Eli before he goes to England to make a movie?

WAGER: My daughter is going to Israel in June to visit my father and mother, and I want to go with her.

LINDFORS: Annie, if I go with George to Fire Island this month, will you do my Jewish-wife scene?

JACKSON: Does that mean I won't get my vacation with Eli? Do you think that is right? Do you think that is fair? Do you think that is just?

WAGER: My father, Meyer Weisgal, who is in Israel, should take precedence over everything else, because he co-produced *The Eternal Road* here, in 1937.

JACKSON: How can we decide? With six actors, six administrators?

LINDFORS: We talk and come to a mature decision.

CLARK: Equality doesn't work. Democracy here doesn't work.

(*The telephone rings. Anne Jackson answers it.*)

JACKSON: Oh, Eli! I heard about a wonderful house in the country. On top of a hill. I immediately saw myself, Eli, running in a dotted-Swiss dress. . . .

TABORI: I want to add some new material to the show. Some poems I just translated. They will make the show even better. Actually, it was Brecht who said, "Nothing is easier than to change a play; nothing is more difficult than to improve it."

LINDFORS: You're fortified in this show by language and ideas. You feel as though you're giving important evidence.

JACKSON (*into telephone*): Yes, Eli, darling, I'll try to get them to take the vote on vacations tonight.

(*She hangs up. Voskovec has been reading a Czech-language magazine. He looks up blankly for a moment and then returns to his reading. Dane Clark nods at him.*)

CLARK: You're always reading fifteen things at once. What are you reading now?

VOSKOVEC (*apologetically*): Sort of a commemorative article. And an interview with my old partner Jan Werich, in Prague. In connection with the thirty-fifth anniversary of the first play he and I did together there—*The Vest Pocket Revue*.

WAGER: Lotte has vast knowledge that we don't have. She's fifty-seven and just coming into her own now.

LINDFORS: She's a very special woman. Whatever she tells you, you pay attention. One day, she said to me, "Don't lose your intensity." Another time, she said, "As an actress, you go out and do your best, but remember, it's not *all* important."

LENYA: I signed a contract in 1959 to write my autobiography. All I have written so far is "I am born." When you write an autobiography, it must be not only a hundred per cent true but it must be three hundred per cent true. Otherwise, it is just a made-up thing.

JACKSON: There is one thing that troubles me, Lotte, about the poem where Brecht lists all the good things.

LENYA: Yes. "The first look through the window in the morning, an old book lost and found, enthusiastic faces, the snow, the change of seasons, newspapers, dogs, debating, taking a shower or a swim, old music . . . comfortable shoes, to write, to plan, to travel, to sing, to be friendly."

JACKSON: Yes, and it seems to me that he left out one very important thing.

LENYA: To be friendly is harder than to make love. When you say "to be friendly," you cover everything. To be friendly.

❧ PIONEERS

LAST WEEK, we accompanied Harris L. Wofford, Jr., Special Representative for the Peace Corps for Africa, as he drove seventy-five miles upstate to greet five dozen freshly recruited volunteers for the Teachers for Sierra Leone Peace Corps Project. Mr. Wofford had just resigned as Special Assistant to President Kennedy on the Peace Corps and on Civil Rights in order to assume his new job. The training site, and our destination, was the State University College, in New Paltz. Mr. Wofford, driving a rented car and accompanied by a young diplomat named J. C. W. Porter, who is Third Secretary to the Sierra Leone Embassy in Washington, picked us up, by prearrangement, in front of the new local Peace Corps office, a store front on East Forty-second Street that is staffed by attractive, steady-eyed young people and festooned with decorative brochures ("TEACHERS in the Peace Corps," "WOMEN in the Peace Corps," "AMERICAN LABOR in the Peace Corps," "HEALTH PROFESSIONS in the Peace Corps," "YOU and the Peace Corps"). We got into the front seat with Mr. Wofford. Mr. Porter told us he had some papers he'd like to spread out in the rear, and after Wofford had dutifully pointed out a traffic jam, an Automat, the United Nations headquarters, and the Triborough Bridge, Porter said he was going to work on his notes for a speech he was scheduled to make to the recruits.

Wofford, a tall, broad-shouldered man of thirty-six, with a ringing voice and a kind of All-America handsomeness, told us that in August he plans to move from Chevy Chase to Addis Ababa, with his wife, Clare, and their three children—Susanne, Daniel, and David, who are ten, seven, and two. "The greatest future of the Peace Corps is in Africa," he said. "I've been to Africa four times this past year. Each time I got there, I felt myself going into high gear. I had the feeling of being in tune with the world. In my new job, I'll be administrator of the Ethiopian program as well as the representative for our work in all the other African nations. I'm campaigning to recruit three hundred teachers for the secondary schools of Ethiopia—that's about as many teachers as they've got now. The population of the country is twenty million. Almost a million Ethiopian children should be in academic secondary schools, but only six thousand are. The population of Sierra Leone is two and a half million, and no more than seven thousand children attend the equivalent of high school. The Peace Corps sent about forty teachers over there six months ago, and of this new batch that we're going to see now we hope to send forty or fifty more. The Peace Corps is only a year old, and we've got a thousand volunteers working now, in fourteen countries all over the world—minimum age, eighteen; maximum age, unlimited. We'll have two thousand, in twenty-seven countries, by September, and five thousand by 1963.

"The Peace Corps is the main embodiment of the New Frontier. President Kennedy says that the Peace Corps is going to restore the American spirit. I happen to feel that the Peace Corps is awakening our slumbering pioneering traditions. As a lawyer, I know that lawyers are all frustrated founding fathers. Lawyers would like to have been around when our Constitution was written. They would like to have chartered all the basic institutions of the country. Well, we've just launched a program to recruit lawyers into the Peace Corps. We've got forty law schools in the country lined up to coöperate with us. We'll give the lawyers a chance to work as clerks in Ministries and in the African courts, to assist in drafting codes, and to teach in the new law schools. But law is just one part of what the Peace Corps can help create in Africa. It's all so wide open. And limited only by our imagination. It's an empty continent. In Asia or in Latin America, the poverty, in a way, closes in on you. But in Africa you can drive fifty miles and not see anybody. You get a feeling there that must be like what the people felt who first saw America. Africans are a young people, making history. They're starting out with a clean slate and writing on it what they want to write. Their No. 1 investment is in education. We in the Peace Corps want to encourage the African countries to think even bigger than they've been thinking so far in terms of moving ahead. By doubling the secondary-school populations this year, we'll develop hundreds of college graduates qualified to teach school in Africa, and we'll really be on our way."

A light glinted in Wofford's eyes. Glancing behind us, we saw Porter completely absorbed in his notes. "Why Africa for you?" we asked Wofford. "Why not stick around in Washington, and go to a few parties?"

"White House social life has added a certain lustre to social life around the country, a certain radiance," Wofford said. "But I believe in forming the world you want to create as well as you can with what's within your reach—a political clue I learned from Gandhi. My whole life so far has been a rhythm between the race question in the world and the race question at home. I call one the big integration and the other the little integration. During the Presidential campaign, I helped draft the civil-rights section of the Democratic platform. I kind of resisted the Peace Corps for a long time, because I felt I ought not to try to do something that was so natural for me. But I couldn't hold out any longer. In my letter of resignation, I told the President that it was time, I felt, to work not from a desk in Washington but from where I want to live, in Africa, where I'll be constantly on the scene. He wrote back with complete understanding and warm good wishes."

"Well," we said, "how did all this start? Where were you born?"

"In New York City, on April 9, 1926," Wofford said. "I grew up in Johnson City, Tennessee, and in Scarsdale. My maternal grandmother came from Little Rock. We were very close. When I was eleven—the last year I was eligible to travel at half fare—she took me out of school for seven months, which we spent travelling around the world on tramp steamers. I saw sixteen countries. In Rome, I heard Mussolini roar from his balcony the night he cancelled Italy's membership in the League of Nations. In India, I saw the poverty of Bombay and Calcutta. After Pearl Harbor, while I was at Scarsdale High School, Clarence Streit's idea for the Atlantic Community took hold of me, and in the name of the Federalists, who transformed the alliance of the thirteen American colonies into a true federation, I founded the Student Federalists. I was its first national president. My wife, by the way, was its third national president. We met at the first national convention. I graduated from high school in 1944 and spent twenty months as an Air Force trainee at

Craig Field, Alabama, after which I attended the University of Chicago, graduating in 1948. Then I got married, went to India and Pakistan with my wife for seven months, came home, and wrote a book with her called *India Afire*. After that, we wanted to go to Israel, and we did. We worked on a *kibbutz* and looked over the country quite thoroughly. When we got home, I decided to study law at Howard University. It was 1950, a very creative period in civil-rights law, and the center of all the litigation was at Howard. Also, I'd never been in a position to know many Negroes, and the chance to be a fellow-student of Negroes appealed to me very much. I didn't think it would hurt me to be a member of a minority for a while. After getting full law degrees from both Howard and Yale, I became a special assistant to Chester Bowles. I also practiced law in Washington pretty regularly, until 1958, with the firm of Covington & Burling. In 1959, I joined the faculty of Notre Dame Law School and taught for a year; I have been away on a leave of absence ever since. The things that interest me are everywhere."

Arriving in New Paltz, we drew up before a brick dormitory building assigned to Peace Corps trainees, and Wofford said, "Mr. Porter, do you have your speech?"

"I will thank the volunteers for leaving all comforts here to go to Sierra Leone," Porter said, "and warn them that the first few months they may be treated with indifference, but the indifference will go away when they show they came to help, not to dominate. I will say, 'Go there with an open heart and do a good job.'"

To the strains of "Home, Sweet Home" piped haltingly on a recorder by some invisible trainee, we went inside, and there we were immediately enveloped by a throng of very young-looking trainees: "I'm Rufus Stevenson, Newman, Georgia, which I left at 6 A.M. this morning." "I'm Judy Salisbury, Westfield, New Jersey, and I'm rather surprised to be going to Sierra Leone." "I'm Thomas Birnberg, Los Angeles, California." "I'm Bill Whitten, Milwaukee, Wisconsin." "I'm Bob Gross, New York City." "I'm Bill Prosch, Birmingham, Alabama." "I'm Bill Graham, Falls Church, Virginia. I'm going to teach history. How can those Africans have a sense of their world without history?" "I'm Bruce Pearson, Greenwich, Connecticut."

Then we met some Peace Corps administrators: "I'm Dr. Joseph

Murphy, and I teach political philosophy at Brandeis University. I decided to spend my summer working for the Peace Corps. One thing that anybody from the academic world finds when he associates himself with the Peace Corps is that the volunteers have more resourcefulness, more intelligence, more energy, more enthusiasm, more of everything than you'll ever see in the average undergraduate." "I'm George Goba. I teach Mende, the main language of the biggest tribe in Sierra Leone. I come from Taiama, a town of three thousand in Sierra Leone. Taiama has the best bridge in the country. I am so proud of that bridge. My mother still lives in Taiama, and many of my friends. They write that a Peace Corps girl came to Taiama, and they asked her to show them how to do the Twist, and she did not know, and they laughed and laughed at her ignorance. I wrote to my friends and said I had met some Americans here who asked me to show them how to do the High Life, the popular African dance, and I did not know, and they laughed and laughed at my ignorance. I left Taiama six years ago, when I was twenty-three, and I hope to go back when I become a doctor. I am studying medicine at Fairleigh Dickinson University. I used to be a houseboy for missionaries in Taiama, and when my father died they helped me come to America to study. My sister Nancy, who is twenty-one, has just come to America. She is in the state of Indiana studying to become a nurse." "I am Dr. David Crabb. I was born in Newark, New Jersey. I am an anthropological linguist. I teach Swahili. Anybody can speak Swahili. There's nothing to it."

And, finally, we attended a dinner in honor of the trainees and listened to the official welcoming speech, given by Wofford: "Everywhere you go in the world you meet American education coming back. . . . In a very real sense, we are going to learn as much as we teach . . . to see whether we of the West, the true minority of the world, can become integrated with the new world, whether we can join the human race. . . . The New Frontiers are not in Washington. . . . They are out where you are going. . . ."

❧ REALISM

THE ANNUAL BOOM in the filming of television commercials for the coming season is on right now, and we were easily lured, one soggy day last week, to a new, fresh-cement-smelling production studio on West Fifty-ninth Street, near the river, to see one made. This particular drop in the TV-commercial bucket—it's a fifty-million-dollar bucket—was to celebrate the virtues of Liberty Mutual Insurance, which was represented, in the usual hierarchy of television, by the advertising agency Batten, Barton, Durstine & Osborn, which, in turn, had enlisted the services of an independent firm known as Elektra Film Productions, and it was the president of Elektra, Abe Liss, a slight man with a modest air, a soft-sell voice, and a black beard like young Dr. Freud's, who took us in tow.

"The move today is toward realism and believability," Mr. Liss said mildly as he led us up to a sound-stage group of sports-shirted movie-makers sitting around on canvas chairs, hovering over a thirty-five-millimetre camera on a dolly, or standing under five-thousand-watt cone lights and seven-hundred-and-fifty-watt spotlights. "What we do at Elektra is try to have some respect for the audience. No talking down. No turning the stomach into a machine. They say that hypochondriacs like to see a stomach that looks like a machine, but not me. The horrible part of this business is it's very competitive, and you usually wind up working for everybody who asks you. Still, I like to think that if you're an artist, you try to find your way in many areas. Every problem has its special solution. We always try for a new and fresh approach—not loud. My attitude is we're imposing on the audience; we have an obligation to entertain it. Here we've been doing industrial-accident-prevention commercials, and now we're working on one that shows how Liberty Mutual rehabilitates injured hands. We put in eight weeks of work on the production, during which we made a story board—drawings showing each sequence of each film. The ad agency's writer went up to Liberty Mutual's Rehabilitation Center, in Boston, and researched the facts, and then worked with us on the story board. The agency's own story board, prepared by its art director, is, as you see, set up here. It winds up: 'The Man Who Sells Protection in Depth Works Only for Liberty Mutual. Call Him In.' Most of these props that you see around—the blood-plasma-transfusion setup, the finger-pulling weight machine—come directly from Boston. We've already filmed 'Exercise,' 'Encouragement,' and 'Cut to Therapist As She Massages Man's Hands.' Those scenes have been crossed out on the board. They're getting ready now to shoot 'Thumb Exercise.'"

"How long will this movie run?" we asked.

"Sixty seconds," Liss replied. "There are two films of one minute each. We spend a day of actual shooting on each film. We get paid nine thousand dollars for each one. The studio rental costs three hundred dollars a day. Camera and lenses, a hundred dollars a day. Film costs about fifty dollars a day. Our cameraman gets paid a hundred and fifty dollars a day. Our makeup man, seventy-five dollars a day—actors are not allowed to put on their own makeup. Assistant cameramen and assistant directors, fifty dollars a day. Electricians, grips, script clerks, and about a dozen of the other people you see standing around here, they get about fifty dollars a day, too. In addition to which we have two Elektra staff men—a director and a camera director—who each get about three hundred and fifty dollars a week in salary. We've got two actors under the lights, as you can see—the worker being given therapy, and a lady therapist. They get about a hundred dollars a day each. Each actor gets additional pay, called residuals, for repeated use of a commercial—it can run into the thousands—which is one fee that the client pays, thank God."

"That li'l old winemaker must be making a fortune," said an assistant director who was standing nearby. "He's been on for years. Every time he's shown, he gets paid residuals."

"I got a friend, a very chic actor," a grip said. "He's the one they always get when they need someone in black tie, because he's so chic, so believable. They always call on him. He just bought himself a yacht!"

"All part of the truth trend," Liss said.

"Realism!" the grip said. "Some of them housewives they show selling stuff, my own opinion is they're so real they're driving the men out of the home, away from the set."

Liss led us closer to the camera and introduced us to a B. B. D. & O. man named Earl McNulty, a Liberty Mutual physical therapist from Boston named Ann Fleishhauer, and the director of the film, Paul Harvey. Harvey was explaining that he wanted what he called "a sober-congenial atmosphere" for a two-second scene of the one-minute movie that would show a therapist giving a worker a thumb exercise. "There's a difference between reality and camera reality," Harvey said. "Through camera reality, we give the impression of more reality."

"The American Physical Therapy Association is going to be watching us," Miss Fleischhauer said. "It's got to be realistic, you know."

"The possibilities are infinite," McNulty said. "We'll shoot and shoot until we get the shot that looks best."

"When they do that thumb grasp, the fingers have got to bend," Miss Fleischhauer said. "The thumb grasp is important. It's the difference between man and the ape."

"We got the finger-weight scene authentic, we'll get the thumb-grasp scene authentic," Harvey said. "Even if I have to go gray."

"That's why I've stressed the Therapy Association patch that the girl wears," Miss Fleischhauer said.

"Action!" called the director, and everybody went back to his station, whereupon the camera rolled on the two-second thumb scene. At the end of it, we fell in with the two principals of the drama. The actor was Bob Pointer, a handsome young man with a Texas drawl, who told us that he is a ninety-nine-per-cent-television-commercial actor, and that he has five children to support. "I smoke cigarettes and puff smoke out for the cameras," he said. "I have played the parts of a new-car owner, a doctor plugging insurance, a smoker of Phillies cigars (they let me dress the way I like, in blue jeans, denim shirt, mackinaw, and one of my Texas hats, which I love so much), a husband in a supermarket buying soap, and a husband kissing his wife in the doorway of his home, for Quaker Oats. The idea of that one is you eat oats and go off to work full of pep. I've had to kiss some pretty old clams in front of the camera. It's my only regret, as an actor. Otherwise, I usually feel pretty real."

"I'm a *real* registered nurse," the actress, an attractive, dark-haired girl named Eleanor Lewis, told us. "I've worked in obstetrics at Doctors Hospital, for people like Hal March's wife and Otto Preminger's wife, but I've also had training as an actress and as a singer. I still do nursing when things get slow."

"Do they ask you if you like their products?" Pointer said to her. "They do me."

"Almost always," Miss Lewis replied. "They want authenticity."

"You see?" Liss said to us. "The move toward realism."

❦❦❦NO NONSENSE

LAST WEEK, over tea at the Algonquin, we had a most sensible talk with Joan Plowright, who is playing one of the leads in the new hit *A Taste of Honey*. Miss Plowright is thirty, big-eyed, hoarse-voiced, energetic, and all set to have a great time in New York. Her hair is gamin-cut, and when we saw her it was wind-blown. She arrived wearing a bright-orange scarf around her neck, small pearl earrings, a Jaeger camel's-hair suit, with a three-quarter-length jacket buttoned up tight, and beige-and-white Italian pointed pumps. She had, clearly, a heavy first-of-the-city's-season cold, and she was, clearly, enjoying even that.

"There's a bit of a wind out," she told us with zest, keeping her jacket buttoned up. "I've just walked over from the Lyceum, where I'm told I have the oldest dressing room in New York. It's sort of like a rabbit hutch. I've been trying to make it look like a bandbox. I waited until the middle of the second week after the opening, then, after all the notices were in, I went over to that big sort-of-everything shop, Stern's, and bought some curtains for the dressing room —some white satin-brocade ones with big roses that go very nicely with the peeling gray walls. I shall have to do something about those walls. For the present, I have these lovely curtains over two sort of cupboards for clothes and sort of around the passageway. Four pairs for fifty dollars. I do suppose that's awfully extravagant, but one's dressing room is really very important. One spends so much time there. I get there at seven and leave about a quarter to twelve. It's really in a way one's home."

The tea arrived, and she put lemon in it and took a sip. "Ah, good!" Miss Plowright said, smacking her lips and giving the single word a reading that made us feel like drinking endless tea. We asked her what she planned to be doing during her free hours. She said

"Ah," took another sip of tea, and replied "Well, I'm going to spend a lot of time in all of your sort-of-everything shops, particularly the ones where you get those marvellous foods all ready to go. I have a flat on East Fifty-first Street. You can see the East River from it if you stand sidewise. Food is so much more easy here—sort of vegetables and salads all done—and as soon as I'm settled in, I plan to try those. Then, I want to go to the art galleries. I go by myself, so I don't have to pretend to talk about it. I like to look at the pictures. I find it satisfying. I find it helpful in my work, actually. It does stir one's imagination. I did a bit of walking around last time I was here, two and a half years ago, in *The Entertainer*. It's so much more exciting now, of course, because now I have a leading part, which I didn't then, and I have so much more responsibility. I come here now without that first thrill at seeing New York, but there is a familiarity one feels now, like coming home. Last time, I did a bit of riding in Central Park, and I hope to get at it again shortly. I wouldn't say that I'm terribly good on a horse, but I'm safe. I used to ride a lot as a child. I had a pony, and later my own horse. We lived near a farm, and my two brothers and I kept our horses there, and appeared in all the local gymkhanas, which I believe you call horse shows. My brother Robert is now thirty-two. He's a lecturer on music at Trinity College, Cambridge, and a composer. He's married and has one child. My brother David is news editor of Granada Television in Manchester. He's married and has two children. I love them all."

Another sip of tea, and Miss Plowright went on, "I was born and brought up in the town of Scunthorpe, in Lincolnshire, about two hundred miles north of London and about thirty miles from Grimsby, a fishing town on the coast. We were in the border country to Yorkshire. It's good, flat land—good for cattle raising, potatoes, sugar beets, that sort of thing. I suppose my speech is characteristic of the North Country. My father has been editor of the Lincolnshire *Star* for twenty-five years. He wanted me to be a journalist or a teacher—of English, presumably. He didn't want me to go on the stage. My mother ran an amateur dramatic society, and still does. She is the shining light of Scunthorpe. Population, sixty thousand. We were always having some sort of rehearsal in our garden, and model theatres and scenery were being painted all over the house. When I was twelve, I played Elizabeth in *Pride and Prejudice*, with David playing Darcy and Mother playing the mother. But Dad wouldn't act for anything. Bob was always round the orchestra. When I was fourteen, I wanted to leave the high school and get a job on the stage, and we had a lot of arguments in the family. When I was seventeen, Dad let me go, when I got a scholarship to the Old Vic Theatre School. He said, 'You'll be back home in six months.' Even when I was in repertory and began to think I could act, Dad said, 'So what? There's plenty about with talent. Don't waste your life.' In 1956, in London, he saw me play my first lead—in *The Country Wife*—and he gave in and said, "Well, all right.' North Country people are famed for saying very little, and that was a lot, coming from him. We're supposed to be rather earthy and a straightforward, no-nonsense type of people. I think I'm fortunate in being from the North Country. For an actress, it's a bit of an asset that stands you in good stead when your nerves are being tried. It guards you against neurosis sort of things overtaking you. You don't get in a great flap about everything. If you make mistakes, you make mistakes, and you don't make them again. You take failure calmly, and you take success calmly. You know how to appreciate success only when you know what it is to fail. I do think my parents gave me a wonderful sort of character training. My father has that guts sort of thing to withstand disappointment and to strengthen determination, and I think I have some of that from him. I do enjoy acting in New York, although the theatre is universal. When you hear the call 'Beginners!' it's the same the world over. An audience is an audience, but the enthusiasm of people here is more openhearted. In London, people don't come round and shake your hand and say they enjoyed the play, but they do here."

🌷🌷MR. KENNETH REVISITED

OUR INDOMITABLE New Frontierswoman Miss Rogers occasionally breaks away from her secretarial desk, runs off on some outlandish reporting assignment she has given herself, and returns to our office with a set of notes. Here is the latest, handed in last week:

"Kenneth just opened his own beauty salon in magnificent Edwardian mansion at 19 East Fifty-fourth Street. Who, in true first-on-moon spirit, was very first client to go through portals and sign in? Me! First under welcoming red-and-yellow plastic canopy! First in wig room, which has frieze of orange and red lacquer stripes interspersed with baguette-shaped mirrors. First to try on pale-pale-champagne-colored, shoulder-length, eleven-hundred-dollar wig for French-roll coiffure! First in front of huge Georgian mirror reflecting staircase carpeted with Indian jungle-flower design and lighted by Chinese-vase lamps! First to take sauna bath! First to get massage! First to have hair cut by Kenneth in new joint! First in everything! First! Was ushered into Royal Dressing Room—mansion's former kitchen. Palatial cold closet of mansion now closet for clients' fur coats. Individual dressing room for everybody, wallpapered in Paisley design on white. Given choice of colored robes. 'These were designed by Kenneth himself,' usherette told me. 'Want the yellow? Red? Blue? Colorful Indian jungle print? The colors blend with the different rooms. Kenneth's own room is yellow Paisley.'

" 'The yellow robe,' I said.

" 'Yellow poncho,' usherette said. 'Kenneth prefers to call them ponchos.'

"In yellow poncho, passed second-floor main styling room. 'A trompe-l'oeil effect here,' usherette said. 'Everything is papered in a bamboo-trellis design. The atmosphere is that of the Brighton Pavilion. The Regency chairs are of bamboo covered in red silky vinyl. The pagodas are of bamboo with straw-cloth roofs, and are lacquered in red inside. That's where we stash the towels.' Glimpsed main drying room. Pack of crazy-eyed clients piling up behind me. Was first to see breathtaking tent of Paisley on red, draped from Paisley walls. Wicker chairs cushioned in black-crocodile-patterned linen, with dryers echoing color scheme. Cries behind me from other crazy-eyed clients: 'Where's Mary Farr? I want Mary Farr to set my hair!' 'Where's William? I want William to set my hair!' 'Where's Ralph?' 'Where's Angela?' Nobody else getting Kenneth first. Reserved.

"Into sauna, on fourth floor. Sauna marvellous. 'Lie down,' nurse-uniformed sauna lady commanded me. 'Hot stones make heat. You sweat from yourself. When you have heat in yourself, Kenneth prefers you take cold shower after. It's healthy.' Reading matter in sauna on poster: 'Cecil Ellis Authentic Finnish Bath. If you are taking a sauna for the first time, don't think you are in for an ordeal.' Some ordeal! Continued reading. 'Sauna is a wonderful place where tensions ease, and aches and pains are soothed with a magical touch. Sauna is more than a bath, it is a way of life. . . . The secret is DRY heat. . . . R-E-L-A-X. Don't be alarmed if the thermometer reads 180 deg or even 212 deg Fahr.' Looked at thermometer. Said 180 deg Fahr. Who alarmed? Continued reading. Directions said to stay as long as felt comfortable, to go in and out of sauna. 'In intervals, rest, read, play cards, swim, take a nap, or roll in the snow,' poster read.

"Out of sauna. R-E-L-A-X-E-D. Into shower. Cheated. Took hot shower. Sauna way of life my way of life. Hot shower my personal touch. Was given yellow towel to match poncho. Off to massage. Slapped around. Toned up. Shipshape, à la directives from you-know-where. Down to shampoo room, on Kenneth floor—third. Clean room. Functional. Crisp. All black and white. Black-vinyl-covered shampoo chairs. 'Kenneth doesn't like shampoos done in his private room,' usherette told me. 'We got a secret private room, on the first floor, where everything can be done, but that's only for top-secret emergencies. Like when we get a wife and an ex-wife in at the same time.' Was delivered glowing to Kenneth in Kenneth's private room. WOW-EE! Nothing but the B-E-S-T. Lacquer-yellow Paisley wall-paper. Indian jungle-flower-print shades. Sconces. Full of antiques. Was seated before antique silver-leaf Regency console table with rose marble top. Custom-made barber-type chairs in lacquer-brown leather. Usherette explained, 'Hair rollers and clips are stashed in covered wicker baskets on rolling stands. Kenneth prefers that beauty-salon-type items be hidden. Note the classy Porthault towels stashed in antique-frame glass cabinets. Only Kenneth clients get Porthault towels—in five patterns. Want a cup of coffee?'

" 'Coffee go,' I said.

"Kenneth showed for No. 1. No glow on Kenneth. Looked like wreck. 'Toothache,' he said. 'I've got to have a tooth pulled tomorrow. Got a headache, too. It will be five whole weeks before everything is perfect. Billy Baldwin was the decorator. He did a wonderful, fast job—eight months. I have associates who gave me enormous financial backing—also a free hand. No interference. No strings. The legal name is Kenneth Beauty Salons & Products, Inc. This is now my salon. Purely, truly mine. For a beauty salon, we're out on an awfully long limb.' My kind of limb. Kenneth started cutting.

" 'Giving me a shell cut?' I asked.

" 'I'm giving you a cut to make your hair controllable,' Kenneth said. 'I don't believe much in names. Your hair is curly. It's strong hair. It almost tells you what it's going to do.'

"I shut up and let hair tell Kenneth.

" 'Stretch,' Kenneth told hair. 'Pull. Soak. Stretch. It looks quite wonderful after it's done.'

"O.K. by me. Usherette put Chock full o'Nuts cardboard container of coffee on table.

" 'It churns me to see a cardboard container on my rose marble silver-leaf console, which I found in a warehouse in New Orleans,' Kenneth said. 'Please put the coffee in Kenneth china.'

"Got coffee back in Kenneth china. 'I want her to have a manicure and a pedicure while her hair is drying,' Kenneth told usherette. Was shipped upstairs to facial room. Put in large chair covered in French-blue linen. Footrest comfy. French-blue dryer lowered over head. Pedicure started by Mirta. Manicure started by Sophie. Closed eyes. Felt cream being spread on face. Opened eyes and saw lady in French-blue smock spreading cream—introduced herself as Mrs.

Read. Very cultured manner. Yum, yum. 'I want to get at your eyebrows,' Mrs. Read said. Said O.K. but wanted vigorous, G-O, healthy look of nineteen-sixties. Mrs. Read started on eyebrows. 'You don't need pencil. Many ladies do. You have a natural healthy look. Your eyebrows are beautiful.' Mrs. Read brushed beautiful eyebrows, then put on makeup. Kenneth lipstick. Kenneth polish on toes. Kenneth polish on fingers.

"Kenneth bells on fingers and toes, returned to Kenneth floor. Finished drying hair on one of many red chaise longues with matching dryers. After dryer was switched off, heard crazy-eyed client talk about getting Alberto's exercises on sauna floor, so when Kenneth was giving me comb-out, asked him how about Alberto's exercises. 'It's a Greek thing he gives to the Green Bay Packers, and this is the first time anybody has got it for beauty,' Kenneth said. 'You need fifteen weeks of it or it's a waste of time.' Hair controllable! Eyebrows beautiful! Bill only fifty-two fifty, not including tips. Did it all for my country."

ꙮ THE FACE OF ANYBODY

ONE NIGHT last week, in a suite on the forty-sixth floor of the Americana Hotel, we stood—along with a half-dozen other admirers—around an upright piano at which sat Charles Aznavour, the French songwriter, singer, and movie star. He was playing and singing his five-hundred-and-eighth, and latest, composition—approximately four hours old—which was entitled "Qui." Aznavour, who is of Armenian descent, is small and tightly put together, with enormous Armenian eyes and a dry little Existentialist face, but he has a strong voice. To a Slavic-Oriental-sounding melody, and with a Gallic inch-long Gitane dangling from his lower lip, he sang:

> "Qui frôlera tes lèvres
> Et, vibrant de fièvre,
> Surprenant ton corps,
> Deviendra ton maître
> En y faisant naître
> Un nouveau bien-être,
> Un autre bonheur?"

The admirers—two men, four women—responded with cries of "Sharl! Sharl!" and bursts of compliments in French. The girls were all very pretty, very alert, and very smily, and all wore new-style flapper hairdos, plenty of makeup, and sleeveless black dresses reaching barely to the knees. They fixed highballs for themselves, lit Gitanes, stamped the cigarette ends with fresh lipstick, and moved restlessly around Aznavour and the piano. He looked at them deadpan and sang another of his songs, also with a kind of Slavic-Oriental melody, but this time with English words:

"You've got to learn
To show a happy face.
Although you're full of misery,
You mustn't show a trace of sadness
And never look for sympathy.
You've got to learn,
Although it's very hard,
The way of pocketing your pride,
And sometimes face humiliation
While you are burning up inside."

When he had finished singing, he listened, still poker-faced, to further cries of "Sharl!" and then he got up from the piano. The admirers put down their drinks, deposited their Gitanes in ashtrays or glasses, and departed in a confusion of "Tout à l'heure"s, leaving us with Aznavour and his American press agent, a chubby hard-fast-talker named Mal Braveman. Aznavour's Carnegie Hall concert, the purpose of his visit to New York, was already sold out, Mr. Brave-man informed us, and he went on to say that Aznavour's American recordings—one album each in English and in French, under the Mercury label—were beginning to sell beautifully over here, as they had been selling in France, in Germany, in Italy, in Spain, and in the Scandinavian countries for years; that his royalties were running to three thousand dollars a day; and that his latest movie, Taxi to Tobruk, which he made after Shoot the Piano Player, would be released here soon. Braveman also said that Aznavour's sixteen-year-old daughter, Patricia, had come over with him for the visit, as had his mother, Mrs. Michel Aznavourian, and that they were at the musical show Mr. President at that moment but would meet Azna-vour later on, to go out on the town and Twist. To all this rundown, Aznavour listened, nodding agreement, and then he remarked, still deadpan, "I have to Twist, because I am the partner of my daughter. But it is finished, the Twist. Now it is the Mashed Potato. So some-times we Twist, sometimes it is the Mashed Potato."

"Trude Heller's is a great place for Twisting," Braveman said.

"I will take my daughter to Small's Paradise, in Harlem," Azna-vour said. "It is her first time here. She will want to go to Harlem.

Mama will go to sleep. While we wait for my daughter, I will go down to Greenwich Village, to Café Society Downtown, where I worked when I first came to America, fifteen years ago."

"Gone!" Braveman said, with what sounded like satisfaction. "Dead. Vanished. Café Society Downtown is no more. Something else is there now. Some play."

"If the building is where Café Society was, I will look at the building," Aznavour said. "I like very much the Village. The houses are small. The night clubs are not big. It is like Montmartre."

Braveman shrugged. "I'll drive you down," he said.

Aznavour gathered up some papers, on which were written some songs, and laid them on top of the piano. "My office is with me," he said. "I am carrying more paper with me than clothes. These songs are for my opening in Paris two years from now. The important thing for me in my songs is the lyric. I always think of myself as a writer. I prefer to be a writer. I am writing songs for all my friends— for Piaf, for Jacqueline François, for Les Compagnons de la Chanson. When they need songs, they call me. My life is my work. I am writing songs like a writer. Not itsy-bitsy-bikini songs. I am writing only about feeling. About love, about death, about youth, about wine. I am very Oriental. But I am not like my songs. Girls always see me in my songs, and they come to me and want me to talk to them like my songs, to cry on their hands, but I do not know how to do it. I am not that man."

The three of us went downstairs, got into Mr. Braveman's car, and started for the Village.

"In Paris, I never go out to night clubs," Aznavour said. "I stay home, in the country, forty miles outside Paris. All my friends come to see me, and we play chess and we talk and we hear music. My father and mother live in the hills of Cannes. Patricia lives with them. She goes to the local school. One of her classmates is the daughter of Picasso. I have been married twice and divorced twice. I have an adopted son, Patrick, who is nine. I have a sister, Aïda, who is one year older than I am. We are a clan, very close. We get together and sing and play music, and we understand each other. We could not live without show business. We are very Armenian. My father and mother met, as actors, in Turkey. My father is a troubadour as well as an actor. There are only two good Armenian singers, and my father is one of them. He sings the songs of the poet Sayat Nova, about love and death and flowers and wine. My father knows nine hundred verses of the poet Omar Khayyám. He plays the *tar*, an Armenian instrument with a long body and a top shaped like a figure eight. When we are together, all day we sing and dance. He refuses to leave Cannes, even to visit America. My grandfather was a cook in the Czar's summer palace in Georgia. After the Revolution, he fled to Paris. My parents came to Paris from Greece. I was born in Paris on May 22, 1924, the day my grandfather and my parents opened a restaurant in the Latin Quarter, called the Restaurant Caucase.

"When I was nine, I played a Negro boy in *Emil and the Detectives*, because I could do a Negro accent, which does not sound the *r*. Then I played Henry IV as a boy in *Margo*, at the Théâtre Marigny, with Pierre Fresnay. When I was seventeen, I wanted to build an act as a singer, together with a piano player named Pierre Roche. But I never found the right songs. The lyrics were very bad. Corny. The-sun-shines-and-I-am-happy kind of song I never liked. So I wrote my own song, 'J'ai Bu,' about a man whose girl leaves him because he drank. It won the Grand Prix du Disque, and I began to write songs every day, for Piaf and others. In 1947, Piaf was coming to America, and she said, for a joke, 'Why don't you come?' So Pierre Roche and I came, without English, without money. We went to Barney Josephson at Café Society Downtown and sang very sad songs for him, and he gave us a job. The people laughed; they thought we were Americans imitating Piaf. But the applause was not bad, and we worked there for five weeks. Then we worked in Montreal for two years, at Le Faisan d'Or, on a bad street. A seven-hundred-seat house. Three shows a day, each show to a full house. We were paid a thousand dollars a week. In New York, we lived at the Hotel Langwell, on West Forty-fourth Street; dined every night at Hector's Cafeteria in Times Square; took a taxi to Café Society Downtown; went to the Village Vanguard to see Robert Clary; then went to Café Society Uptown to see Piaf. As, there it is! Café Society! It is now playing *The Hostage*."

"I told you," Braveman said.

"I like to see it anyway," Aznavour said. "I like it here in the Village," he continued as Braveman made for Bleecker Street, where the coffeehouses were sending an overflow of patrons out to the curb. "It is like Saint-Germain. The beards. The polo shirts. No neckties. They play chess. The hair of the girls falls down."

"You *like* that?" Braveman said. "I *hate* that. I like a girl to look pretty."

"For me, they have a personality, and I think personality is better than beauty," Aznavour said. "I cannot be with an actress who always is thinking about her face. Also, if I have a girl I want to be with her all the time, and an actress has to work. I am a little bit of Pygmalion. I like to choose what my girl will wear. When you choose a dress for an actress, it is nothing. When you choose a dress for a girl who is not an actress, it makes her happy, and I like that."

"Had enough?" Braveman said, turning uptown again.

"We rendezvous now with my daughter," Aznavour said. "Today we went to the Buitoni restaurant and we ate spaghetti. She is too young to see too good places. I don't want her to feel that she is the daughter of a rich man. I do not care what I eat. I am not like some French people, who cannot eat strange food. I can live with two eggs a day, but I cannot live without show business."

"Lots of actors feel that way," Braveman said.

"I am an actor only when I sing," Aznavour said. "In the movies, I am not a real actor. I am only a movie actor. I play the situation. The public puts you in the situation. It is not my business. I am simply there. I am empty. Others put things in me. It is an art to be empty."

"That how come you're so popular in France?" Braveman asked.

"I am popular because I am like everybody in France. My face is the face of anybody. My voice is the voice of anybody. My face is the face of their hope. I do not care how small is the part I play. I will play it if it is human."

At the place of rendezvous, Braveman went in to collect Aznavour's daughter. He returned in a few minutes, followed by the earlier group of pretty, nervous French-speaking girls, and announced that Aznavour's daughter had been too tired and had gone to sleep. The eager fans piled into the back seat, sitting one on top of another, laughing, calling "Sharl! Tweest, Sharl!" Aznavour stared straight ahead, without expression, as Braveman started the car.

❦ THIRD RACE

WHILE MOST PEOPLE were talking Kentucky Derby, we got off to a cool May start for Aqueduct one day last week in the company of Alfred G. Vanderbilt, owner of a two-year-old colt named Seat of Honor, who was scheduled to run in the third race. At the age of fifty, Mr. Vanderbilt is, we're happy to report, as gentlemanly and romantic a figure as ever—light-voiced, light-mannered, light-hearted. He was sporting a belted raincoat and Tyrolian hat, and showing only faint evidence of extra poundage.

"I never weighed over a hundred and thirty pounds till I quit smoking, fourteen years ago, but now I weigh about a hundred and sixty," he said, somewhat apologetically, as he drove us through the Midtown Tunnel toward Queens. "This morning, a stranger stopped me on the street and sternly asked me, 'Where's your old hat?' I had to explain that I started going without a hat after the war, and then, a few years ago, my wife bought this hat for me. I'd never worn anything as gay as a Tyrolian hat before. I've been asked quite often today if I'm going to the Derby, and everybody says 'Too bad' when I say no. A lot of the things people do are done out of habit. Actually, I've been to two Kentucky Derbys—both times when I had horses running. One was Discovery, who came in second in 1934, and should have, because he was the second-best horse, and the other was Native Dancer, who came in second in 1953, but who should have won, and would have if it hadn't been for a fluke. I have only fifteen horses in training now. This has been a sparse year all around. I have about thirty brood mares on my farm in Maryland, where I breed and raise horses, and I have only nine two-year-olds, but next year I expect to have seventeen. I'll never again go through the kind of bad time I had when I was twenty-one and had

a stable of seventy or eighty horses. Before I went into the Navy in
the Second World War, I was putting in a good long week training
my own horses and being active in track management. Now I'm a
trustee of the New York Racing Association, which operates Aqueduct, and I'm president of the Thoroughbred Owners and Breeders
Association. When I became president of Belmont Park—I was
twenty-eight—I did a lot of worrying about how things were for the
customers. I used to put on dark glasses and a cap and mingle with
the crowds to see that the customers were being treated with the
proper courtesy. Now, I understand, there's a service you can get to
do that for you—or so my father-in-law, who's in the restaurant business, tells me—and you don't have to do it yourself. In thirty years
of racing, I've had horses in about ten thousand races—I just happened to check the figures the other day—and I've won nine hundred and ninety-eight. My colors are cerise and white. They haven't
changed. I may be still racing out of habit—the habit of just liking
to win. Do you like Aqueduct?"

"Well, it's very modern, and it's got escalators," we said.

"Sort of cold, though—like a machine," Mr. Vanderbilt said.
"Aqueduct is basically concrete. I like Belmont. Now, there's a very
pretty track. It came as a great surprise to me when Belmont was
condemned. I hope when we rebuild it, it won't be like a cold machine. I'm very fond of Saratoga, which is charming, and, of course,
Pimlico, because that's where I saw my very first race, when my family took me to see the Preakness. I knew then what it was that I
wanted to do. There was something about the over-all excitement
that got me—not the horses so much as the race. I'm not crazy
about riding horses myself. Every summer, when I take my family
out West, I get hijacked into getting on a horse, but I get off as soon
as I can. Western saddle, of course. I like to have something to hold
on to."

As Mr. Vanderbilt drove into the parking lot at Aqueduct, we
asked him about Seat of Honor, and he said that the colt had made
his début about three weeks earlier and had run fourth in a field of
seven, and that he showed real promise. "I have hopes for him as a
useful horse," he said. "Some horses will tell you they're good earlier
than other horses will. About ten years ago, my horse Find made his

first start as a three-year-old when I entered him in a claiming race. He hadn't shown anything, but he won, and then he won six or seven races in a row. He was a gradual surprise. He raced till he was eleven—one of the hardiest horses I've ever had. He won eight hundred thousand dollars, which made him the third-biggest money-winning gelding of all time. Sometimes they fool you. I've learned not to get excited till I know. Native Dancer is the best horse I've ever had. He's at stud now, at the farm, where we give him about forty mares a year. He has around a hundred and twenty offspring, the eldest of whom is now seven or eight, and he's the grandsire of about ten. The best two-year-old in France last year was his—Hula Dancer, owned by Mrs. P. A. B. Widener. Hula Dancer is a filly, but she's better than the colts. I have only two complaints about that filly—she's in the wrong country, and she's under the wrong colors. Nine of my active horses are by Native Dancer—Ring Around, Look Ma, Footloose, Goose Step, Heel and Toe, Restless Native, Last Leg, Local Color, and Charity Dance. I used to feel as though nobody had a right to call any other horse any kind of Dancer at all."

Going up in the Turf and Field Club elevator, we asked Mr. Vanderbilt whether he intended to bet on Seat of Honor, and he said he never bet on any horses, and hadn't since 1940. "I used to just about break even over the years when I bet," he said. "If I won, I'd be winning the purse anyway, and if I lost, I'd be that much madder. I don't have much of a gambler's instinct. I just like to win races. I'm worried today about the coughing sickness that's going around. I hope Seat of Honor doesn't have the cough. Up to yesterday, the only other stable that hadn't caught it was Ogden Phipps's. The Phippses have a hatful of horses—about forty in training—and they're doing very well. Seat of Honor is running against a Phipps horse—Atomic, by Bold Ruler out of High Voltage." He handed us a program. Listed for the third race, by number, were Niloric, Tanwood, Atomic, Bartow, Admiral Todd, Harbison, Woolie, Seat of Honor, Brave Lad, and Solar Stance. We read that Seat of Honor was by Citation out of Sit This Out by Native Dancer—a Native Dancer grandson—and was to be ridden by a jockey named John L. Rotz. "A good rider and a very intelligent boy," Mr. Vanderbilt told us.

After placing—under Mr. Vanderbilt's restraining influence—a minimum bet of two dollars on the daily double, and losing it, we accompanied him to the saddling paddock, where the horses for the third race were being led into the stalls. Seat of Honor, in Stall 8, looked mighty handsome to us—a bay, with an alert expression on his face. Mr. Vanderbilt conferred with his trainer's foreman, who told him that the horse did not have the cough and that his legs had been bandaged. Over in Stall 3, Atomic was being fussed over by Mr. and Mrs. Ogden Phipps, and also by Mrs. Henry Carnegie Phipps. Then the jockeys came out, and Rotz, wearing cerise and white diamonds, with cerise sleeves and a white cap, shook hands with Mr. Vanderbilt. The trainer's foreman came over to Rotz and said hello. A moment later, the horses, according to ritual, were brought into the walking ring, and the jockeys took positions to their left.

"Hustle him out there. Get a good position, and ride him accordingly," the trainer's foreman said to Rotz.

"Good luck," Mr. Vanderbilt said to him.

"Thank you," Rotz said.

"Riders up, please!" the paddock judge in charge called out.

The riders mounted the horses and rode slowly out to the track, heading for the starting gate. We accompanied Mr. Vanderbilt to his box, overlooking the finish. Our palms started to dampen, and we slid out and back to a betting window, where we placed two dollars, at five-to-one odds, on Seat of Honor to win. When we returned to Mr. Vanderbilt's box, we found him looking through binoculars at the horses in the starting gate.

"We're being a little balky," he said, with a calm that impressed us. Then the horses were off.

"We're third on the outside," Mr. Vanderbilt continued, in the same calm manner, as he watched the runners through his glasses, which he then offered to us.

"Please, no," we said, pushing them back at him.

Mr. Vanderbilt peered again. "We're second and not looking too good," he went on, with no change of tone. "I'm not crazy about it right now. We're backing up a little."

The horses galloped past the finish line.

"I think we were second," Mr. Vanderbilt reported.

"He looked good," we said. "Even if he did run second. Woolie won, but Seat of Honor beat Atomic."

"Basically, you win or you lose," Mr. Vanderbilt said. "Running second, I wouldn't expect you to congratulate me."

❦❦ THE PROFESSOR

DR. NIKOLAI TROFIMOVICH FEDORENKO, the new Soviet Ambassador Extraordinary and Plenipotentiary to the United Nations, is fifty years old, a Doctor of Philology, and a former professor of history and Chinese literature at the University of Leningrad. The other day, at the restaurant called Danny's Hide-A-Way, on East Forty-fifth Street, we attended a United Nations Correspondents Association luncheon for Dr. Fedorenko, who is very professional-looking, with a lot of wavy hair, and eyeglasses that have upper rims of tortoise shell and lower rims of steel. As soon as the Professor assumed his role as Ambassadorial speaker, we were beset by the same mixed feelings that used to tear at us in the classrooms of college teachers who were, one way or another, pushing a little too hard. (The early part of the luncheon was fine. No tearing at all during Danny's Special for the occasion: borscht, turkey with cranberry sauce, and chocolate pudding with plenty of whipped cream.) We sat next to Oleg Kalugin, the Radio Moscow correspondent, a handsome, confident young man with a quick smile, who was wearing sharp British (or British-looking) tweeds, an English (or English-looking) striped shirt, a maroon-and-navy Old School-type tie, gold cufflinks, a flat gold wristwatch, and bitten fingernails. He took notes with a fountain pen that contained red ink. Mr. Kalugin explained to us the Soviet government's policy toward Russian musicians with inclinations to play jazz and Russian painters with inclinations to paint abstractions. "The State wants to express its opinion about jazz. Right?" he said, over the turkey and cranberry sauce. "So the State *expresses* its opinion about jazz. Right?" He said he had learned to speak English at the University of Leningrad, had picked up his Mort Sahl rhythms during three years in New York, and had never seen any abstract art in the U.S.S.R. himself but had heard that abstract painters had been invited by Nikita Khrushchev to leave the country. "Half in jest, half serious. Right?" he said to us.

When Dr. Fedorenko was introduced to the ninety-odd correspondents at the luncheon, he immediately struck a pedagogical note by addressing them as "ladies and gentlemen of the Fourth Estate." Then, having noted that a few months had passed since his appointment as Ambassador, he said, in excellent English, "It would be natural, therefore, to be guided by the philosophy of the East: 'Open up your eyes fast, but make no haste in opening your mouth.'" He also said that it would be appropriate to recall a Japanese proverb: "The tiger is careful with his claws, the sage with his tongue." The Professor got some pretty good classroom laughs with both these sayings. Then, to our surprise, he said that his "English articulation system" was "not in best form," so he was asking his neighbor to his *right* (another classroom laugh) to help him out by reading his prepared speech. The neighbor, a U.N. interpreter named Basile Yakovlev, thereupon gave us the old one-two about how "the Western Powers—members of NATO—do not stop their interference into domestic affairs of the Congo, preventing it from adopting a course of free national development," and how "American neo-colonialists are pursuing their expansionist policy in the Congo under the banner of anti-Communism."

As we listened to Mr. Yakovlev's reading of the Professor's speech, it seemed to us that the new Ambassador had found a fine pedagogical key to classroom popularity: Tell the jokes yourself, but get the section man to do the dirty work. In a question-and-answer period, questions asked in English were answered in Russian by the Professor and translated into English for the class. Again the Professor was once removed from whatever was ungracious or ungainly. When Miss Pauline Frederick, the charming and knowledgeable U.N. correspondent for the National Broadcasting Company, asked, "How can the Soviet Union say it is for the United Nations when the Soviet Union refuses to pay its share of U.N. costs?" the Ambassador's chastising reply came as though it were not from him. The interpreter said, "You are guilty of a fundamental inaccuracy. . . . You are not conversant with U.N. affairs. . . . The Soviet Union has abided by the regulations and regularly paid its assessment. . . . This may be sensational news to you, but the Soviet Union is second only to the United States in the size of its contribution. . . . Even though we live in the age of electronics, it is difficult for me to penetrate into your mind. . . . What is written with a pen cannot be struck off with an axe. . . . Wasn't the Soviet Union right in refusing to foot the bill for illegal operations in the Congo?"

We looked at Kalugin.

"Right?" he said.

This went on for some time, and then, in the tradition of the professor who wants to leave his students laughing, Ambassador Fedorenko seized upon the last question, from Mr. Michael Littlejohn, of Reuters, who wanted to know whether Khrushchev would attend the Eighteenth General Assembly of the United Nations, next September. "The question is an excellent one," Professor Fedorenko said, all on his own, in exemplary English. "And to this excellent question about Nikita Sergeyevich Khrushchev, I can only say that the most brilliant answer will be provided by him."

✿✿ CONDON UPTOWN

AFTER TWELVE YEARS on West Third Street, Eddie Condon has moved the jazz institution known as Eddie Condon's uptown to the Sutton Hotel, at 330 East Fifty-sixth Street, and we dropped in on him the other afternoon while he was getting the place in order for the opening, which was scheduled to take place this week. The new night club, which is on the ground floor of the hotel and has its own entrance, is small, trim, cheerful, and easy to get into and out of, and, behind a gay orange-colored awning, it has a number of surprisingly, but not alarmingly, elegant fixtures: a red-carpeted cocktail lounge, a black bar shielded by a pink canopy, walnut panelling, a main dining area with pink cloths on the tables and pink-and-black chairs, globular white-glass light fixtures on the walls, a roomy bandstand protected by a brass rail and decorated with a photo-montage mural depicting events in the many lives of Eddie Condon, pink curtains, a high ceiling painted red, and slate-gray carpeting—wall, of course, to wall. We found Condon looking quite elegant himself, in a black topcoat and a pearl-gray Cavanagh hat, and slightly unnerved by the hammering, painting, carpet-tacking, arm-waving, and yelling of a crowd of overalled workmen surrounding him. As we joined him, he was gazing at the red carpet in the cocktail lounge and shaking his head in admiration.

"You know what the color of the carpet is called?" he said to us in greeting. "Ecclesiastical red. Isn't that a hell of a name for a carpet? You know what we call the color on the ceiling? Persimmon red. Isn't that a hell of a thing? The main drink we're going to have in this saloon will be called wet paint on the rocks." He jumped as a carpet-tacker asked him to move his feet. "The color system downtown was sort of yellow and green, with a black ceiling, but the motif was not exercised to the hilt," Condon went on, picking up

one foot and then the other as the carpet men worked around him.
"This motif"—he paused to throw us a starry-eyed glance—"is what
we call *exercised.* This place used to be entitled Bourbon Street, but
all that's left of Bourbon Street is the ceiling, the walls, and the
floor. We moved the bandstand from the side to the front. The
music used to acoustically bounce off the walls. Now it goes all the
way to the door. We're going to have our first rehearsal this afternoon: Cutty Cutshall, trombone; Rex Stewart, cornet; Herb Hall,
clarinet; George Wettling, drums; Gene Schroeder, piano; Leonard
Gaskin, bass; Eddie Condon, guitar. See that picture frame over
there near the door? Maybe I'll fill it with a closeup of Eugene V.
Debs."

One of the workmen on the floor looked up at us and said, "This
is the only night club in town that has a real hi-fi set for the playing
of records. Isn't that right, Mr. Condon?"

Condon gave the man a stern look. "All we say is we open at five
and start playing live at eight-thirty. Before that, we'll play records,"
he said.

"Eddie Condon records," said the workman.

"To move a saloon is a project," Condon said to us. "First, you
need a new location, and, second, you need to transfer your liquor
and cabaret licenses. All I can tell you is I haven't slept in several
weeks. I haven't slept since I signed the lease with my landlord, the
Sutton Hotel. What I'd like is to work out some way I won't have to
show up opening night. I will not wear white tie and tails. I'll wear
the usual sackcloth. Opening night is a combination of pleasure and
displeasure—displeasure because we can't fill the requests for reser-
vations. This place is smaller than the old place—more intimate
seating. A capacity of a hundred and twenty seated, and maybe
thirty more standing in the bar. Well, opening night is opening
night, whether it's Sing Sing or the Alvin Theatre. Oh, yes, I haven't
eaten in several weeks, either. I'm strictly a yoghurt-and-wheat-germ
man, so it's easy. I've been doing a MacSwiney. Hey!" he shouted to
the room at large. "How long was MacSwiney's hunger strike, in
Ireland?"

"Fifty days!" one of the carpenters shouted back.

"It was longer than a weekend, anyway," Condon said. "Go
ahead, Jackson!" he yelled to his informant. "I can hear every word

you're hammering. Here's an interesting story," he went on, turning back to us. "Anyway, it happened. You don't open a saloon in fifteen minutes, you know. Two years ago, we got word downtown that we'd have to move to make room for a housing project and some N.Y.U. buildings. Well, our neighbors, mostly hatmakers and so on, moved to New Jersey and places like that, and their problems were solved. We were the only ones left on the block. Pete Pesci, my manager, and I started looking at places. The first place we saw was this basement place, Martinique, at Fifty-seventh and Sixth. Actually, it's La Martinique, and it was the 'La' that I didn't like. Anyway, I dread basements. It's bad enough to have to go into a saloon on the ground level. At least thirty people called me up and said I should go into Childs in the Paramount—another basement. You know the décor? Solid granite! A tomb, with wonderful acoustics. I kept telling Pete I wasn't going to open any swimming pool. Anyway, Pete and I were getting discouraged, and we were being enveloped on Third Street by this housing project. Then, about six months ago, my wife and I went to the Waldorf for Lionel Hampton's opening, and around two in the morning we decided to drop in on Bourbon Street, where I had never been, to hear Turk Murphy. In there, I looked around, and I thought, Would I love to have this room! It's beautifully located in—shall we coin an expression?—the fantastic Fifties. And it was atmospherically attractive. A *hell* of a room. I went back there twice, looking around, and thinking, Mmm. Well, here's an 'Mmm' that turned out. Murphy went back to San Francisco, and the ownership of Bourbon Street, for one sudden reason and another, also departed. I knew a couple of lawyers that have degrees, and got hold of a lease and signed it. Want to see the kitchen?"

We followed Condon back to the kitchen. More pounding and painting. "Pastry oven!" Condon shouted above the racket, putting a hand on a black stove. "All we need is a pastry oven! This kitchen is more capacious than the old one, and more modernly equipped. We even got an electric dishwasher. Ah, here's Pete," he said as we were joined by his manager, a handsome man who very much looked the part of the muscular maître-d' and bouncer.

"The ashtrays will be here tomorrow, Eddie," Pete said. "Black and pink."

"Pete's wife and her pal, both ex-showgirls, chose all the pink stuff, as well as other stuff, for the place," Condon said.

"It's all so beautiful," Pete said breathlessly.

"Take it easy, Pete," Condon said. "We're going to be here for a long, long time."

Condon led the way out to the main room again, where we found the musicians assembling on the bandstand. He took off his coat and hat and joined them onstage. "Now let's see how the place sounds," he said.

✿✿✿ THURSDAY

AT THE MOMENT when Astronaut Cooper was firing his retro-rockets and heading back from space, we were entering the Waldorf-Astoria with United Nations Ambassador Adlai Stevenson, who was on his way to his ninety-first reception of the year 1963 and what we have estimated to be his one-thousand-one-hundred-and-seventy-sixth reception in line of duty since he assumed his present post. The occasion was a party celebrating the admission of Kuwait to the United Nations. Kuwait, No. 111 in the assembly of nations, is a very rich oil country, of 5,800 square miles (approximately the size of the state of Connecticut), bordering on Iraq, Saudi Arabia, and the Persian Gulf, and its ruler, His Highness Sheik Sir Abdullah al-Salim al-Sabah, like other Kuwait government employees, gets a salary—in his case, twenty-eight million dollars a year. The country has a daily income of one and a quarter million dollars, and just before joining the United Nations it signed up for the purchase of a million dollars' worth of United Nations bonds. Kuwait's Foreign Minister, His Excellency Sheik Sabah al-Ahmad al-Sabah, who was giving the party, was at the head of the receiving line; he was wearing Arab costume—white cotton-and-silk *hattah* and *dushdasha*, with an impressively regal black *oghaal* over the *hattah*. Beyond the line, the diplomatic, well-wishing, economic, political, social, and special-interest elements of the party stood talking, drinking, eating, watching, and waiting.

"Now, you stick with me," Ambassador Stevenson told us, making first for His Excellency the Foreign Minister. "I just go in there, hands open, ears open. Expect a concentrated period of handshaking and whispering." His Excellency gave Ambassador Stevenson a great big happy grin and passed him along quickly to the couple beside him—Talaat Ghoussein, Kuwait's Chargé d'Affaires in Washington, and Mrs. Ghoussein—who, in turn, passed him on to Saeed Yacoob Shammas, Kuwait's Consul General in New York, and Mrs. Shammas. They all greeted Ambassador Stevenson, it seemed to us, not in the usual formal manner of present-credentials-and-hello-and-goodbye but in the *gemütlich*-reunion manner of people who see each other every day at the office but rarely meet outside it, and, when they do, manifest a special joy, as though it were a couple of years since they had seen each other last.

"Now I just let myself be drawn in here," Ambassador Stevenson told us, steering us toward the rest of the party. "Ah! Sir Muhammad Zafrulla Khan," he said, shaking hands with the President of the General Assembly. Sir Muhammad, twinkle-eyed and twinkle-bearded, promptly whispered a few things into Ambassador Stevenson's left ear. A couple of other diplomats, including Ernest Thalmann, the Permanent (U.N.) Observer from Switzerland (which is not a member of the U.N.), came over and rejoiced with Ambassador Stevenson at his being there. The Permanent Observer and Ambassador Stevenson plunged into what seemed to be a running exchange about the possibility of Switzerland's becoming, after all these years, a joiner. Then Ambassador Stevenson found himself in the custody of a very talkative young American, who, after whispering things into his right ear for about ten minutes, turned out to be a party crasher with strong diplomatic opinions.

"Do you really *listen* to everybody?" we asked after Ambassador Stevenson had disengaged himself from the crasher.

"I'm meat for those people," he said, with the well-known Stevenson laugh.

"Don't you have bodyguards or something?" we asked.

"I've never cared much for elbow men," he said as the crush moved in on him.

"I merely want to say thanks for everything you've ever done, Mr. Stevenson—and I mean *everything!*" one young man called out quickly, in passing.

"Thank you," Ambassador Stevenson said. "And here's Oumar Sow, Ambassador from Mali to the United States," he went on, introducing us to a very young-looking man. "And there's one of the most beautiful women in the world," he added, extending a hand, over several intervening heads, to shake the hand of Mrs. Jeanne

Rousseau, the Counsellor of Embassy of Mali. She was wearing a lovely native costume, called a *boubou*, of delicate peach-colored silk. "Mali," Ambassador Stevenson repeated, as though savoring the name.

A fat-faced, hearty-voiced gentleman wearing rimless spectacles took Ambassador Stevenson's hand and shook it, saying he was from Texas. Ambassador Stevenson replied that he was always delighted to meet a Texan, especially in a place where oil was in the air.

At that point, someone shouted for silence, and a hush fell over the party. His Excellency the Foreign Minister of Kuwait took up a position at a microphone on a dais, and motioned to Ambassador Stevenson to stand alongside. His Excellency made a little speech, in Arabic. The whole party applauded and cheered. Then Chargé d'Affaires Ghoussein stepped up to the microphone and delivered an English translation of His Excellency's speech, which informed the rest of us that Astronaut Cooper had landed safely and that His Excellency, on behalf of the nation of Kuwait, wanted to congratulate Ambassador Stevenson. The party applauded and cheered again. Ambassador Stevenson thanked him and went on to say, "It is our job now to try to keep pace with the programs of science."

A little while later, the Ambassador left the reception, and so did we. Someone in the lobby had a portable radio, and we heard an announcer say that Astronaut Cooper had climbed out of his capsule. "Thank goodness he's back with the rest of us," Ambassador Stevenson said.

❦ DIRECTOR

WE HAD A TALK last week with Tony Richardson, the thirty-five-year-old English director of the new hit play *Luther* and of the forthcoming Brecht play *Arturo Ui*. Catching him when he had just emerged from the opening of the first and was preparing to submerge himself in rehearsals for the second, we pinned him down briefly in his suite at the Algonquin, where, wandering around in white socks, All-American chino pants, and a black wool pullover on top of a white shirt open at the collar, he looked like a combination of all those gaunt, underfed student-poet characters in Chekhov plays, though not tortured.

"Performances sometimes go down on opening nights, but everyone in *Luther* was in peak form," he told us, speaking with a slow, soft Oxford accent that contained one or two North-of-England overtones. "And the critics are much better here than in England. They have a sort of literateness and perception, an awareness of the play, and a sense of responsibility that we don't get in England, where the critics—in the tradition of belles-lettres, supposedly—write just in order to write an amusing piece. Critics here seem to be especially good about English plays; perhaps they're not quite as good about American plays, possibly because they're too close to them. I don't like critics much, actually, in any of the arts. There are times when they don't seem to have the foggiest idea of what it's all about. They don't get it. Critics and creative people are bound to hate each other. They can't help it. They're on different sides of the fence."

As soon as his opening was over, Mr. Richardson told us, he had got started on the sets, costumes, and auditions for the next play. "I like to have several things going at the same time," he said. "I work best when I can switch from one thing to another."

Pressed for a rundown on some of the switches he would make during the next week or so, he said he'd be working on the New York opening of *Tom Jones*, the movie he directed for Woodfall Films, which he founded with John Osborne in 1958 (the work would include examining the print of the movie that was sent over here, to see if its color matched the original); he'd be working on the cutting of another Woodfall movie, *Girl with Green Eyes*, which he produced just before he came over here for *Luther*; he'd be preparing to direct *The Sea Gull* and Brecht's *Joan of the Stock-yards* in London this winter, and possibly *The World's Baby*, by a new playwright named Michael Hastings, all three starring his wife, Vanessa Redgrave; and he'd be greeting her and their six-month-old daughter, Natasha Jane, who were coming over from London soon for Natasha Jane's first visit to this country. At some point in the early summer, he added, he would be in Hollywood, directing *The Loved One*, a movie based on Evelyn Waugh's novel.

"I like being in the States," Mr. Richardson told us. "I like New York. I feel at home in New York. From the minute I first saw New York, in the summer of 1953, I knew it was the place I liked best in the world. I was just a kid, down from Oxford. I came over on one of those student trips, travelling on a hundred dollars, and lived in some crummy little hotel in the Village. There was a heat wave, and I couldn't afford air conditioning. I just wandered around the city, walking and looking and loving New York. I stayed here a week, and then, for the next six months, with the help of friends who'd been with me at Oxford, sort of Jack Kerouac'd around America—drove to Texas and Mexico City, up the West Coast to San Francisco, and back through the Dakotas. One's personal responses are always inexplicable. It's like that marvellous thing that Henry James felt about London from the moment he went there. He left after a few days and lived in Paris and Geneva, but all the time he knew in his heart that the place where he felt at home was London. That's the way I feel about New York. I love the excitement and fun of Broadway, the unexpectedness of the whole city, the feeling that something can happen at any moment. And the sheer physical beauty of it. The way all those buildings look all lit up when you're driving down through Central Park. However much I'd like to *be* an American, I'm not. Everything about me is English. Mainly, I'm stuck."

We urged Mr. Richardson to fill us in on what he is stuck with, and he told us that he was born in Shipley, Yorkshire, on June 5, 1928, an only child. His father is a pharmacist, now semi-retired, he added, and went on to say, "Shipley is a small town, sort of a suburb of Bradford, the *Room at the Top* town. It's like Wuthering Heights around Shipley, and just a tram ride away from this great big heavy, prosperous industrial city. I wanted to be a movie director from birth. I went to movies—American movies—endlessly, and, other than that, lived a sheltered life. I never grew up with other kids. I went to a very small private school and was then sent to boarding school—Ashville College, which had been evacuated from Harrogate to Westmorland, in the Lake District. Boarding school was such a traumatic shock that I didn't get to know any of the kids there, either. I spent my free time alone, wandering around communing with nature. I learned one thing. If you absolutely refuse to do anything you don't want to do, they can't touch you. All they can do is chuck you out or give you your own way. You can always force other people to come to terms with you, and they always do. I directed my first play, *Everyman*, for the drama festival at school, when I was twelve, and continued directing at Oxford, a very good place for taking three years off at a time when it's terribly important to be free of all pressures except those of doing all the things you want to do."

In 1956, Richardson, having settled in London, helped found the English Stage Company—with, among others, George Devine—at the Royal Court Theatre, where, that same year, he directed John Osborne's *Look Back in Anger*. The play had been sent to the producers cold, and when they looked up the author they found him living, on practically nothing, in a barge on the Thames. Richardson at the time lived in a small apartment a few blocks away, overlooking the river. Osborne was working sporadically at odd acting jobs, and Richardson, who was then connected with television, was able to help keep the young playwright going by getting him some work as an extra until *Look Back in Anger* was produced. After that, Richardson directed another Osborne play, *The Entertainer*, and, with the formation of Woodfall, the movie versions of both plays.

In 1957, by invitation, Richardson took *Look Back in Anger* to the Moscow Art Theatre. "I loathed the conformity and the drabness of Russia and the endless sort of bureaucracy that was present everywhere—except in the Moscow Art Theatre, where the people were most extraordinary," Mr. Richardson said. "Electricians learned the whole play in English and worked the whole show with very complicated lighting effects. But you didn't meet many young people who were alive. They were so very, very conformist. I didn't like East Germany, either. You get that feeling that the Communist Party is running the country and despising the people. West Germany, on the other hand, is disgusting and degrading and materialistic. A real spiritual wasteland. Just terrifying. I am uneasy about the culture boom in the States. The culture boom and everything that goes with it is sham. There are some words in *Luther* that describe it: 'Shells for shells, empty things for empty men.' I'd rather see one performance of Martha Graham than all the boom put together. It's a sham concocted by the same people who put labels on things because they have no other way of grasping things. It's a convenient way of stopping living, instead of responding at every moment to whatever experience is there for you at that particular moment. It's a lot of people just walking around dead. It's all like some of the English theatre companies and that certain English group that thinks that if you create an institution, the institution automatically creates art. The truth, of course, is that art creates the institution. Work should speak for itself. I love working. I love working with people. The communication should be in the work. I'm not drawn to television. That's just nothing. It's good for reporting things at the moment. It's a very fast and rough means of producing film, but nothing that you can't do better in a movie. I just absolutely love being on a movie set or on a stage, trying to make something come to life."

❦❦ ❦ WHO'S?

THE PLAYERS: *The entire cast of Edward Albee's Who's Afraid of Virginia Woolf?—Uta Hagen, attractive, hoarse-voiced, volatile, energetic, youthful-looking veteran of twenty-five years on Broadway; Arthur Hill, tall, thin, loose-jointed, scholarly-looking, no-nonsense man; Ben Piazza, blond, boyish veteran of Albee's The American Dream and The Zoo Story; Rochelle Oliver, ingénue with long blond hair, who won the Clarence Derwent Award as the outstanding young actress of the 1960 season for her performance in Toys in the Attic—plus Ugo Betti, eight-and-a-half-year-old black cocker spaniel belonging to Miss Hagen; and Herbert Berghof, stocky, temperamental, Russian-intellectual-looking actor, husband of Miss Hagen, and co-head, with Miss Hagen, of the H. B. Studio school of acting.*

THE TIME: *Around midnight on a Tuesday, following Performance No. 418 of Who's Afraid of Virginia Woolf?, the second performance of the second year of its Broadway run.*

THE SCENE: *Apartment of Miss Hagen and Mr. Berghof, at Washington Square and Macdougal Street. A large living room with four white-curtained windows, one of them in the right wall, behind a grand piano. To the left are a long sofa, three soft armchairs, and a round coffee table. On the table are a tray of sandwiches, cans of beer, soda bottles, a bottle of Scotch, and a bowl of fresh daisies. Bookshelves line the wall behind the sofa. A desk stands behind one of the soft chairs. Alongside the coffee table, the dog is amusing himself vigorously with a squeaking rubber boot.*

Miss Hagen enters, wearing tight black pants and a hound's-tooth jacket. She places a bowl of ice on the desk. Mr. Hill en-

ters slowly behind her. He wears a neat blue suit, a conservative blue-and-black striped tie, and black-rimmed glasses.

MISS HAGEN (giving Ugo Betti a dazzling smile): That dog is happy, because he was raised with love. (Mr. Hill presses his lips together and nods quickly, several times, in agreement. He sits down on the sofa, and, as with all tall men, his knees poke up awkwardly.)

MR. HILL: Yes.

MISS HAGEN (examining the sandwiches): They're all the same. Pastrami. With pickles. Don't they smell delicious?

MR. HILL (sniffs and draws deep breath): Mmm. (He takes one and bites into it.)

MISS HAGEN: Have something to wash it down. You want to see how I open these lethal pop-top beer cans? You have to have a pot holder, or else you cut yourself to ribbons. One time— (She breaks off to greet two latecomers—Mr. Piazza, wearing a gray wool sweater and blue jeans, and Miss Oliver, wearing a yellow sweater, a black straight skirt, and red pumps. They take chairs, and Miss Hagen fixes drinks for them.)

MR. PIAZZA: This is a real celebration. Sandwiches and everything!

MR. HILL: It isn't every night we have an anniversary. It's like being on the road. A little band of brothers. (He removes his coat, places it on the back of the sofa, and loosens his tie before taking another sandwich.)

MISS OLIVER: Yes. (She gives a little sigh and lights a cigarette.)

MISS HAGEN: We're the family. You make a new family in every new play.

MR. HILL: Your families onstage and off are as separate as can be.

MISS HAGEN (to Miss Oliver): That's why I make you come up and say hello to me before curtain. I'm so mean to you first thing onstage. I don't want something mean to be the first thing I say when I see you.

MR. PIAZZA (thoughtfully): Macy's delivered my new bed to my new apartment today. But they didn't deliver the frame. I told the delivery man I'd have to sleep on the floor. You know what that man said? He said, "Oh, you actors are never satisfied!"

Miss Hagen: They treat us like an ethnic minority. (*She bursts into hoarse laughter.*)

Mr. Hill: *Caveat emptor.*

Miss Hagen: I'm always fighting with Macy's, and then, when I have to buy something, I say, "Well, I think I'll go to Macy's."

Mr. Hill: Altman's is a great place. No matter what happens, they take it back. (*Mr. Piazza gets up and goes to the desk, where he helps himself to some fresh ice. Ugo Betti growls at him.*)

Mr. Piazza: That dog is growling at me.

Miss Hagen: He's got a cookie. He's growling at his cookie. Arthur! (*She points a finger at Mr. Hill.*) I heard you went out in your boat and capsized! On our anniversary!

Mr. Piazza: It would have been terrible if you'd missed the anniversary performance. That's the trouble with living out there in White Something.

Mr. Hill: White *Plains.* With my wife and two kiddie-winks.

Miss Hagen: I thought Edward [Edward Albee] was awfully nice when he came back to see us after the anniversary performance—when he said he'd been told by other playwrights not to go when the anniversary came up. The performances go stale, they told him. But he said he was as proud of the play as he was when it first opened.

Miss Oliver: It was nice, the way he thanked all of us. (*There is a moment of silence.*)

Mr. Hill: The audience was dead tonight. The laughs were all wrong. We weren't on top of the play.

Miss Hagen: We had a good audience last night—a quiet house, but they had great alertness.

Mr. Hill: Even tonight, though, I got a laugh I hadn't got in a long time—when I come in in the third act and say, "Flores; flores para los muertos. Flores." There were people out there tonight who knew it was from *Streetcar.* I'll never forget the day I got a wire from my agent telling me to get hold of a copy of Who's Afraid of Virginia Woolf?—spelled W-o-l-f. Well, I did, and sent my wife and kiddie-winks off to see a movie, and sat down, and—pow! (*There is a murmur of appreciation all around.*)

Miss Hagen: I'm a long-run girl myself. If the play is marvellous, as this one is, to have that challenge of keeping it spontaneous, keeping it alive!

MR. HILL: It's the job of the actor. To produce that thing.

MR. PIAZZA: We've got the good fortune to have a good cast, good people.

MISS OLIVER: Oh, yes!

MR. HILL: If one of us were hateful . . . (*He shudders.*)

MISS HAGEN: When the stars or leading players are wonderful, everything is great. If the stars or leading players are terrible, the cast is abominable. They get mean, nasty, and dig and knife each other. I've played with people when we had a terrible director, but we all banded together and supported each other, and it went all right, because the leading players are the ones who set the tone.

MR. HILL: They impose the climate.

MISS OLIVER: Maybe one reason it started off so well was that you didn't go out of town. You could go home after rehearsals and relax, the way I go home every night now.

MISS HAGEN (*with one of her laughs*): You know, the audience thinks you and Ben are married. (*To Mr. Hill*) After the show, Rochelle and Ben come out fighting; he accuses her of taking too long to get out of her costume.

MR. PIAZZA: I hate to be kept waiting. We share a cab going downtown, where she meets her husband, and the audience sometimes hears us when we come out.

MISS HAGEN: Fighting. The other night, I heard somebody in the audience say, "I *told* you they were married. I *told* you."

MR. HILL: Why didn't anybody before this show think of having previews instead of going out of town?

MISS HAGEN: That out-of-town routine creates so many lousy tensions, with all the New York hawks coming to see what they can pick up. With every new tryout town, there's a set of hysterias.

MR. HILL: All that hippety-hop!

MISS HAGEN: By the time you get to New York, you're nuts. Every show should open in New York. (*Everybody nods. There is another brief silence. Berghof enters. He has black-rimmed glasses on and is bald except for a monklike fringe of white hair around* the back of his head. *He is wearing black slacks and a black turtleneck sweater. He looks from one actor to another before speaking.)*

MR. BERGHOF: All these good actors! The sandwiches! Can I have one?

MR. PIAZZA: They're pastrami. Terrific sandwiches.

MR. HILL: We're honored. (*Mr. Berghof takes a sandwich. Again he looks from one actor to another.*)

MR. BERGHOF: I just ate something outside. (*He sighs.*) All these good actors! (*He leaves.*)

MISS HAGEN: We should feel flattered. He never does this. Herbert is happy. Ugo is happy. Everybody is happy tonight. (*Ugo runs up and starts licking Miss Hagen's face and pawing at her arm.*)

MR. HILL: One thing I like about this play is you never feel tied to any particular mood. It bounds around.

MISS HAGEN: The parts are extraordinary, enormous. I've played Lady Macbeth on television. I don't know how often I've played Lady Macbeth, and all I can say is you can have Lady Macbeth. It's a ghastly part. It should be played by a man.

MR. HILL: It's all on one note.

MISS HAGEN: All on one note. Ambitious venom. My part here is one of a human being.

MR. HILL: She doesn't serve only one purpose. She has all the problems of the American woman today. This play isn't a one-hole golf course. This is an eighteen-hole golf course. It's a *thirty-six-hole* golf course. Not that we've ever sat around talking about the "inner meaning of the play." (*Laughter all around.*)

MISS HAGEN: When the audience gets crude, though, it's hard to take.

MR. HILL: It's shocking.

MR. PIAZZA: There was one night last week that was weird. They were quiet and completely unresponsive in the first act. Then they came back, and—boy! They must have got crocked in the intermission.

MISS OLIVER: They were awful.

MISS HAGEN: It's a good thing we're all O.K. among ourselves.

MR. HILL: You couldn't play a neurotic play like this if you weren't.

MR. PIAZZA: You're either a psychotic or an actor.

MISS HAGEN: If an actor is working, he should be the healthiest person alive. Why does somebody who works in Wall Street go home and get potted every night? Because he can't express all those feelings onstage.

MR. PIAZZA: I used to take the Zoo Story part home with me every night.

MR. HILL: I never did that. Never.

MR. PIAZZA: I hated the way it made me feel. It was awful. I don't do that now, though.

MISS HAGEN: You don't do it once you have experience and know exactly what you're doing. (She pauses and laughs her laugh.) Thank God we all know what we're doing!

⚘ ROCKY IN MIAMI BEACH

OUR MAN Stanley is in Miami on some enterprise of his own, having to do with sizing up the coming season at Hialeah, and when we heard that Governor Nelson Rockefeller was going down there for a day to make a campaign speech, we managed to persuade Stanley that he could safely abandon his project long enough to send us a report on what happened. Here's the dope that Stanley wired in:

"Temp., 78 deg. Ocean, 74 deg. Wind, 8 m.p.h. Pools heated. Far cry from cold rain Rocky got in New Hampshire. Miami *Herald* banner headline: 'ROCKY MAKES PITCH TO EDITORS TODAY.' Miami *News* banner headline: 'ROCKY HERE TO WOO EDITORS.' Meaning Rocky slated to address Thirtieth Annual Convention of Associated Press Managing Editors Association, at Miami Beach's Americana Hotel. Five hundred and five editors just drop in bucket of sixteen thousand conventioneers expected in Miami Beach, now at height of convention season. Convention of osteopaths—American Fracture Association—is also at Americana. Gathering of truckers is at my hotel—Roney-Plaza. 'The Roney is still the class of the Beach,' taxi driver told me. 'The Hialeah race-track crowd stays at the Roney. Real high society.' Taxi driver knows onions. Took me out to meet Rocky at airport by way of Arthur Godfrey Road, which taxi driver explained as follows: Arthur Godfrey gave Miami Beach publicity, so they named it in his honor.

"Rocky due Miami Airport 11:30 A.M., via Eastern Airlines Flight 607, departed Idlewild 8:45 A.M. Found Rocky advance man named Arch Gillies (tall, skinny, friendly) in charge of advance festivities at Eastern's arrival gate. Found participants in festivities to include two babies (one boy, one girl, in strollers) with mothers; Associated Press greeting committee; Dade County Republican Executive

Committee greeting committee; couple of dozen loose Republican greeters carrying signs reading, 'SOS Save Our South Rocky,' 'Welcome Rockefeller Our Next President,' and 'Miami Welcomes Rockefeller;' couple of dozen screw-loose Republican teen-agers carrying signs reading, 'Go Back to N.Y. Police State,' 'Rocky vs. Jack Is No Choice,' 'Liberate New York and Cuba,' and 'Yellow Whites Appease Red Blacks;' three people wearing buttons that bore handsome photo of Rocky and words 'Always Looking Ahead;' television cameramen with cameras labelled 'WTVJ-CBS, Ch. 4, Miami,' 'WLBW-ABC, Ch. 10, Miami,' and 'WCKT-NBC, Ch. 7, Miami;' and haphazard-looking twenty-two-piece uniformed brass band of schoolboys blaring what sounded like 'My Heart Belongs to Daddy,' followed immediately by peculiar rendition of 'Anchors Aweigh.' Big bass drum bore legend 'Pan Am World Airways Vanguards State Champs Miami Florida.' Arch Gillies looked pleased at rendition of 'My Heart Belongs to Daddy.' 'Very peppy band!' he shouted in my ear. 'Real welcome music!' He pointed out fellow wearing shiny black pin-striped suit, and said, 'Marcus A. Kyle, chairman of the Dade County Republican Executive Committee. They just endorsed Goldwater. I don't know why. Shows lack of confidence. Who does the County Executive Committee represent, anyway?'

"Rocky plane still not in, so went over, gave Marcus Kyle big hello, got big hello back, along with information that Dade County Republican Executive Committee endorsement of Goldwater represents result of poll of eighty-four per cent of Republican leaders throughout state. Also information that Dade County has fifty-five thousand registered Republicans, three hundred and fifty thousand registered Democrats. 'We've expressed our preference,' Marcus Kyle told me. 'We're going to greet Governor Rockefeller courteously, and that's it. I'm not nasty. I'm a Republican first. Being nasty is not good politics. Not good sportsmanship.' Learned Marcus Kyle works for National Airlines. Rocky flying in on Eastern. Salt in wound. Kyle put comb through his hair to make himself shipshape to greet Rocky like good sport.

"A Republican shouted, 'Rocky's plane has landed!' Two minutes later, Rocky showed up. He looked sleepy, bleary, cheerful. Another good sport. He was accompanied by four more Republicans, all look-

ing wide-awake, cheerful, good sports. Everybody gave Rocky big
hello. Introductions started: 'Mr. Brinkman, Mrs. Brinkman, Mr.
Keller, Mr. May, one of our most distinguished . . .' Vanguards
band rendered rerun of 'Anchors Aweigh' and 'My Heart Belongs to
Daddy.' Airport guard told carriers of signs to put signs down—not
allowed. Signs were put down. Rocky gave A.P. committee big
hellos. Mustached A.P. committeeman with badge reading 'Tippen
Davidson, Daytona Beach, Fla., News-Journal' tried to get close to
say hello. 'I really don't belong,' Tippen Davidson said to me with
good-sport shrug. 'I'm an Adlai Stevenson man.' 'Hi there!' Rocky
said to Tippen Davidson, delivering great campaign smile. 'Hi
there!' Rocky said to Republican National Committeewoman busy
telling other Republican greeters, 'Be sure to introduce Leon and
Mortimer and Dave.' Marcus Kyle was busy introducing. 'Hi there!
Nice to see you!' Rocky said to loose Republicans, to kids, to Mr.
Brinkman, to Mrs. Brinkman, to Marcus Kyle.

" 'There aren't enough Republicans to go around,' man wearing
'I'm on the Rockefeller Team' button told me. 'That's why we
brought out the Goldwater men.' Festivities began moving out of
airport. Brass band encored 'Anchors Aweigh.' Rocky said something in Spanish to man in a brown suède jacket, tapped him,
hugged him, waved him goodbye. Man reported to me, 'He speak to
me in Spanish. He say he expect to liberate Cuba if he will be President.' Rocky began to talk to supporters and TV cameras: '. . .
offer constructive alternatives based on principles . . . failures of
Kennedy administration . . . and we're going to see a Republican
victory in '64!' Talk ended, he proceeded toward three-car motorcade to go to Americana. TV man stuck mike in front of walking
Rocky, asked, 'What'd you think of the reception?' 'Hi there! Very
nice,' Rocky said. 'Was it what you expected?' TV man asked.
'More than I expected,' Rocky replied. 'Rockefeller for President!' a
new spectator shouted. 'Thanks!' Rocky shouted.

"I fell in step with Arch Gillies on way to third limousine. En
route to Americana, via Arthur Godfrey Road, asked him what kind
of Republican Rocky is and why. His answer: He's a Republican like
Teddy Roosevelt, that's what kind, and also why. 'No motorcycle
escort?' I asked Arch Gillies. 'The Governor doesn't like that sort of

stuff,' he said. On to Americana. Expensive hotel; not like Roney. 'Hip! Hip! Hooray!' a crowd of eight at Americana's entrance yelled to Rocky. 'Hi!' Rocky yelled. His bleary, sleepy look gone. Conventioneers from American Fracture Association were in lobby of hotel, clapping for Rocky. Rocky waved. Arch Gillies audibly wished he could go swimming. Rocky's mob went into Bal Masqué Room for lunch—three-fifty per person, all-inclusive—of Fresh Florida Fruit Cocktail au Maraschino en Supreme Silver, Potted Brisket of Prime Beef Madère (Handsome Garnishing to Compliment), Key Lime Sherbet, and Coffee, and a Rocky speech. I skipped lunch and had glass of pineapple juice at pool. It cost eight-five cents (thirty cents at Roney). Got back to Bal Masqué in time to see Americana management trying to keep Fracture conventioneers from merging with editors to hear Rocky.

"In Bal Masqué, Rocky said something about how his grandfather saved money—no argument there—and then went on to subject of how State of New York has little debt but City of New York has *big* debt. (Aha, here we go!) 'We want every young person in any state to have the best possible education, regardless of financial means,' he said. There was more about fundamental principles, then references to being threatened on one side by extreme Right of Republican Party and threatened on other side by you-know-who-and-what. And 'We need twenty million new jobs.' Charged you-know-who with 'lack of understanding of the nature and gravity of the Communist threat.' (Big hand.) Then there were questions and answers. Question: How do you assess your chances in the South? Answer: The South is moving to a two-party system, and Republicans will get a strong vote in the South. Question: What about Goldwater's proposal to sell T.V.A.? Answer: T.V.A. is great as it is; in fact, the Power Authority in the State of New York generates even more power than T.V.A. through a similar public-private relationship. Question: Do you expect to win the New Hampshire primary? Answer: I'm the underdog now, but it's a long time between now and March. Question: Is your strong civil-rights plank going to hurt you in the South? Answer: No. (Big hand.) Question: Nixon? Answer: Well, he's offstage but peeking around the corner. Question: Are you in favor of the Peace Corps? Answer: Yes. It's the best single program that the Kennedy administration has undertaken. No further questions.

"Beat it back to Roney in time to catch television news program (WCKT-NBC, Ch. 7), with announcer saying, 'Hopeful Nelson Rockefeller took Miami Beach by storm today.'"

❧❧ THE PRESIDENT

OUR LAST GLIMPSE of President Kennedy was in Miami, where, four days before his death, he was engaged in the same kind of mission that took him to Dallas. He was slated to arrive at Miami International Airport at 5 P.M. on Monday, November 18th, to speak there to a crowd of voters, rounded up mostly by local Democrats, and, a couple of hours later, to address a convention of the Inter-American Press Association at the Americana Hotel, with appearances at a couple of social-political gatherings squeezed in between—all this after Saturday at Cape Canaveral, Sunday at Palm Beach, and all day Monday at Tampa, there inspecting MacDill Air Force Base, lunching at Army–Air Force Strike Command Headquarters at the base, journeying by helicopter to Lopez Field, in downtown Tampa, and speaking there on the fiftieth anniversary of commercial aviation, addressing the Florida State Chamber of Commerce, addressing a meeting of the Steelworkers' Union, and riding around the Tampa streets, shaking hands through it all with everybody he could reach. The main danger that crossed our mind as we went out to the Miami airport that Monday afternoon with the press was that, in his eagerness to make himself accessible, he was probably coming in contact with scores of colds, and we marvelled at his physical stamina.

The Miami Beach *Daily Sun* had kept the public posted with banner headlines like "SPECIAL VISITOR IS COMING HERE TONIGHT," and the Miami *Herald* Spanish-language section carried a headline reading, "ARRIBA HOY KENNEDY A MIAMI—HABLARA A LOS EDITORES LATINOS." There were signs everywhere at the airport of the precautions that the Secret Service, the F.B.I., and the local police had taken to reconcile maximum handshaking with maximum security. There were also signs everywhere of Democratic Party rifts, dissatisfactions, and antagonisms, all of which the President himself would be trying, by sheer will and the force of his personal presence, to reconcile. We encountered Congressman Claude Pepper before he left Miami to meet the President in Tampa. He planned to fly back to Miami with him on the Presidential plane, along with Senator George Smathers, Governor Farris Bryant, and Congressman Dante Fascell. Pepper told us he was very hopeful that Kennedy would carry the State of Florida in 1964, having lost it by only 46,776 votes in 1960. "Some Democrats didn't fight too hard for him in 1960," he said. "I want to see the Democratic Party fight harder in '64." Pepper didn't know definitely whether he would introduce President Kennedy to the crowd at the airport. That was still to be decided, he told us—probably on the plane. He added, "All you're supposed to say is 'Ladies and gentlemen, the President of the United States.' Sam Rayburn always used to say, 'It is my distinguished honor to present the President of the United States.' What I'd like to say is 'My fellow-countrymen, it is our honor now to hear our friend the President and the next President of the United States.' "

The President's plane was scheduled to land in the Delta Airlines area, and a Delta hangar had been festooned with a red-and-white banner reading, "WELCOME MR. PRESIDENT." Among the Secret Service men and the police and the political planners, we came across a planner who was passing out identifying badges of various colors to members of the V.I.P., official, platform, and press groups, along with diagrams showing the position of each group (including a group of two dozen Florida mayors), and also of a hundred-and-forty-five-member band, the Band of the Hour, from the University of Miami. Another planner—a Democratic State Committeeman for Dade County, of which Miami is the seat—was passing out placards to the public, stationed behind a wire fence. The signs read, "WELCOME PRESIDENT KENNEDY BISCAYNE DEMOCRATIC CLUB" and "POLISH-AMERICAN CLUB WELCOMES PRESIDENT KENNEDY" and "SENIOR CITIZENS' COUNCIL WELCOMES PRESIDENT KENNEDY." Milling about in the V.I.P. section were a number of V.I.P. children, wearing cardboard buttons that proclaimed, "MY MOM AND DAD ARE FOR YOU PRESIDENT KENNEDY."

Just behind the wire fence stood a pretty young Negro woman, who was herding a small group of Negro children. She was Mrs.

Lillian Peterson, she told us, and the children were part of her fourth-grade class at the Lillie C. Evans Elementary School. She said that no one had invited them to come to the airport; they had just come. The children looked at us solemnly and, at their teacher's prompting, identified themselves as Barbara Laidler (wearing a green ribbon bow in her hair), Anthony Shinhoster, Ietta Odom, Gregory Gill, and William Ingram. "We've just finished studying the United States of America and our three chief executives," Mrs. Peterson told us. "I drew a diagram for the children showing the Mayor in a small circle on the bottom, the Governor in a bigger circle over him, and the President in the biggest circle on top. The fourth grade, you know, is really the foundation grade for the rest of your life. These children have the responsibility of sharing the President's visit with others in the class, who could not come. They have the responsibility of writing a report about what they see today."

Around four-fifteen, four helicopters arrived and sat waiting to take the President and his party from the airport to a secret landing area near the Americana Hotel. In the V.I.P. section there appeared a group of women wearing Uncle Sam hats—red-and-white striped crowns, brims with white stars on blue, and the words "WIN WITH KENNEDY." An F.B.I. man instructed the band's conductor, a man with white hair, to play ruffles and flourishes when the President arrived, and then "Hail to the Chief." At four-twenty-two, the band broke into "On the Square," and it got through "The Colossus of Columbia March," "The Crosley March," "Nobles of the Mystic Shrine," "God Bless America," and "March of the Mighty" before the blue-and-white Presidential plane, bearing the words "UNITED STATES OF AMERICA" and the Presidential seal, finally landed, at five-twelve.

President Kennedy emerged from the tail of the plane, looking relaxed and good-humored, and got to work immediately at what he was expected to do, and more. With the Congressmen, the Senator, and the Governor sticking close to him, he extended his hand wherever he was directed to extend it, and he seemed to find a number of hands to shake on his own, too. He varied his "Hello" and "How are you?" and "Glad to see you" with an occasional "Nice going, boy." When the President appeared on the platform, there was a big cheer from the crowd (it numbered about eight thousand), and though he had yet to be introduced, he came forward eagerly to smile and wave and give a little bow. Pepper, on the platform, introduced Governor Bryant, and the Governor, it turned out, had the privilege of introducing the President. The Governor said that they were all proud of what President Kennedy had done for Florida, and that he felt a special pride and pleasure in presenting the President of the United States.

President Kennedy took it from there, in his own ebullient way. "I've been making nonpartisan speeches all day, and I'm glad to come here as a Democrat," he started off, in old-fashioned campaign style. The crowd loved it. There were cheers from both sides of the wire fence, and all the politicians on the platform appeared happy and satisfied. The President went on to talk about the national purpose—among other things, taking care of seven or eight million boys and girls who will want to go to college in the year 1970. The President said he was going to go on fighting for Congressional enactment of his program, even though certain people "oppose what I am trying to do, just as they opposed everything Franklin Roosevelt tried to do and everything Harry Truman tried to do." The crowd cheered again. The President wound up by saying that the Democrats had won in Dade County by nearly sixty-five thousand votes in the last Presidential election, and he was convinced that the State of Florida was going to be Democratic in 1964. At that, the V.I.P.s, the politicians, the public—everybody—seemed to be united in cheers and smiles.

President Kennedy then left the platform and started walking among the people, smiling, shaking hands, and saying hello. He made a special point of going over to the conductor of the Band of the Hour and thanking him. Behind the President, the politicians piled up, greeting each other joyously with cries of "Hey, Sheriff!" and "Hey, Judge!" and "Hey, Mayor!" We ran into the State President of the Young Democratic Clubs of Florida, a young man named Dick Pettigrew, who had flown in from Tampa on the President's plane. He was glowing. "I never saw so many people in my life as I did in Tampa," he told us. "The President made a brilliant speech before the Chamber of Commerce. He did a beautiful job of explaining why the administration is not anti-business. The Secret Service man next to me on the plane said that the applause the

President got was not just polite applause, it was genuine." Then we ran into Congressman Pepper, and he, too, was glowing over the reception in Tampa. "If President Roosevelt, at the heyday of his popularity, had been riding through Tampa, he never would have got such a reception!" Pepper told us.

We noticed that Mrs. Peterson and her fourth-graders were crowded against the wire fence, their hands outstretched, and we noticed that the President kept trying to pull away from the Secret Service men and head in their direction. A white man was holding Barbara up high to get a better look (her green hair ribbon was now untied and fluttering), so that she could give a responsible report to the rest of her class and share with them everything that she saw that day.

The next afternoon, we telephoned Mrs. Peterson to ask her how the children had carried out their responsibilities. Barbara, she told us, reading from their reports, wrote, "The first thing we had was music. They took the President's picture many times. The President has reddish hair and had on a suit. People enjoyed seeing President Kennedy." Anthony reported that he had seen "lots of policemen," and ended up, "I enjoyed seeing our President." Ietta wrote, "We waited and waited and waited. At last we saw some airplanes and four helicopters. We saw a lot of people. John F. Kennedy finally came. He said a little speech." Gregory wrote, "I was glad to go and see our President because this was my first time seeing him and I admire him and his speeches. I think Mr. Kennedy is the greatest man in the world!" William wrote, "He went on the helicopter. Crowds and crowds of people began to say goodbye as he flew away. The crowd of people began to yell louder and louder and it sounded like one thousand people saying goodbye."

FUGUE

Mr. Glenn Gould, the pianist, held a private showing one recent morning, for Mr. Yehudi Menuhin, the violinist, of a movie starring himself. The movie, which had been made from an hour-long video-tape recording, was entitled The Anatomy of Fugue. It was projected on a screen the size of a pillowcase, in a room the size of an average closet, in the local office of the Canadian Broadcasting Corporation, which had broadcast the tape. Mr. Gould, unslept and unbarbered, was in town for a couple of days from his home, in Toronto. He had on his usual baggy dark-blue suit with outmoded overpadded shoulders, a raggedy brown sweater, and a worn-out bluish necktie. A yellow pencil protruded, eraser end up, from his coat pocket. He was burdened with a baggy brown overcoat, a brown wool muffler, and a navy-blue cap. Mr. Menuhin, pink-cheeked, chubby, trim, and serene, had come to town from his home, in London, to start on a three-month, twenty-eight-city recital tour that would include several benefit appearances and one appearance on the Bell Telephone Hour. He was neatly encased in well-tailored pin stripes and well-laundered supplementation. Mr. Gould sat on a straight-backed office chair, with his coat, cap, and muffler on his lap, and with his arms crossed and his hands tucked under his arms. Mr. Menuhin sat on a straight-backed office chair right behind him, his fingers intertwined over his midriff.

"I'm so glad you could come, I'm so glad you could really make it," Mr. Gould said, turning around, to Mr. Menuhin. "I want you to see this one. This one is a special pet."

"Such a nice thing to do in New York," Mr. Menuhin said, in a light, warm voice, and gave Mr. Gould a gentle, warm smile. "Seeing a movie, at eleven o'clock in the morning! I'm so happy you suggested it."

"I like making these films," Mr. Gould said. "I've always felt this terrible frustration in concerts—you do it and it's gone. Why not put it on film and have it? So that it will be there."

"Wonderful idea. Wonderful," Mr. Menuhin said, his smile broadening and a look of appreciation coming into his eyes.

Mr. Gould grinned.

"I did a television film on Bartók, covering the musical influences in his life, and playing some of his arrangements of Hungarian folk tunes and excerpts from the solo violin sonata he wrote for me, and speaking in between, and I did another one about Yoga," Mr. Menuhin said. "I find it rather difficult when they put you in front of the camera and say, 'Do something.'"

Mr. Gould bobbed his head in agreement. "We had a very good director for this one, and we even built a set, as you'll see," he said. "We shot the whole thing in two days. After two months of conferences, of course."

"Was it dreadfully expensive?" Mr. Menuhin asked. "These things do cost so much."

"Thirty thousand dollars, about," Mr. Gould said. "But I wanted to do it right. There's no point in doing it at all if you can't get what you want." He waved a hand at the projectionist, who was peeking out of a square hole in the back wall. "We're ready any time you want to start," Mr. Gould said.

Mr. Menuhin gave a little sigh and tightened his hands around his middle. "I hope this will be made available to television in this country," he said.

Mr. Gould grinned again. "Well, they've got Leonard Bernstein," he said. "I don't do it the way he does it. Not that I don't admire the way he does it. He has the ability to communicate on a great many levels at once. My way is different." He bobbed his head vigorously. "I don't know if my film is for the mass public. Sometimes I think they don't know what the hell I've said, but they feel elevated."

Mr. Menuhin's eyes twinkled.

"Roll it," Mr. Gould said to the projectionist behind the wall. He turned back toward the screen, and tossed his coat, muffler, and cap on the floor. The lights went out, and the movie started, showing Mr. Gould at the piano playing an improvisation based on "Do Re

Mi," from Richard Rodgers' score for *The Sound of Music*. When he had finished it, he looked up, on the screen, and said to the camera, "For hundreds of years, musicians have been doing the sort of thing that I was attempting just now. They have been taking little bits of musical trivia, like that theme from *The Sound of Music*, and trying to find complicated equations into which, like a common denominator, these tidbits will fit. In fact, there is some part of almost every musician that longs to experiment with the mathematical quantities of music and to find forms in which these quantities can function most successfully. And perhaps the long-time favorite of such forms is that special musical mix we call the fugue. The fugue is normally conceived in a number of voices, a number of individual lines that, up to a certain point, may lead a life of their own. But they must have in common a responsibility to some special material that is examined in the course of the fugue, and consequently each of the voices is first heard announcing, in its most comfortable register, the same theme. . . ."

As Mr. Gould elaborated on the give-and-take between the voices in the fugue—each musical voice, he said, went off on "some pretty wacky tangents of its own"—Mr. Menuhin listened intently, and when Mr. Gould explained that the relation of the subject of a fugue to its countersubject would be something like that of "God Save the Queen" to "The Star-Spangled Banner," Mr. Menuhin made a soft sound of concurrence. "They ought to combine and complement their personalities in a manner that, as Johann Sebastian Bach once said, suggests three or four civilized gentlemen conducting a reasonable conversation," Mr. Gould continued. "And the conversation that they carry on does not necessarily always deal with particularly imposing matters. . . . In fact, in certain cases the more ordinary the subject the better."

"Good," Mr. Menuhin said. "Very good."

The offscreen Mr. Gould got up and went right up to the pillowcase screen, shaking his head ruefully. "Can you get a slightly sharper focus?" he called back to the projectionist.

Nothing changed in the focus. Mr. Gould sat down again. Onscreen, he was saying, "When we hear a fugue like the one in E flat from Volume II of Bach's *The Well-Tempered Clavier*, we hear a composition that not only disciplines four profoundly beautiful lines but makes them more compelling by having them work within a superbly disciplined harmonic regime." He then played the fugue on the piano.

"Lovely," Mr. Menuhin said when he had finished. "Lovely." The offscreen Mr. Gould gave Mr. Menuhin a pleased look. Then he got up and went back to see the projectionist. When he returned, a moment later, the image on the screen was sharper. "Better?" he asked Mr. Menuhin.

"Much better, yes," Mr. Menuhin said.

Both men settled back more easily in their chairs. Mr. Gould crossed his legs. He hunched forward as he heard himself say, on the screen, that he was now going to play a much more intense fugue from Volume II of The Well-Tempered Clavier—the B Flat Minor, one of the finest of Bach's fugues.

"Wonderful," Mr. Menuhin said at the end of the fugue.

"It's a great piece," Mr. Gould said.

Mr. Menuhin commented on the lightness of the piano sound, and Mr. Gould said that this particular piano had almost no after-touch.

At one point, when the camera zeroed in on Mr. Gould as he was playing, the watching Mr. Gould shuddered. "God, that's a nasty shot," he said. "It's like Cornel Wilde in A Song to Remember, with Merle Oberon leaning over the piano."

"Oh, no, it comes over beautifully!" Mr. Menuhin said.

Every time Mr. Gould finished playing something on the screen, Mr. Menuhin would lean forward slightly, Mr. Gould would turn around to him, and Mr. Menuhin would say, "Wonderful performance, wonderful performance." Near the end of the movie, Mr. Gould said, onscreen, "Paul Hindemith is one of the few composers of our own time who can undeniably be called a fuguist to the manner born. Hindemith has developed a very special language of his own, a language that is contemporary in the best sense of the word but in its attempt to provide harmonic logic uses what you might call a substitute tonality." Then he played the fugue from Hindemith's Third Piano Sonata, which Mr. Menuhin immediately said was a wonderful piece.

"And now!" the offscreen Mr. Gould said, standing up. "We come to what we've all been waiting for!" He adjusted a knob near the screen that turned the sound up. "We have to have *this* louder, that's for sure," Mr. Gould said, laughing and shaking with his laughter.

Mr. Menuhin smiled.

On the screen, a quartet—a baritone, a tenor, a soprano, and a contralto—started singing a composition in fugue style by Mr. Gould:

> "So, you want to write a fugue,
> You've got the urge to write a fugue,
> You've got the nerve to write a fugue,
> The only way to write one is to plunge right in and write one.
> So go ahead."

"Lovely, lovely," Mr. Menuhin commented.

The movie ended. The lights came on.

"Wonderful program!" Mr. Menuhin said. "Beautifully done!"

Mr. Gould suddenly looked shy. "Thank you," he said. "It was really quite fun to do. But it took a hell of a lot of work."

"I love your approach to the music and the completely unmechanical way you play," Mr. Menuhin said, beaming at Mr. Gould with admiration. "And you spoke throughout so *smoothly*. Was it impromptu?"

"I had it on the TelePrompTer," Mr. Gould said. "I looked at it often enough to pick up all the cues, but I forced myself to invent phrases as I went along, to keep it sounding natural and not too formal."

"Yes, wonderful," Mr. Menuhin said. "Especially if the words are your own."

Mr. Gould laughed shyly.

"For the one I did on Bartók, I had quite good dialogue, but not quite as good as yours," Mr. Menuhin said. He gave a little sigh. "Most enjoyable!" he said.

"Next year, if you're going to have some time, we might do one together," Mr. Gould said. "You ever done the Schoenberg Fantasia?"

"Oh!" Mr. Menuhin gave a little gasp. "What a splendid idea! I must look at the music."

"It's a dry work—one of his last things," Mr. Gould said.

"I have the music," Mr. Menuhin said. "You're not coming to England next summer? We might do it there."

"I'd love to come and visit you," Mr. Gould said. "But I'm finished with concerts. You know my feeling about concerts. I'm bored with them."

Mr. Menuhin smiled wistfully. "On the screen, it does gain dimensions," he said.

"Some people say that every performance is an experience, but it's not that for me in concerts," Mr. Gould said. "It's animals. It's all a circus. It's immoral."

"Yes, I do know what you mean," Mr. Menuhin said mildly.

"When I'm onstage, I can shut them out, but I don't like it," Mr. Gould said. "I won't do more than six concerts a year. My view of the future is the end of the concert experience and the revitalization of the home experience. I haven't gone to a concert in months. When I'm in the audience, I'm completely distracted, I'm acutely uncomfortable. I don't feel the therapy of private listening."

"You are recording, though?" Mr. Menuhin said, beginning to look alarmed.

Mr. Gould said of course, and laughed. "I want to send you the 'Six Bach Partitas' that just came out," he said. "I'm rather proud of that record."

Mr. Menuhin appeared relieved. "Would you come to England in July?" he asked. "To make the film?"

Mr. Gould bobbed his head and grinned. "The Schoenberg," he said. "In July."

Mr. Menuhin got up to go, smiling and looking utterly at peace. He gave Mr. Gould his hand. "It will be lovely," he said. "We will do it, and then it will be there."

❧ REDEDICATION

AT 12:28 P.M. on December 4, 1963, in the Security Council Chamber of the United Nations, our Ambassador, Adlai E. Stevenson, who is presiding over the Council this month, spoke on a draft resolution by Norway that is known in the archives as S/5469 and was identified on his typewritten address as "Statement on Apartheid." Governor Stevenson (as he is still called by his friends) began by saying, "Last Wednesday, the new President of the United States, speaking to a joint session of our Congress, rededicated the Government of the United States—and I use his words—'to the unswerving support of the United Nations.' I speak today in the spirit of that rededication, in the spirit of his plea for an 'end to the teachings and preachings of hate and evil and violence,' and in the spirit of his determination that 'it is'—to use his words—'our responsibility and our trust in this Year of Our Lord 1963 to strike the chains of bias and prejudice from minds and practices as Lincoln, a century ago, struck down slavery.' President Johnson's first message to our Congress included an urgent call for action to wipe out the remnants of racial discrimination in this country. No less firm is our opposition to racial discrimination anywhere. . . ."

Four hours before Governor Stevenson spoke, we called on him in his Waldorf suite as he was starting his usual breakfast-cum-work, a half grapefruit before him, the Times at his plate, the dining room filled with sunshine, the forty-second-floor view of the city unfogged, the telephone in the next room jangling, his housekeeper, Mrs. Viola Reardy (white-haired, pink-cheeked, cheerful), hovering over him, and the Governor himself, his hair freshly slicked and a crisp white handkerchief protruding from his breast pocket, looking wide-awake and eager to meet the day. When we remarked on how well he looked, he explained that he had had a vacation: three and a half

days, over the Thanksgiving weekend, at Chelsea, an ancient planta-
tion in Ridgeland, South Carolina, in the company of his sister, Mrs.
Ernest L. Ives; his sons Adlai, Jr., and Borden; Adlai, Jr.'s, wife; and
some friends. He had gone duck and quail hunting, he said—had got
up at five every morning, put on heavy boots and corduroys, had
breakfast, ridden horseback through the pine forest, dismounted to
follow the hounds, and started shooting at sunup. "It's the longest
rest holiday I've had in 1963," he told us. "I had none at all this past
summer. In July, I was in Paris and Geneva, with the Economic and
Social Council, and at the end of a couple of weeks of work I set out
to visit friends at Lake Como, and was going on from there to visit
my sister in Florence. My first day at Lake Como, the President—
President Kennedy—called me. There were immediate decisions to
be made about our policy in sundry places, including the Portuguese
colonies in Africa. He said, 'If you can't come back, we can talk on
the phone,' but I felt I ought to come back."

Mrs. Reardy removed the grapefruit shell, set in its place a plate
of poached egg sprinkled with diced ham, offered the Governor
some thick whole-wheat toast, and poured coffee into his cup. The
Governor asked her if she would, at some point that morning, take
an envelope he had addressed to the President of the Philippines
down to the thirty-fifth floor, where the President of the Philippines
happened to be staying, and just hand it to the guard there. He had
scarcely made a dent in the poached egg when Mrs. Reardy asked
him if he would take a call from our Ambassador to NATO,
Thomas Finletter. The Governor said he would indeed, had a quick
bite of toast, and excused himself to take the call. When he reappeared, he told us that he expected to speak on the Apartheid Resolution at the Security Council meeting scheduled to start at 10:30
A.M. but would first go to his office at the United States Mission,
across First Avenue from the U.N.'s General Assembly Building, for
his daily meeting with his aides. "My speech should be waiting for
me, with suggestions for possible changes," the Governor explained.
"I finished writing it last night and sent it down to the State Department on the wire for the team there to go over it. I wrote a good
part of the speech while presiding the past three days; I sit there and
listen, and, during translations, try to get some of my own work
done. This has been a bitter business with South Africa, working

against her policy of apartheid—the total separation of the white
and nonwhite populations. A resolution was drawn up while the de-
bate was going on, and we may take the vote this morning."

We asked the Governor whether he didn't get discouraged by the
bitterness inside as well as outside the country, and he said quickly
that he was still optimistic. "The murder of President Kennedy was
the act of a maniac, an individual maniac, and there's no evidence
that it was political," he said. "There have been other shocking mo-
ments in our time, such as Pearl Harbor and the death of F.D.R.
But there was a special poignancy to this tragedy: President Kennedy's youth, his promise, his vitality, his blithe spirit, all snuffed
out so suddenly. There was the sense of incompleteness. He demonstrated that brains have some place in politics. One felt his sense of
commitment to the rational, and to the possibility of doing something. Probably his firm stand for equal dignity for all people, not
just white people, also contributed to the burst of sympathy, so universal, from friend and foe alike. After the tragedy, there were many
eulogies—some brilliant—at the United Nations General Assembly.
I had to speak last, and used the opportunity not only to talk about
President Kennedy but also to affirm President Johnson's support
for the U.N. and the continuity of American foreign policy. It was
important to reassure the other nations quickly."

The Governor lit a cigarette over his coffee and, after a quick puff
at it, said, "Somehow, I still have a complete sense of the importance of the United Nations, in spite of the frustrations and the
exhausting trivia. I think of the United Nations, in the political
field, as one of the great experiments of man. My job has become an
exciting one. There's no issue in the world now that doesn't affect
the United States. We're involved in everything. There are a hundred and ten other nations in the U.N., and I have to receive and
talk with representatives of almost all of them, and there's no problem any more on which we can take the position that we're going to
sit this one out. In my own day-to-day life, it's very much the way it
was when I was campaigning for President; it's campaigning perpet-
ually. The worst thing about running for President, for me, was that
you had to shave twice a day, and you have to do that in this job,
too."

He put out his cigarette, picked up his *Times*, grabbed his coat and hat, said goodbye to Mrs. Reardy, and urged us to come on. Going down in the elevator, he said we'd have to take a taxi, because he had given his car to a lady from the Peace Corps who had to make an official trip to the Bronx. His speech that day, he told us, would be his third important policy speech since Lyndon Johnson became President. "Last week, I stated President Johnson's views on the U.N. and the search for peace. I also had to speak on Outer Space to the First Committee—the first expression of our policy as it has been laid down by President Johnson—and I had some good quotations from past Johnson speeches that I could use," he said. "It was so very important for me to make known the continuity of our policy, such as the United States proposal for a joint effort by the Russians and the Americans to reach the moon, and the freedom-of-the-skies policy that we have laboriously worked out with the Russians over the past two years. Kennedy and Johnson, of course, had exactly the same policy. After the President's funeral, Johnson asked me to come back to the White House with him, and we talked a bit about it then, and we talked again after his address to the Joint Session of Congress, and then we had another conversation on the telephone, and after I'd made the speech he told me he'd heard it on the radio. It's an area he's been interested in—at first, as Senate leader—since the beginning. Few know more about it than Johnson."

Going down Second Avenue in the taxi, we asked the Governor how long he has known President Johnson. "Since 1933," he said. "I was assistant counsel in the Agricultural Adjustment Administration and he was the bright, energetic, and liberal secretary of Congressman Dick Kleberg, with whom I played golf occasionally. Then, during the Second World War, when I was assistant to the Secretary of the Navy, my recollection is that after Pearl Harbor Lyndon wanted to get into the Navy and I handled his application for a Reserve commission. When he was elected to the Senate, I was Governor of Illinois. I was nominated for President by the Democrats in 1952 and 1956 while he was our majority leader in the Senate. So we met often in those years, while I was the Party's leader. And, of course, constantly during the Kennedy administration. We've found common ground on most of the issues since the New Deal. President Johnson is a much better politician than I ever thought of being. He knows that the important thing is the objective, and you try to get as much as you can of it. He has incomparable managerial skill and is extremely mature. There's an old saying that the best politics is the least politics. President Johnson understands that. At the same time, I think the bold thing is the best politics. For a politician to be both right and bold is not easy."

At the United States Mission, we accompanied the Governor to his office, on the eleventh floor, where he put his coat and hat in a closet and sat down in a high-backed green leather swivel chair behind his desk, with his back to the picture window overlooking the U.N. He put on his glasses and started reading his mail and some papers on his desk while several secretaries and aides moved into his office. An hour later, after he had worked out appointments with the Korean Foreign Minister and twenty-six other people for the rest of the day and got through his daily session with his staff, he again said come on, and led us out to the elevator and down to the street, where he hurried us across First Avenue against the lights, dodging traffic. He practically ran up the drive to the General Assembly Building and into the Security Council Chamber. There, saying "hello"s, and a couple of "bonjour"s, and greeting Secretary-General U Thant with a wave, he took his place in the center of the horse-shoe-shaped table, behind the plaque reading "President." To his right sat U Thant, Sir Patrick Dean (United Kingdom), N. T. Fedorenko (Union of Soviet Socialist Republics), Privado G. Jiminez (Philippines), Sivert Nielsen (Norway), and Dey Ould Sidi Baba (Morocco). To his left sat Vladimir P. Suslov (Undersecretary-General), Tulio Alvarado (Venezuela), Carlos Bernardes (Brazil), Liu Chieh (China), Roger Seydoux (France), and Alex Quaison-Sackey (Ghana).

We went up to the gallery and took a seat just in time (10:45 A.M.) to see Governor Stevenson give a gentle tap of the gavel and hear him say, "The thousand-and-seventy-eighth session of the Security Council is now in session. . . . If I hear no objection, I shall take it that discussion is in order on Document S/5469. . . ."

The speeches started at 10:57 A.M. Sir Patrick Dean led off (sixteen minutes; for the resolution, with objections on procedure), and was followed by Seydoux (seven minutes; for the resolution) and then by Fedorenko (eleven minutes; for, also with objections on procedure). In almost every case, equal time was occupied by translations.

At 12:28 P.M., Governor Stevenson began to speak. He started off by saying, "Inasmuch as all the members of the Security Council have now spoken, I shall exercise my privilege of speaking on behalf of the United States," and ended by quoting President Kennedy as having said "Is not peace, in the last analysis, a matter of human rights?" and declaring that the United States would vote for the draft resolution. (Eighteen minutes.) During the translation of his speech, there was a great deal of wandering around by the delegates and their aides, and several of them went over to Governor Stevenson and conferred with him. A few minutes later, Governor Stevenson announced that five more delegates had asked for, and been granted, time to speak. They were representatives of Liberia (". . . All that we ask is justice for the nonwhite majority. . . . In his recent, eloquent Thanksgiving Day address to the American people, President Lyndon B. Johnson declared, 'God made all of us, not some of us, in His image. All of us, not just some of us, are His children' "), Sierra Leone, Tunisia, India (". . . The resolution is, in our opinion, a step forward, perhaps a small one, but nevertheless a step forward"), and Ghana ("In view of our desire to coöperate with our Scandinavian friends . . . my delegation would not press its request"). Ambassador Nielsen, of Norway, then spoke a few words of thanks to Ghana for "the new sign of coöperation." The Ambassadors of the United Kingdom and the Union of Soviet Socialist Republics both declared that they withdrew their objections to the resolution.

At 1:27 P.M., Governor Stevenson asked if anyone else wished to be heard, and when it appeared that no one did, he asked if there was "any objection to proceeding forthwith to a vote."

No one objected.

"All those in favor, please raise hands," Governor Stevenson said.

All representatives on the Council raised their hands. The Security Council was thereby appealing for a world-wide embargo on the shipment to South Africa of equipment for arms, as part of the drive to force her to abandon her policy of apartheid, and was, for the second time, condemning her for that policy.

"The result of the vote is unanimity," Governor Stevenson said. "I would suggest, therefore, that we adjourn."

As the representatives on each side of him arose, looking pleased, he sat quietly for a moment and then quickly gathered up his papers and left the Chamber.

❧ LASSIE'S FUTURE

LASSIE, our favorite television star, was in town last week for personal-appearance shenanigans at the Coliseum Sports Show, and, with all the rumors going around that the *Lassie* program was going to dump the kid stuff and go adult, we took the opportunity to get at the truth about Lassie's future. A telephone call to the vice-president-in-charge-of-Lassie of the Wrather Corporation, producer of Lassie's TV program (and owner of, among other things, Muzak), got us an interview with Lassie in her midtown hotel suite, which she was sharing with her trainer, Rudd Weatherwax, and with a friend, a two-year-old silky terrier named Silky, who is also an actor. We took a friend of our own along—a pretty little girl named Amy, who is ten. It was a joy to Amy and to us to find Lassie looking —unlike everybody else in television—a hundred per cent secure and untroubled. She looked great—exactly like her golden image, except for an expression in her eyes which strongly resembled Cary Grant's. After graciously permitting Amy to shake her paw and granting five straight minutes of ogling time, Lassie stretched out on the sofa of her suite, with Amy lined up alongside and Silky establishing a claim on Amy's lap. This arrangement left a small space at the end of the sofa, which we grabbed. Mr. Weatherwax, a handsome, hard-muscled, flat-stomached man with a salt-and-pepper crew haircut, took an armchair, stretched his legs and arched his back, and said crisply to Lassie, "Lassie, put your head on your right paw." Lassie did.

Amy got straight to the main and burning question. "Is it true about Lassie not belonging to the little boy Timmy any more and not being on the farm and being taken away from Timmy?" she asked.

"Get it right, now, for God's sake!" Mr. Weatherwax said to Amy, in the same crisp, commanding tone. "I'll tell you the way it will be. Timmy's father, Mr. Martin, gets a government job to go to Australia to show American know-how to the Australian farmers, and he accepts, not knowing the law that says you can't take a dog into the country. Then the kid is brokenhearted—and all this you will see next September—so the kid leaves Lassie with the old neighbor, Cully, where Silky lives. And the forest ranger, Corey, comes to the Martin farm after the kid has taken off for Australia with his folks, and finds them gone, and so he goes over to Cully's, and there Cully asks him to take Lassie back to live with *him*. That's the way it will be. The old crowd appears once, in the first episode, and then they're all out of the picture. All except Lassie. Course, I'm going to miss that little kid, but he's made enough money to live in comfort for the rest of his life, and his mother wants him to go to school, even if he is rich at fourteen."

"Does he get *paid?*" Amy asked.

"God, the kid makes sixty thousand a year," Mr. Weatherwax said.

"Does *Lassie* get paid?"

"In excess of a hundred thousand a year," Mr. Weatherwax said. "The kid won't miss Lassie, because he comes to the ranch every weekend to play with Lassie, and Lassie won't miss the kid, because Lassie has his own family. Me and my wife are Lassie's real family. Why, this dog before he had his eyes open was sleeping next to my skin. Every three hours at night, I'd get up and feed him his bottle, and when he got his eyes open, the first one he saw was me. This dog is the grandson of the original Lassie, who was in the movies seven years and lived to be nineteen. This one's father, who was also Lassie, is twelve, and he'll be in the house while I'm giving commands to this one outside, and he'll be doing everything in the house that this one does outside. Lassie, here, is going to be five in November. By now I guess everybody knows we use a male collie for Lassie, because the males are bigger than the females and, also, the males don't shed. I'm always training two or three collies to be Lassie. But you can train one for a couple of years and still you don't get a *Lassie*. You can't have a Lassie who is scary or spooky. And you can't have a vicious dog, but still you need a dog with nerve enough to fight forest fires and jump cliffs and swim the rapids and buck the snow avalanche and save Corey's life and—"

"And save Timmy's life," Amy said.

"Not any more," Mr. Weatherwax said. "I *told* you. Lassie will be with Corey, the forest ranger. They've gone into the problem thoroughly back home, and everyone feels it's time to go on to more adult programs. We've outgrown two kids, and for ten years we've written about the Martin farm. We want to get away from the Martin farm. They've gone into every aspect of the problem as a show for adults, and you can be sure they know their ground. This series is Lassie's series. Bob Bray, who plays Corey, doesn't resent working with a dog—which a lot of actors do, because the dog steals scenes from them. Bob Bray is going to be a real popular type, along Clark Gable lines. He's a very happily married man of forty-two, has eight kids, lives up at Lake Arrowhead, follows nice, clean living, and keeps himself in marvellous condition. He doesn't mind it when he has to carry Lassie—ninety-two pounds. I can tell when people like dogs."

"Was Lassie's mother an actor?" Amy asked.

"No, just the father," Mr. Weatherwax said. "I wouldn't have anything but a great strain of collie for the mothers, but the only two great dog stars have been male. When I was a kid, it was Rin-Tin-Tin, and although Strongheart, a German shepherd, and Buck, a Saint Bernard, got to be well known, they never became stars, like Rin-Tin-Tin and Lassie. Wherever I take her, Lassie gets start treatment or I won't go. I do rodeos and fairs with Lassie when we're not working on the series, which we do from the end of June to the first week in February, but I won't go anywhere unless Lassie can be the top star. I know there's a big adult audience for Lassie, because I see the way the grownups look at him when I walk him around. Their eyes dance. They all push the little kids out of the way so *they* can touch Lassie. Come here, Lassie."

At the abrupt summons, Lassie slid slowly off the sofa and ambled over to the trainer.

"You're my baby, aren't you?" Mr. Weatherwax said, like any other dog-babier. "Turn to your left," he said conversationally to Lassie. Lassie did. "Turn to your right," he said. Lassie did.

"Does he know left from right?" Amy asked.

"Don't you?" Mr. Weatherwax said. "Watch this one. Lassie, yawn." Lassie did.

Mr. Weatherwax went to the kitchen and returned with some raw ground steak. He put the steak on the coffee table. "Snarl," he said to Lassie. Lassie snarled. "All right, eat it," Mr. Weatherwax said. Lassie complied.

"Watch this," Mr. Weatherwax said, setting an empty ashtray on another table. "Push it off the table," he told Lassie, and Lassie stood on her hind legs and nudged the ashtray off with her nose.

"That's my baby," Mr. Weatherwax said, and, turning to us, continued, "This dog is taken care of better than most kids. When we go anywhere on a plane, she has her own seat. Even though she lies on the floor of the plane. But she pays half fare, because she's under twelve. She doesn't eat on the plane, and doesn't drink, either, so the airlines save money there. She has an award from one airline for having flown more than a million miles, and another airline has given her its most-coöperative-passenger award. I always bring bottles of distilled water for Lassie wherever we go, and I always get a suite with a kitchen, so I can fry two pounds of ground sirloin for her supper. I bring Silky along so Lassie can have company. Lassie doesn't mind traffic in New York. If he can fight forest fires, he can negotiate the New York taxis."

"Sometimes you call Lassie 'he' and sometimes you call Lassie 'she,' " Amy said. "Why?"

"Because Lassie is in a class by Lassie's self," Mr. Weatherwax said.

FOURTEEN LAPS

OUR MAN Stanley has taken us up vigorously on our cavalier reference to him last week as our "aging" operative, in contrast to his "youthful" nephew Hiram. Stanley turned up in the office wearing black cycling shoes, plaid Bermuda shorts, a bright-green turtleneck pullover with horizontal white stripes, and a dashing white linen cap pulled low on his forehead, and we thought he had never looked better. "Kids!" he muttered, tossing his latest report on our desk. He had just spent a couple of hours cycling in Central Park, he said, and if we wanted him, he would be on the tennis courts the rest of the afternoon and at Shepheard's frugging and mashed-potatoing and Watusiing the whole night, and after that he was going to drive out to Jones Beach for a swim at dawn. Having been infected by his energy, we rush into print with his copy, which follows:

"Just did fourteen laps around bicycle path in Central Park. Each lap mile and half. Made speed equal to going Olympics rate. Bike rented from brand-new Parks Department concession called Bicycles in the Park, a division of Arnold Kaufman Incorporated, 72nd Street on the Mall. Attractive innovation. About time. Gets going every noon. Red-cum-white candy-striped booth has been set up at Mall entrance, overlooking Bethesda Fountain. Red-cum-white candy-striped wooden police barriers mark rental area. Red-cum-white sign on booth reads, 'Renters ride at own risk and are responsible for loss. Stay on bicycle paths. All bicycles must be in 6:00 P.M.' Bunch of shining new English bikes stationed behind barriers. Found proprietor, Arnold Kaufman, stationed behind small red-topped-cum-white-legged table, reading *Wall Street Journal*. Kaufman handsome, affable, athletic-looking fellow with shining, curly black hair, horn-rimmed glasses. Wearing oxford-gray pin-striped business suit with crease in trousers, dark Paisley necktie. He dropped *Wall*

Street Journal to give bikes to girl renters signing in as Hallee Schein and Francine Markowitz. 'Both our own personal bikes were stolen out of the baby-carriage room, so now we have to rent,' Hallee Schein told Kaufman. Francine Markowitz told him, 'We can't take our bikes into our apartments, because when you try to take your bike into the elevators, the people give you dirty looks and say, "The elevators are for *people*." ' Kaufman sighed and handed over two racers. Said boy who had been managing rentals had left for college, so he had to do it himself. Said he was planning to get new manager. 'My father-in-law is coming in for the weekend, and then I can go out and play golf,' Kaufman said. 'I never intended to be doing this work myself. I'm a full-time business broker. This morning, I was involved in discussions leading to the sale of the assets of one company listed on the Stock Exchange to another. That's what I do. I got into this rental thing because one mild, beautiful day last February I wanted to go bicycling with my fourteen-year-old daughter, Ellen. We had to go way over to the other side of town to rent bikes, when right here there was a million-dollar property not being fully used. So I sat down and wrote a letter about it to Newbold Morris, suggesting this operation. I have yet to meet him, though I've met all his assistants. We arranged to set up the concession on the same basis as the concessions for rowboats, skates, tennis lessons, and refreshment stands, giving the Parks Department a percentage of the gross. My investment was only five or six thousand dollars. Very modest. We have a hundred and fifteen bikes, about eighty per cent of them three-speed racers and the rest foot-brake models. Not nearly enough. I've ordered more. You ought to see this place on weekends; we move to a bullpen on the Mall because of the crush. Weekends I have a working staff of eight people. After next week, when school begins, we will be open only on weekends. We've got our own air compressor, spare parts, and tools, and we keep them in our workshop and storage room, in what used to be the Union News restaurant at the Bethesda Fountain. Every bike has a bell. Baskets are available, if desired, for ten cents. By the end of the year, we'll be self-supporting. This thing is extremely profitable. A five-dollar deposit is required, and the rental is a dollar twenty-five per hour for racers, a dollar-ten for foot-brake models. Which?'

"Ordered three-speed racer with high seat. Wanted plenty of leg action. Kaufman said most people made lap around bicycle path in twelve, fifteen minutes. Made first lap in about six minutes. Then relaxed, did it in seven next time around. Took in all terrific Park sights. Shifted to low speed at Mall. Bunch of people making filmed television commercial. Charles Ross Lighting truck. Theatrical Transfer Theatrical Equipment truck. Two motorcycle cops supervising. Director waiting for lights. Meanwhile playing guitar. Playing 'Malagueña.' Beautiful model waiting for call of 'Action!' Shifted to second speed. Young fellow in gray wool track outfit standing with foot on park bench, combing ducktail hair. On next bench, man in undershirt asleep sitting up, handkerchief tied over his head. Shifted to third speed. Caught up with club cyclists racing each other. Put on steam. Got past entire mob. Central Park Wheelmen wearing blue-and-gold color scheme. French Sporting Club, red, white, and blue. German Bicycle Sporting Club, black and red stripes on white. Unione Sportiva Italiana, blue and white. All wearing black tights. Bermudas more comfortable. Leave black-tights conforming to kids. Took it easy passing statue of Daniel Webster, hand inside coat: 'Liberty and Union, Now and Forever, One and Inseparable.' After that, felt I could make Olympics. Park looking great. Fellows sleeping on grass. Squirrels hopping around them. On road leading in from Seventy-second Street, whole football team of twelve-year-olds trotting toward Sheep Meadow, sweating. Sunlight flickering on them. Sunlight flickering through browning leaves on trees. Park smelled like country. Approached young couple riding tandem. Used bell. Went by them at fine clip. Just north of Sheep Meadow, came to fenced area for bowling on green. Splendid idea. Passed drinking fountain. Little girl holding up long line of thirsty kids. Little girl trying to fill empty beer can through pop-top aperture. Crowd in line looking pessimistic. Sheep Meadow spotted with games—two soccer, two football, one baseball, one tag. Eight picnics. Thousands of baby carriages. Counted four sets of twins. Scores of lovers. Counted sixteen pairs asleep. Baseball diamond. Going too fast to read names on uniforms. Players yelling in Spanish. Came to sign: '7th Ave. 59th St. Last Exit Southbound Keep Right.' Headed north. Almost ran into young couple walking illegally on bike path, holding hands. Stopped. Told them path for bikes, not *people*. Girl dark, beautiful, smiling. Young fellow with freckles, red hair, wearing black skullcap with Hebrew letters embroidered on it in white. Asked what Hebrew said. Fellow said, 'My name in Hebrew. It's Samuel, after the prophet.' Thanked him. Got going again. Carrousel mobbed by screaming children. Wollman Skating Rink deserted. Three small sailboats making trips on Conservatory Pond. Elderly Japanese man with camera hanging around neck yelled at me, 'Get a horse! Get a horse! Hee-hee-hee!' Hysterical. I paused at Boathouse. Lots of rowboats out on water—fifty cents an hour for one person, twenty cents an hour for each additional person. At snack stand, had quick bite of bean soup, franks, potato salad, fried eggs, blueberry pie, frosted chocolate, popcorn, Chiclets. Got going again. Was stalked by six-year-old infantryman with toy rifle and wearing helmet camouflaged with green leaves. Lost him at Mall. Hundreds of benches set up facing bandstand. One old man sleeping on bench at rear. Stage deserted except for two little girls jumping around, one behind other, singing 'Hello, Dolly!' Giggling. Knocking selves out. Bronze plaque on side of stand read, 'In Memory of Elkan Naumburg Who Inaugurated Orchestral Concerts in the Old Band Stand on the Mall 50 Years Ago and Donated This Stand in 1923. May 30, 1955.' Did some figure eights around benches. Went over to statue of Beethoven facing bandstand. Cop told me to scram. Cop said, 'I wish they'd put signs up where to ride. I guess signs cost money.'

"Back to bicycle path. Raced midnight-blue Rolls-Royce on other side of wooden rail separating path from Park Drive. Only passenger in Rolls Siamese cat. Reached Bethesda Fountain area again. Commercial had got further along. Director had stopped playing guitar, was now directing model to stand in silhouette, throw hair product to boy friend, tell boy friend if he wants to stay boy friend he should use hair product. Young fellow in gray wool track outfit still stalling. Now fixing shoelaces. Club cyclists at standstill at corner of Mall, chewing fat. Daniel Webster unchanged. Still 'Liberty and Union, Now and Forever, One and Inseparable.' Sleepers still sleeping. Squirrels still hopping. Couple on tandem gone. Team of twelve-year-olds now third football game on field. Little girl at water fountain still struggling to fill beer can. Line behind her had different personnel but was just as long, just as discouraged. Picnics. Twins. Lovers. Switched to third speed. Going good thirty m.p.h. Flying. Ciao, Hiram, old sock!"

AUDITION

ABOUT FIFTY TEEN-AGERS turned up the other evening at the offices of Station WNDT (Channel 13), at 1657 Broadway, to audition for *The Comers*, a new television program that features a permanent panel of four boys and two girls sitting around informally and talking about anything they like. Waiting to select the best combination of talkers for the panel were Charles Schultz, a scholarly-looking young man, who is the director of programming for the station; Lee Polk, the producer-director of *The Comers*; Frank Leicht, its executive producer; and Mr. Polk's staff: Michael Kerr, assistant to the producer; Dick Christian, who will take over in a couple of weeks as the director; and Peter Davis, who presides onstage when the boys and girls perform. He is called the host. The men had assembled in a badly ventilated conference room to look at and listen to several prospective Comers at a time, around a rectangular table loaded with cookies and soft drinks. At the head of the table, wearing a red bow tie and a brown corduroy suit, sat Mr. Davis, who has a turned-up nose, a perpetual expression of innocence, and a voice that is somewhat cracked, as though it had only recently changed. He is, however, twenty-seven. "This will be a program of, by, and for teen-agers," he said to the first group of applicants when they had seated themselves around the table. They included a girl named Judy, from the Dalton Schools, who wore tortoise-shell-rimmed sunglasses pushed up on the top of her head; a high-school boy named Tom, from Summit, who was wearing a navy-blue blazer and a shirt with a tab collar, and was holding a paperback edition of *Seven Days in May*; a prim and pretty girl named Joyce, with hair falling to her shoulders, who came from the School of Performing Arts; a tall, skinny boy named Tim, whose hair repeatedly fell over his forehead, and who also came from the School of Performing Arts; a very proper, neatly suited young man named Philip, from George Washington High, in upper Manhattan; and a couple of watchful girls named Barbara and Andrea, both of whom came from a new school in Westchester. The teen-agers eyed both the soft drinks and the men from Channel 13 with cool interest.

Mr. Polk, who had been sitting over near one wall, stood up, grinned at the teen-agers in a wry, knowing manner, and said, "We want you to be as free with your language as you feel. Have no respect for *anyone*." His listeners, including the ones from Channel 13, gave little laughs. Mr. Polk gave the final little laugh, and said, "We want this to be a program in which teen-agers can talk to *teen*-agers. He"—Mr. Polk grinned in the direction of Mr. Davis—"is not the usual sort of moderator, so don't expect a David Susskind act of him."

Everybody laughed again, and Mr. Davis cleared his throat and said, sounding almost puzzled, "We don't want you to be a Youth Forum kind of thing, talking about Should-Communist-China-be-admitted-to-the-U.N., although it's an important problem. We don't want pontifical statements—that kind of thing. You know?" He looked in a friendly way at the group around the table, and they looked back at him evenly.

With considerable urging from Mr. Davis, the talkers got off, rather haltingly, on a consideration of the problems of vandalism, cheating, and stealing in their schools.

Judy, in the manner of a practiced and never-rejected talker, pushed her sunglasses up a bit higher on the top of her head and told the others that the approach in *their* schools to the matter of books swiped from the school library was probably quite different from what it was at Dalton. "At Dalton, the teacher just stands up in front of everybody and says, 'Now, dear ones, we all love you, and you know we all love you, and all we want you to do is sneak back and put the book back, and no one will know and no one will criticize you, and everybody will love you just as much as before,' " Judy said. "That's the way it is at *Dalton*."

The other teen-agers around the table began to stir, a few smiling with forced compassion.

"Nobody likes our school, so at basketball games the kids throw things at the other kids," Andrea said.

"Does this happen *often?*" Tom asked, sitting up straight.

"They don't care about athletics at our school," Barbara said, glancing at her schoolmate for reassurance. "They don't care about who wins the game. They just want to throw things. It's a brand-new school, and we have no school spirit."

Joyce put in quickly that Performing Arts was very old. "Every time we do a *plié* in dance class, the plaster falls down on us," she said, with calm self-appreciation. "The whole school is falling apart, but everybody takes our school spirit for granted."

"The whole question of school spirit baffles me," Judy said. "Everybody at Dalton acts as though it's not chic to have school spirit. Like who needs it?"

"I can't agree with this," Tom said. "I was at Harvard this summer. At Harvard, it's fashionable to pretend that you have no school spirit. You don't find this at Yale. I like Yale much better. I don't mean to knock Harvard. It just didn't appeal to me."

"I think we ought to define school spirit," Tim said. "How open or verbose are you about your spirit? That's what we ought to understand. It has always been and will always be fashionable to knock your school."

Mr. Davis looked at Philip, who had been quietly attentive, turning from one to another of the teen-agers as they spoke but saying nothing himself. "What about your school, Philip?" Mr. Davis asked. "Do you have school spirit at your school?"

"Well, if we have a basketball game, everybody is going to go," Philip said.

Philip started to open his mouth again, but Judy was talking, with indignation. "That's not *true* about Harvard," she said. "A lot of young men who are taking me out are running the houses at Harvard and working on the *Crimson* and are involved in a lot of activities at Harvard, and I know from my own personal experience, by going with Harvard men, that they have a *lot* of school spirit."

As Andrea tried to bring the talk back to how it was hip at her school to hate the school, Mr. Polk passed a note to Mr. Schultz. It read, "We have new ones to bring in. Maybe we can keep a couple of these to provide security."

The changing of teen-agers was accomplished deftly. Tom and Barbara were held over to provide security, and the others were replaced by a group who immediately shook everybody up with their noticeably different attitudes. They wore bright-colored heavy sweaters or windbreakers, and they were smoking, kidding around, laughing, and looking at the men from Channel 13 with keen observation and an air of fun. They came from a West 147th Street neighborhood social center. Their names were Bernard, Winton, Valerie, John, and Willie.

"We have been talking about vandalism," Mr. Davis said, in his cracked, puzzled voice. "I don't know if you have those problems in the center. Is the center as important as your school? Valerie, what do you do in the center?"

"We have sewing, photography—things like that," said Valerie. She shrugged and looked across the table at John.

"We don't have a center in Summit," Tom said stiffly and deferentially. "What is it, exactly?"

"You know, you go there," John said. "You play basketball, pool, checkers—you go to dances. You know?"

"I don't go much," Willie said. "It's boring. They don't want you to dance here, to dance there. They don't want you, when you're dancing, to have the lights low."

"Let me ask you," Mr. Davis said. "Why do girls seem to like the Beatles?"

"Why, all their publicity," Willie said. "All that publicity on WINS, C.B.S.—that would make anybody like them."

"I don't see why the girls flip over them," Winton said. "I think a lot go to see them because they want to see their haircuts."

"They're O.K. for a rock-'n'-roll group, although I don't care for rock 'n' roll myself," Barbara said.

"I hate them," Willie said. "I think more of Elvis than I do of the Beatles. Because Elvis made it himself. The Beatles made it with all that publicity."

Mr. Schultz and Mr. Polk left the room for a brief conference. "You can tell right away," Mr. Schultz said. "It'll be Tom. He can be counted on always to say the right thing, the proper thing, the accepted thing."

"And Willie," Mr. Polk said, grinning. "The combination of Tom and Willie. Right?"

"Right," Mr. Schultz said, looking delighted.

"Keep in mind who will be the catalyst, who will make lots of enemies, who can draw the others out, who can lecture each one," Mr. Polk said. "And do we have the luxury of having kids who will argue for argument's sake? No."

"I agree," Mr. Schultz said.

"And we need real kids," Mr. Polk said. "Kids who will reveal themselves."

"Right," Mr. Schultz said. "I agree."

The two men returned to the conference room.

The next batch—very mixed—consisted of Maria, Carlos, Bob, Ed, Charlie, Roderick, Hiram, Louis, Elizabeth, Diane, and Joan.

In response to prompting from Mr. Davis, Roderick, who looked like an even handsomer Cassius Clay, informed the group that he didn't go to school but, when he wasn't sleeping, spent a lot of his time working, even though he somehow had more money when he wasn't working.

"Don't you get bored?" asked Diane, a pretty, theatrical-looking girl from James Madison High, in Brooklyn, who had told Mr. Davis that she wanted to be an actress.

"Uh-uh," Roderick said. "Go to parties. You don't get bored going to parties."

"But don't you want to go to school?" Diane asked.

"Why? What for?" Roderick said.

"Well, to learn a trade, or something. Don't you want to get married?" Diane said.

"Uh-uh," Roderick said. "I got enough trouble by myself."

There followed a discussion of how Roderick and Hiram spent their time—a discussion that involved definitions of words in their special vocabulary, such as "Jitterbugging is when a group of guys fight to protect your territory," and "Bluebellies, they pick you up and take you to the station, they're cops."

"You just stand on corners?" Elizabeth asked. "Why stand on a corner?"

"Because we got no place else to go," Hiram said.

"You have fights?" Diane asked. "Why do you get into fights?"

"It's like this," Roderick said. "When you get a reputation, everybody wants to take it away from you."

"Isn't it frustrating, just fighting every day?" Elizabeth asked.

"No," Hiram said. "Every day we got a *different* fight."

Mr. Polk and Mr. Schultz turned to each other. Both of them looked triumphant.

❧ THE TABLE

LAST FRIDAY, we went over to the United Nations, arriving at 6:15 P.M., forty-five minutes after the adjournment of the hastily called 1,141st urgent meeting of the Security Council (requested by Adlai Stevenson, the Permanent Representative of the United States) and twenty-six hours before the even more hastily called 1,142nd urgent meeting of the Security Council (requested by Orhan Eralp and Zenon Rossides, the Permanent Representatives of Turkey and Cyprus). The evening was unseasonably cool, and a high wind from the east was blowing prematurely brown, dry leaves in swirls around "Single Form," the twenty-one-foot-high bronze sculpture in front of the Secretariat. Nobody was in sight as we headed for the Security Council Chamber.

The delegates' anteroom was completely deserted, the only immediate evidence of the meeting being the smell of tobacco smoke. Just inside, on the floor of the Chamber, to the left of the entrance, the Conference Officer's desk had a white note pad pushed to one side, a standard yellow pencil lying diagonally across the scribbled notation:

> QUANG BINH
> HON NGU and HON ME
> KHANH HO

At the Council's horseshoe table, we made a quick inventory of the places of the Security Council delegates. From left to right, facing the gallery, were Brazil, one half-filled glass water pitcher and an empty glass; Bolivia, one half-smoked L & M cigarette butt in a glass ashtray; United States, two cigarette butts in an ashtray, smoked thriftily down to a quarter of an inch, and a mimeographed document headed "Provisional Agenda for the 1,141st Meeting of the Security Council (to be held in the Security Council Chamber at Headquarters, New York, on Friday, 7 August 1964, at 3 P.M. 1. Adoption of the agenda. 2. Letter dated 4 August 1964 from the Permanent Representative of the United States addressed to the President of the Security Council [S/5849]);" United Kingdom, one white note pad with standard yellow pencil, the point still sharp, the eraser pink and unused, and a mimeographed copy of Security Council Document Number S/5849, entitled "Letter Dated 4 August 1964 from the Permanent Representative of the United States Addressed to the President of the Security Council" and continuing "On behalf of the United States, I request that you convene an urgent meeting of the Security Council to consider the serious situation created by deliberate attacks of the Hanoi Regime on United States naval vessels in international waters. Accept, etc. [Signed] Adlai E. Stevenson;" Union of Soviet Socialist Republics, an ashtray filled with ten L & Ms very well crushed and a TASS wire-service news-ticker report, baby-blue type on a two-foot-long sheet of paper, the top bulletin starting out, "Statement One: Moscow August 5 TASS Follows the Text of TASS Statement: On the order of President Johnson, the United States naval forces increased the other day the number of their ships in the Gulf of Tonkin . . ." (Statement Four, at the bottom of the page—"Competent Soviet circles resolutely denounce the aggressive actions of the United States in the Gulf of Tonkin which lead to a dangerous exacerbation of the situation in Southeast Asia, tense as it is"—had been marked for emphasis with a bracket in pencil); Undersecretary, one water glass, half filled, and a mimeographed agenda in Russian; Norway, one water glass, quarter filled, one white note pad and yellow pencil, unused, and presidential wooden gavel, the pounding side pockmarked and worn; Secretary-General, two cigar butts, each an inch long, ditched in the tray; Morocco, three note-pad sheets torn neatly into quarters, the top quarter with the tantalizing pencilled notation "Monsieur le Président, c'est avec beaucoup . . . ," and a mimeographed agenda in French, "Ordre du jour provisoire de la

1141ème séance du Conseil de sécurité (qui se tiendra dans la salle du Conseil de sécurité au Siège, à New York, le vendredi 7 août 1964, à 15 heures. 1. Adoption de l'ordre du jour. 2. Lettre adressée au Président du Conseil de sécurité, le 4 août 1964, par le représentant permanent des États-Unis d'Amérique [S/5849]);" Ivory Coast, one cigar butt half an inch in length, alone in an ashtray; France, two sheets from a pad, half torn, the words "délégation j'assume" running crookedly around the crumpled paper, and a copy of Document S/5849 in French ("Lettre adressée au Président du Conseil de sécurité, le 4 août 1964, par le représentant permanent des États-Unis d'Amérique: 'Au nom des États-Unis d'Amérique, j'ai l'honneur de vous demander de convoquer d'urgence le Conseil de sécurité pour qu'il examine la situation grave créé par les attaques délibérées du régime de Hanoi contre des navires de guerre des États-Unis dans des eaux internationales. Veuillez agréer, etc. [Signé] Adlai E. Stevenson'"); Czechoslovakia, one empty water pitcher and one empty glass; China, one note pad and an unused yellow pencil.

There was a stir at the rear of the gallery, and a group of twenty visitors trooped in, led by one of the U.N. girl guides, who directed them to take seats and started the usual description and explanation of what the Security Council is. The guide was tall, stately, and beautiful, and one we recognized as being from Sierra Leone. She wore a blue linen native robe and headdress and gold earrings, and as she talked she waved her hands, the fingers long, tapered, and with long, lacquered fingernails, at the horseshoe table, where we stood. "What they do here is maintain international peace and security," she told the visitors, in a soft accent that sounded to us like a soothing blend of Jamaican and French. "The members of Security Council must be ready to meet at any time." The visitors turned their faces to her with hypnotic attention. We, too, stood transfixed. The guide from Sierra Leone waved gracefully at the horseshoe table. "If you count the chairs around the table, you will count twenty. We have eleven members in Security Council, but other countries are invited to sit here and present their views in disputes. Security Council is empowered to send United Nations troops and to take enforcement measures by members' decision. These actions are taken only when everything has been done to keep the people from fighting."

The girl's matter-of-fact tone sounded strong and highly confident. The visitors looked from her to the horseshoe table and seemed satisfied.

❧❧ HOMAGE

ONE RECENT AFTERNOON, Sir John Gielgud, Dame Edith Evans, and Margaret Leighton met in a Columbia Records studio on Thirtieth Street near Third Avenue and spent three and a half hours making a record entitled "A Homage to Shakespeare." The record consisted of selections that they felt would give delight and so help celebrate the four-hundredth birthday of the Bard. The three actors stood side by side in front of three microphones, about eight feet apart. As seen from a glassed-in control booth where Charles Burr, Columbia's director of special projects, was stationed, Mr. Gielgud was at the right, Miss Evans in the center, and Miss Leighton at the left. Mr. Burr, a sharp-faced man who was wearing horn-rimmed glasses, alternately sipped black coffee from a cracked white porcelain cup and helped himself to yellow candy drops from a cellophane bag, which was labelled "Le Bon Bonbon Napoleon" and was passed around from time to time among his assistants. Mr. Burr studied the three actors with solemn approval. Mr. Gielgud was holding a pair of horn-rimmed glasses in one hand and was in his shirtsleeves, the shirt being crisp and white, with a light-blue pin stripe; his tie was crisp and dark blue, and was clipped to the shirt by a straight gold pin, and his trousers were crisp and gray and somehow or other more splendid than other gray trousers. Miss Evans, gray-haired and wearing an equally splendid gray wool dress and a three-strand necklace of pearls, had steel-rimmed spectacles pushed down on her nose. Miss Leighton, very, very slim and straight in a sleeveless, narrow-skirted cocoa-brown dress, wore a jewelled gold pin on one shoulder and a jewelled gold ring. Her hair was dramatically blond, and she stood with folded arms.

Mr. Gielgud started the session off by giving a Gielgud reading of Sonnet CXLIII:

"Lo, as a careful housewife runs to catch
One of her feather'd creatures broke away,
Sets down her babe, and makes all swift dispatch
In pursuit of the thing she would have stay;
Whilst her neglected child holds her in chase,
Cries to catch her whose busy care is bent
To follow that which flies before her face,
Not prizing her poor infant's discontent:
So runn'st thou after that which flies from thee,
Whilst I thy babe chase thee afar behind;
But if thou catch thy hope, turn back to me,
And play the mother's part, kiss me, be kind;
     So will I pray that thou mayst have thy will,
     If thou turn back and my loud crying still."

Mr. Gielgud's fellow-actors regarded him with admiration, and in the control booth Mr. Burr flipped a switch and expressed his own admiration, then flipped the switch back. One of Mr. Burr's assistants tossed a Bon Bonbon Napoleon into his mouth and said, "This one will be a ball. Sir John is a one-take man." During a playback of Sonnet CXLIII, another assistant noted on a chart marked "Tape Identification Data" that it had a running time of forty-five seconds.

Miss Leighton and Miss Evans went on next, as Lady Capulet and the Nurse, respectively, in Act I, Scene 3, of *Romeo and Juliet* (running time, three minutes twenty-seven seconds), and afterward Mr. Gielgud paid them his compliments. After the playback, Mr. Gielgud took over again, giving his introduction to *Richard II*—"King Richard II, who has been living in a world of fantasy and self-conceit, deposed by his cousin Bolingbroke, awaits his death in Pomfret Castle"—in one Gielgud voice, and then declaiming in another Gielgud voice:

"I have been studying how I may compare
This prison where I live unto the world:
And for because the world is populous,
And here is not a creature but myself,
I cannot do it; yet I'll hammer it out.
My brain I'll prove the female to my soul . . ."

(The running time was four minutes fifteen seconds.)

The actors went bounding on, with appropriate changes of voice, mood, humor, and passion, to play scenes from *Macbeth* and *Henry VIII*. They listened carefully to the playbacks of their readings, the ladies usually looking to Mr. Gielgud for a final O.K. "I thought it was all right, Johnny, if you think so," Miss Evans said of her Queen Katharine in a scene from *Henry VIII* in which Mr. Gielgud played Cardinal Wolsey, and he told her he thought the scene sounded fine. All three actors were really swinging by the time they got to *King Lear*.

Mr. Gielgud asked Miss Evans if she would read the introduction to the *King Lear* scene (Act IV, Scene 7): "Would you mind doing it, darling? It's only two sentences."

"No, no, of course I don't," Miss Evans said, and read, "King Lear is reunited with his daughter Cordelia. He is carried into her presence, still sleeping, after his madness."

And Miss Leighton, as Cordelia, went on:

> *"O my dear father! Restoration hang*
> *Thy medicine on my lips, and let this kiss*
> *Repair those violent harms that my two sisters*
> *Have in thy reverence made!"*

Then Mr. Gielgud came in as King Lear:

> *"You do me wrong to take me out o' the grave:*
> *Thou art a soul in bliss, but I am bound*
> *Upon a wheel of fire, that mine own tears*
> *Do scald like molten lead."*

They gave their readings plenty of action; Mr. Gielgud hugged himself as he read, and Miss Leighton raised her head and hands in pleading gestures as she implored:

> *"O, look upon me, sir,*
> *And hold your hands in benediction o'er me.*
> *No, sir, you must not kneel."*

And Mr. Gielgud read, in a crying, shaking voice:

> "Do not laugh at me,
> For, as I am a man, I think this lady
> To be my child Cordelia."

And Miss Leighton read:

> "And so I am."

By the time the actors had finished and were listening to the play-back, Mr. Burr and his assistants had abandoned the Bon Bonbon Napoleons. They looked like an audience that had been shaken up.

At the microphone, Miss Leighton glanced at Mr. Gielgud and said, "Can we have some coffee now, Johnny?"

"Coffee time," Mr. Gielgud said.

"Jolly good!" Miss Evans said.

The actors retired to a side control room, where a small table was neatly set with a silver coffee urn and a silver tray of small sandwiches. All three of them went at the sandwiches with enthusiasm. Nothing was left of the atmosphere of *Lear*.

"I saw *Hello, Dolly!* last night," Mr. Gielgud said, pouring coffee into a cup and offering it to Miss Evans.

"Did you see *Barefoot in the Park?*" Miss Leighton asked. "I adored that."

"I saw *Yesterday, Today, and Tomorrow*, and loved it, but I haven't been to the theatre this time here," Miss Evans said.

"I liked *To Bed . . . Or Not to Bed*," Mr. Gielgud said. "It was awfully funny."

"You should see *Funny Girl*," Miss Leighton told Miss Evans. "Do you remember Kay Medford, the one who put her head in the oven in *Bye Bye Birdie?* She's in it, and she's marvellous."

"You know, I sort of like *not* going to the theatre," Miss Evans said.

"Yes, there's something about *not* going to the theatre that's like being on holiday," Miss Leighton said, quickly eating a cucumber-sandwich sliver and reaching for another.

"I have to keep saying what I haven't seen," Miss Evans said. "I've been over here now for six weeks—two weeks in Hollywood. I'm longing for London. I'm longing to get home to my garden."

"Did you go to Disneyland?" Mr. Gielgud asked Miss Evans.

"Oh, I loved Disneyland!" Miss Evans said.

"Didn't you adore the Alice in Wonderland things and the Snow White things and Peter Pan?" Mr. Gielgud said. "And there's a divine thing called the crocodiles. You didn't miss that, did you?"

"I went because you told me to," Miss Evans said. "I thought it would be all Donald Ducks and things."

"I suppose it's like Battersea Park in the evening, when you went with a lot of chums and you went on things and screamed," Miss Leighton said.

"Yes, but there's so much more than going on roller coasters and things," Mr. Gielgud said. "I really hate roller coasters. Disneyland is so pretty and clean, and so well arranged, and I loved talking with all the out-of-work actors there who work as spielmen."

"I started off rather cross in Disneyland," Miss Evans said. "There was a couple there. With a baby. The baby couldn't have been over three weeks. Imagine bringing a baby to see the crocodiles! It was hardly a mite." She sipped at her coffee.

"It will probably grow up and go out and conquer the world," Miss Leighton said, reaching for another small sandwich.

"A child that age ought to have peace and quiet," Miss Evans said. "It will probably have a nervous breakdown."

"I was at the Guggenheim last Sunday, looking at the van Goghs," Mr. Gielgud said. "There were at least thirty-five children there." He put down his coffee cup and brushed the palms of his hands together. "It's sonnet time!" he said happily.

"Sonnet time!" Miss Leighton sang out.

"Sonnet time it is," Miss Evans said.

They went back to their microphones, and Mr. Gielgud, shifting voices, launched into Sonnet XIX:

> "Devouring Time, blunt thou the lion's paws
> And make the earth devour her own sweet brood;
> Pluck the keen teeth from the fierce tiger's jaws
> And burn the long-liv'd phoenix in her blood;
> Make glad and sorry seasons as thou fleet'st,
> And do whate'er thou wilt, swift-footed Time,
> To the wide world and all her fading sweets;

But I forbid thee one most heinous crime:
O, carve not with thy hours my love's fair brow,
Nor draw no lines there with thine antique pen!
Him in thy course untainted do allow
For beauty's pattern to succeeding men.
   Yet do thy worst, old Time! Despite thy wrong,
   My love shall in my verse ever live young."

🌸 CAMPAIGNING—I

ROBERT FRANCIS KENNEDY has been campaigning for fifty days for election to the United States Senate from New York, and we joined him at eight one morning last week at his home in Glen Cove and drove in to town with him for the start of another day. (We have every hope of giving equal time to Senator Keating.) His car, a rented white Chevrolet sedan, had a campaign-dented roof, a telephone, and a driver named Jim King, who informed Mr. Kennedy that his first appointment was a television interview. "You might want to put on your black shoes instead of those brown ones, as long as you're wearing the gray suit," Mr. King told Mr. Kennedy as we drove down Glen Cove Road toward the Long Island Expressway. "We've got the black shoes on the seat back there."

Mr. Kennedy said he'd change his shoes as soon as we reached the city.

"And change the cufflinks," Mr. King said.

Mr. Kennedy nodded, and showed us the cufflinks he was wearing—a handsome gold pair embossed with the Department of Justice seal. "People sometimes pull them off when I'm in crowds," he told us. "My brother and sister-in-law Jackie gave them to me about a year and a half ago. I lost one in Syracuse last week at the airport, but I found it a few seconds later myself, on the ground. A couple of weeks ago, I lost one in the ballroom of the Americana, and thought it was gone, but somebody picked it up and sent it back anonymously a couple of days later to my apartment at the Carlyle. The experience was very lifting. Now, just before I go into crowds, I put on substitutes—cloth ones."

We asked Mr. Kennedy how he found the energy to do morning television interviews in addition to regular campaigning. He said that energy was no problem—that he had always felt he needed

eight hours' sleep but found now he was getting much less than that
and still didn't mind taking on interviews. "People have so many
questions about me, and I have an opportunity on TV to give them
the answers," he said. "This is an awfully big state, and basically it's
a matter of communication. I've been involved in a lot of campaigns, but this one is so different in so many ways. In previous
campaigns, our family was so closely bound up together. There was
one candidate, but we were all sort of involved, including my father,
of course, who felt so strongly about it. Now my brother isn't here,
and my father can't speak, and my younger brother isn't around.
The whole operation is different. Everything is different. In a campaign, somebody has to think about all the speeches at all the
dinners, about the debates, about how to use TV, about who might
be helpful, about what kind of ads to use, about whether the literature gets out properly, about the right kind of message to send upstate. You think about a lot of things when you're running a campaign. Ideally, the candidate should be thinking about what he's
going to say in his next speech, and not about the mechanics of the
campaign—not about where the suitcase is or whether somebody is
going to meet the plane. But it's never that ideal. There's such a
short period of time in which you must function and function efficiently. It's about like establishing General Motors—getting hundreds of thousands of people working, deciding who's taking on certain responsibilities, and getting the cars out in a short time."

"Well, how's it going?" we inquired.

"It's a relief, in a way," Mr. Kennedy said. "I like being out of
Washington. That's first. And I like seeing so many other people. I
like communicating again with that part of American life. I like
looking at people, in all the towns and all the cities all over the state.
They smile. They don't have an angle. It's very lifting. They're just
ordinary American citizens. Washington is so inbred. Washington is
a one-industry town. Everyone reads the columnists. Everyone reads
the editorial page. Something disturbs them each day. Here, the
people that come to an airport to meet you just seem to have sort of
a basic confidence that the country is in good hands. They represent
the United States so much better than what we have in Washington. They smile. The impression you have is that they look happy,
and yet serious at the same time. And they *listen* to you. It's just

nice, that's all. It's just the way they look. That's what makes it worthwhile."

"Any surprises?" we asked.

Mr. Kennedy considered the question for a while and then said, "The intensity, I suppose, is greater than I would have anticipated. I don't go in much for thinking about all the incidents along the way. I'm not great at that sort of thing. But I did get a lift out of something that happened in one of the parades on Long Island the other day. A man of about thirty-five who was with his wife yelled out at me, 'Carpetbagger!' His wife was carrying a rolled-up newspaper, and when he yelled at me, she hit him over the head with it. I find I'm doing better in some places than in other places. In my speeches, I haven't done as well as I should do, on occasion. In Buffalo one night, I had to speak at a Democratic dinner at eleven o'clock after a morning that started out at five-thirty, and I know I might have made my points sharper in that speech. I know when I make a good speech, just as I know when I play a good game of tennis or swim well. You do the best you can. I try to make an effort all the time. If you started out thinking you had to keep yourself feeling well rested and up to this or that, you'd hardly ever move."

We asked Mr. Kennedy whether he preferred one kind of audience to another.

"College audiences, usually," he said. "They usually ask the best questions, and when there's opposition in the audience, it's basically more stimulating. I'm always trying for communication. Yesterday, I was supposed to make a speech before a group of teachers—eleven hundred nuns. I was handed a speech written for me at one in the morning, and I was supposed to speak at ten. I found I didn't like the speech. It was very pedantic and routine. It just didn't have any idealism. It was just vaguely about youth. So I spoke extemporaneously about some of the issues, and how we needed intelligence to make the right decisions. They listened."

"How's the campaign as a campaign?" we asked.

"I expected this campaign to be on a higher level," he said. "I find myself being charged with making deals with Nazis and running out on Negroes and being anti-Italian and being a crook, covering up for Bobby Baker, and I just didn't expect it would be as bad as that. When you bring the campaign to that low level, it lowers the opinion of people about the people involved in politics. In a national campaign, you couldn't get away with it. If you made charges on that low level, they'd be answered immediately, but in the state campaign nobody bothers to answer, nobody gets very horrified at it. They print what somebody says, but nobody bothers to answer the false charges or writes what the facts are. On the other hand, in a campaign, people make such efforts for you. One young guy gave up his job in the Justice Department, in Washington, and came to New York with his wife. They have no money, and they're working as volunteers. There are a lot of people like that. They run out to a factory at five-thirty in the morning and open a door and take your coat, and you never see them again. That's inspiring. It's a difficult campaign. I may have a difficult time winning. I'll do the best I can. There are terrific problems facing the country, including problems of whether people are going to live or die. I'd like to play a role in the future. I'd like to do something about it. If things work out, I'll be in the United States Senate. If they don't, I'll teach or something. Either way, I'll be glad I made the effort. It all pales in significance in the light of the events of the past year."

❦❦ CAMPAIGNING—II

Last week, we reported on the start of a day of campaigning with United States senatorial candidate Robert Francis Kennedy, and a few days later we set out on a similar jaunt with the incumbent, Senator Kenneth Barnard Keating. We met the Senator, by prearrangement, in his suite at the Roger Smith Motor Hotel, in White Plains, as he was finishing breakfast and being briefed for the activities of the day by several aides. The hotel was old but sort of modernized. The suite consisted of two small rooms with low ceilings, fluorescent lighting, and jazzed-up air conditioning. The Senator's aides were young and tense, and, like the Senator, wore dark, sedate suits and sedate ties. The Senator's breakfast, set out on a modern, plastic-topped table, had for a background wilting chrysanthemums and a tired-looking bowl of hotel fruit. The Senator looked untouched by his surroundings. His face was pink and his white hair unruffled, and he listened calmly as his aides conducted him downstairs in a self-service elevator and told him that he was going first to a breakfast-and-coffee hour in Scarsdale, at the residence of a Mr. and Mrs. Benjamin Berkey, and would next be due at the Beach Shopping Center, in Peekskill, for the second of thirteen rallies scheduled for the day, with the Senator handshaking, greeting, and speaking.

"How do you do all this?" we asked him. "And what would happen if you didn't?"

"You'd probably be defeated," he said. "You'd give the impression that you were cold and didn't want to meet people. The people don't want anyone like that for their senator."

"What do you do to keep going?" we asked.

"I take vitamins," he said. "Want one?" He handed us an inch-long brown capsule and gave us a small smile. "I've been taking them for twenty years."

"You ought to see some of the places we've been!" one of the aides said. "That health spa in Dansville we had to stay over in! Surrounded by hikers! Health diets! Carrot juice! You couldn't take a shower! You couldn't get a drink! Old-fashioned wall telephones!"

"It was all right with me," the Senator said evenly, and went on, "The pace now is faster. We're covering more ground. All there's time for now is the campaign. I've got a pile of books a mile high at home, but I haven't been able to look at them. There are so many people to meet, and only fourteen days to go. I don't know how many speeches I made yesterday—from five to fifteen. Last night, in Syracuse, the people were yelling, showing their feelings. 'We want Keating!' 'Keating is our man!' 'Keating! Keating! Keating!' " The Senator didn't change his tone for the cheers but gave us another small smile. "At Syracuse University, the *Daily Orange* came out for me, and I understand that in polls it conducted the students favored me two to one."

Outside the hotel, the Senator's aides ushered him into the front seat of a white Cadillac sedan, and then all but one aide ran to cars that had formed a motorcade behind. We were invited into the rear seat of the Cadillac, along with Ogden Reid, an incumbent Congressman who is up for reëlection in Westchester, and the remaining aide, Dick Nathan, who appeared to be about thirty and was holding a large, worn briefcase. The driver, a chipper man with a small mustache who had on a tan Glen-plaid suit and a tan bow tie, turned around and shook our hand. "I'm Herb Grimsey, commonly known as J. Herbert," he said. "I'm the Republican campaign chairman for Westchester County."

"Let's go," Senator Keating said mildly.

Led by an escort of Westchester Parkway police, we started for Scarsdale.

"Berkey," Senator Keating said. "Now, let's see . . ."

"He's president and chairman of the board of Berkey Photo Incorporated," Mr. Nathan said. "And you know her. She's a personal friend of yours."

"Senator, you have a lot of personal friends," Congressman Reid said.

"All of Westchester County is a favorite of mine," Senator Keating said.

"And you're a favorite of Westchester," said Congressman Reid.

"This is my twenty-ninth appearance in Westchester since I've been a Senator, other than for social functions," Mr. Keating said.

"The Senator works like a tiger. He wears all us young fellows out," Mr. Nathan said. He had been studying a large card headed "Basic Speech Card," and now he handed it to the Senator. "You're going to speak from a stairway at the Berkeys' breakfast," he told Mr. Keating. "You'll have to adjust."

"I don't mind," the Senator said, staring at the card.

"Is there anything about this campaign that's different from past campaigns?" we asked the Senator.

"I've never been in a campaign like this, where my record has been so distorted," the Senator said. "Why, there was a letter in the World-Telegram yesterday saying that I was against the school-lunch program. That is preposterous! In 1958, we had a relatively clean campaign. My opponent was Frank Hogan. Very able. Very much the gentleman. I've been a candidate seven times, and this is the first time I've been up against such distortion."

"Is anything else different?" we asked.

"There are certain complications," the Senator said. "I'm not supporting Goldwater. But that cuts both ways. Some are happy about it, and some are not."

We asked the Senator if there was anything he liked about this campaign, and he replied that he liked getting out in the air. "October of '58 was the worst weather," he said. "We had only five days when it didn't rain or snow. This October has given us the best weather that I can recall."

We had reached the Berkeys' residence, a large red brick house with large white Georgian pillars flanking the entrance, and as Senator Keating stepped out of his car and went inside, a three-piece combo (accordion, saxophone, guitar) started playing "Oh, What a Beautiful Mornin'" and a couple of hundred women, all wearing suits, all with fresh hairdos, sang along with it: "We've got a wonderful feeling/Keating is going to stay." Senator Keating stood under a large crystal chandelier, not far from a wide circular staircase with a turquoise carpet, and shook hands with the women, many of whom were carrying cups of coffee and toasted bagels covered with cream cheese and Nova Scotia salmon, and many of whom asked the Senator to forgive their sticky fingers. On the walls were a couple of large tinted photographs of Mr. Berkey and one of Mr. and Mrs. Berkey together. A tall woman who was wearing ivory earrings in the shape of elephants said that invitations to the breakfast had become a genuine status symbol in Scarsdale, and that the affair was a big success. "It's a great omen," she said. "If only they could go from here to vote!"

We sampled a toasted bagel with cream cheese and salmon, and recommended the dish to the Senator, who told us that he never gets a chance to eat anything at campaign breakfasts. "I don't even get a sip of coffee," he said, and then he hastily touched our arm. "But I *like* bagels," he added.

It was time for the Senator to make his speech, and he stepped to the turquoise circular staircase and told the women he was delighted to be there on such a beautiful morning. The women applauded, and one called out, "You're in!"

Senator Keating gave them a small smile and said calmly, "I'll try to be a good senator for those who vote against me as well as for those who vote for me."

❧ TRUFFAUT

IN THE WINTER OF 1960, when we met François Truffaut, the French director-producer-writer of the movie *The 400 Blows*, on his first visit here, we resolved to have a talk with him every five years or so, and we acted on that resolve last week, when Truffaut, now thirty-two years old, was here for a few days for the opening of his new film, *The Soft Skin*. We called on him at his midtown hotel suite, and it was a pleasure to find him looking just about the same—slight of build, no more than a pound or two heavier, and as keen and alert and unnoisy as ever. He still speaks no English, and, as before, his American friend and colleague Mrs. Helen Scott, who did the English subtitles for *The Soft Skin*, served smoothly and unobtrusively as his English voice. He quickly brought us up to date on the major developments in his life: he now has two daughters, aged four and six, whom he has trained to cry out "Vive Papa!" as soon as he comes home; he still has his own film company, Carrosse, in Paris; he has made three films besides *The Soft Skin* since we first saw him—*Shoot the Piano Player*, *Jules and Jim*, and a half-hour untitled movie that was one part of an international five-parter called *Love at Twenty*, produced by French, Italian, and Japanese filmmakers and including segments by a Pole and a German; and, in collaboration with Mrs. Scott, he has been writing a book about Alfred Hitchcock. In addition to making five trips to the United States, he has left France for working visits to Argentina, Brazil, and Canada.

"All right," we said. "Now, to begin with, will you explain why and how you are writing a book about Hitchcock?"

"Because I have long been sure that he is the greatest director of films in the world," Truffaut said. "And with every passing day I am surer than ever. Each week for the past few years, I have been going to see at least two of his pictures. *Vertigo* I see at least every two months. When I undertook to write the book, I went to the Cinémathèque in Brussels—the best archives for Hitchcock—to see all his pictures over again. The more I see of Hitchcock's pictures, the less desire I have to see pictures other than his."

"And the book?" we asked.

"It will be published in six months, and it will be published simultaneously in France and America, as *Conversations with Hitchcock*," Truffaut said. "It will have a unique aspect—two hundred and fifty photographs, each appearing at exactly the point in the book at which the scene in the photograph is being described. In the summer of 1962, I wrote a letter to Hitchcock, which Helen translated into English, and I told him I wanted to write the book. I suggested a series of interviews over a period of eight days. He agreed. On August 13th, Hitchcock's birthday, Helen and I arrived in Hollywood. We stayed at the Beverly Hills Hotel. Every day, Hitchcock would come and pick us up at eight in the morning and take us to his office at Universal City Studios, and we would sit in his office and talk until six at night. We spoke to him with microphones around our necks, and a sound engineer stationed in the next room recorded what was said. We kept the microphones on even during meals. Every day we ate with Hitchcock, and every day we ate what he ate—steak, fried potatoes, and ice cream."

"Well, how did you like Hollywood? What else did you do there?" we asked.

"In the evening, at the hotel, Helen and I sat up until midnight and talked about Hitchcock," Truffaut said. "Many people called up and invited me to come to parties and to meet producers and to see actresses and to see studios. Many columnists wanted to interview me. But I didn't want to do any of this. Out of respect to Hitchcock, I didn't want to see anybody else."

"What about your pictures?" we asked. "What did Hitchcock think of them?"

"I gave instructions to Helen never to mention my pictures to him, and he did not bring them up," Truffaut said. "Hitchcock has made forty-nine pictures. I have made four real features, in addition to *Love at Twenty* and my very first attempt, a short film called *The Mischief Makers*. I had come to see Hitchcock and talk about his pictures and talk about Hitchcock—only Hitchcock."

"How did it go?" we asked.

"I think Hitchcock was happy that I knew his pictures so well," Truffaut said. "He had never before had an opportunity to speak of himself and his work in forty years—since he began making pictures. We talked about all his pictures—how he had come to make each one, about the actors, about the construction of the scenario, and about the technical problems of shooting. From the third day on, his sensitivity emerged. He became self-critical. He described scenes in which he thought he had done something that was foolish or pretentious or careless. I was struck by the contrast between the public man, so sure of himself, so cynical, and what seemed to me to be a very vulnerable man, very emotional. And I learned what I needed to know—all the things I had sensed but had never clearly formulated. For instance, the principle, extremely important, that an emotion must be created on the screen and then must be sustained—on the technical level as well as on the scenario level. Many can create an emotion on the screen, but very few know how to sustain it. It is so important to sustain it, even after the character eliciting the emotion leaves the room, goes off the screen. There is so much to learn from Hitchcock—how to keep the camera on the character you want the audience to be interested in, and not cut, even when the character walks all the way across a room. That is just one small example of what one learns from Hitchcock."

"Will you talk about your own pictures now?" we asked.

"Freely," Truffaut said. "I am very critical of my pictures. I would like them more if they had been made by somebody else. Because I used to be a film critic who wrote strongly about pictures, people say that if I had been a critic of my own films I would have knocked them strongly. Quite the contrary. I think I prefer *Love at Twenty* to my feature films. Perhaps because it lasts only thirty minutes, I don't see any weaknesses in it. In *Shoot the Piano Player* I can see now that the story is not well narrated. If I were to make *The 400 Blows* today, I might be more indulgent toward adults, a little more shaded. In *Jules and Jim*, the first half hour is the best; the rest of it should have been as good. The book it was based on, by Henri Pierre Roché, is truly a hymn to life. The author wrote it when he was seventy-four. Up to then, he had spent all his time living. There are forty women in the book—enough for forty pictures. I wanted the picture, too, to be a hymn to life, but I'm not sure it's as complete as the book. Perhaps I made it too early in my own life. You are at a disadvantage when you choose too large a subject. The picture has everything—all the seasons, war, fights, reconciliations, farewells. It is a résumé of life. I made *Shoot the Piano Player* as a sort of antithesis to *The 400 Blows*. And *The Soft Skin* I made as a violent answer to *Jules and Jim*. It's as though someone else had made *Jules and Jim*—as if I were now saying *Jules and Jim* is a lie. To some people *The Soft Skin* might seem to be sordid, but to me it is about love in the city, instead of love in the country, as in *Jules and Jim*, and love is necessarily less beautiful in the city. *The Soft Skin* is truly modern love; it takes place in planes, in elevators; it has all the harassments of modern life. It may be too early for me to criticize the picture, but I think I did not establish the man's profession clearly enough; he is a specialist in the history of literature, he has published a book about Balzac, he is supposed to enjoy fame, because he has been on television broadcasts, but I think I did not show enough of what he *is*."

"Is there anything different about the way you work on a film these days?" we asked.

"I am less worried about what will happen to the picture, and I have more of a sense of continuity," he said. "When I was here in 1960, I was very anxious about choosing my next picture; I thought the choice was very important. Now I am philosophical about it. I no longer have doubts. I know that whatever picture I choose to make will inevitably contradict the one I have just made. I work harder on a scenario than I used to. I am less instinctive as I try to be more professional—about the music, about the sound. To be a film-maker, you are almost forced to be surrounded by contradictions. It is a social act, unlike the work of the painter, who attempts to impose his individuality on society. As a film-maker, you must work alone, and yet you must handle actresses, you must deal with producers who may work against the best interests of your picture, you must face technicians who only want to go home. You must have talents of so many different kinds—talents that are contradictory. You must be timid and bold. You must be modest, in order to create scenes that are intimate, that are delicate, yet you must be authoritative and arbitrary, to enable yourself to do it as you must."

✿✿ ALBEE REVISITED

EDWARD ALBEE's new play, *Tiny Alice*, is in rehearsal at the Billy Rose Theatre, where the line of people waiting to buy tickets is very, very long, considering that the tickets are for a still not opened straight play, and the other morning we called on Mr. Albee at his home, an eight-room duplex on West Tenth Street, to accompany him to a rehearsal. We hadn't seen him since his *The Zoo Story* days, almost four years ago, when he was thirty-three. We thought he was looking somewhat leaner now and, for a man wearing corduroy slacks, a tweed jacket, and a shirt open at the collar, impressively dignified and reliable. He instructed a gray Persian kitten, whom he addressed as George, to get down from a bookshelf, and then to get off a French library chair. After taking the chair himself and pulling another one up for us, he lit a cigarette and, at our urging, gave us a quick rundown on the past forty-odd months.

"I'm a couple of plays older, and I'm learning more—a *little* bit more—about how to write for the theatre," Mr. Albee said. "And I now own a house, for the first time. It's in Montauk—on three acres, on a hill, sixty feet above the ocean. There are two bedrooms, a living room, a dining room, and a kitchen, and there's a guest house. There's plenty of grass and trees and flowers. I have three cats now, and they love it out there. I drive them out in my car, a Lancia, which I bought in Italy last spring. The cats run about and climb trees. The house is a year-round one, with central heating and with fireplaces, too, and it's great in the fall and winter. The air is fine to breathe. I do a lot of walking on the beach. I stayed out there all last summer, while I was writing *Tiny Alice*. *Who's Afraid of Virginia Woolf?* has been opening all over the world, and I suppose I could spend my time now just travelling around to see the various productions. Ingmar Bergman did it in Stockholm, and Zeffirelli directed it in Rome and in Paris, where it's just opened. It's been put on in London, Berlin, Prague, Budapest, Brisbane, Tokyo, Mexico, and a couple of places in South America—I've forgotten exactly where. And I'm not sure about Israel; I get a little confused. In October, 1963, it opened in Stockholm, and two days later in Berlin, and in Venice two days after that, and I wanted very much to go over, but the time coincided with the last week of rehearsals of The Ballad of the Sad Café, and I couldn't leave it. Besides that, I don't like to fly. And when you're in Europe you want to spend a lot of time there. I managed to get to the opening in London. I spent half my time fighting with the Lord Chamberlain's office. They wanted to make seventy-five cuts in the play, including deleting the line 'Jesus H. Christ!' I suggested substituting 'Mary H. Magdalene!' and they said that was fine. Their suggestions for cuts were preposterous. I got them down from seventy-five to three." Mr. Albee laughed.

"How did the play do there?" we asked.

"It was received beautifully," he said. "Better than most American plays in the last ten years. The leads at the moment are being played by Constance Cummings and Ray McAnally. It opened in February and it's still going, which is quite remarkable."

"Any trouble anywhere else?" we asked.

"No," he said. "In Australia, the church people were pretty much upset about it, but the critics said, 'Stop being silly,' and that was that."

"Haven't you seen any of the other productions?" we asked.

"I saw the rehearsals of the play in Prague, on my way back from that two-month trip I made last winter to Russia and Eastern Europe," he said. "The Czechs were good actors. I couldn't understand a word of the language, but I'm used to that. I know who speaks after whom in the play and exactly what they're saying. I know Who's Afraid of Virginia Woolf? so well I sometimes think I could rewrite the entire play from memory."

Mr. Albee looked at his wristwatch and said we'd better get going to the rehearsal. He quickly got into a camel-colored duffel coat with a hood and picked up a large package wrapped in brown paper. "Rug samples, for the staircase of the set," he told us, firmly tapping the package into position under his arm. "I'm up at six-thirty every morning, and today I spent all morning going around to wholesale rug houses looking at rugs. I like to help. It's interesting, if you do a play, to watch what's happening with the set, with the lighting, with the props. But I don't pretend to be a professional."

"What about rehearsals?" we asked.

"I didn't go until the actors began to know their parts," he said, leading the way downstairs and taking two steps at a time. "This week I'll start spending more and more time there. Plays have been known to get away from their authors, but that's no problem here— not with Alan Schneider, our director. I like to go and see if I contradicted myself in the middle of the play, or if I created confusion. The play exists in its total and real form on the typewritten page, where it's three-dimensional. When you start working with it on a stage with actors, it becomes artificial, and then it's gradually brought back to reality."

"Is there any disparity between the first reality and the final one?" we asked.

Mr. Albee laughed again. "You get so involved in watching that you can't quite tell," he said. "In any event, you find that a reality has emerged. I hope you don't mind taking the subway," he added, heading for the Independent. "It's the fastest way uptown."

"Not at all," we said, and urged him to tell us the history of *Tiny Alice*.

"I never know how long a play is going to be until I start to write it," he said as we hopped aboard a train. "Last spring, I was working on two plays—*Tiny Alice* and *The Substitute Speaker*. At the time, I didn't know how long they'd be. It turns out now that *The Substitute Speaker* is going to be in two acts, and *Tiny Alice* in three. It's a little shorter than *Virginia Woolf*—maybe by twenty minutes. I can't remember what started me thinking about it. Probably something I read in a newspaper a year or so ago—something that turned into other things once I started thinking about it, and eventually, as I thought about the play, turned into still something else. The actual writing time was very short. It took about three months. I finished it on September 15th—rehearsals started a month later—working four hours a day, five days a week. I can't go for more than four hours. I still use yellow paper, and I work on the typewriter. For one thing, I can't read my handwriting. For another, I get the rhythms of the speeches by listening to the typewriter."

"Are you still stuck on the theatre?" we asked.

"I like the sense of immediacy, of the present," he said. "I'm not a very good poet, and my prose is tortured." He gave another laugh. "You can get nice tensions going on the stage," he said.

"What's been the best part of working in the theatre so far?" we asked.

"Being able to do something and have it go well," he said. "I enjoy that. I like being a writer."

We got off the subway and headed for the theatre. Mr. Albee shifted his package of rug samples from one arm to the other, and said, "I keep wondering when the real nervousness is going to start. Everybody is just beginning to show signs of strain."

We asked Mr. Albee how he had gone about casting Sir John Gielgud, who plays a character named Julian, a lay brother, in *Tiny Alice*. Before replying, he told us that the other characters are a cardinal, a lawyer, a butler named Butler, and Miss Alice, the richest, most powerful woman in the world. "And they become entangled," he said, looking amused. "When people ask me if they're like the characters in my other plays, all I can say is they're different, and so they talk in a different way. 'Naturalism,' 'stylism'—those terms don't mean anything to me. Most of that cataloguing is meaningless. Anyway, I thought of Gielgud after the play was finished. If you start writing a part for a particular actor, it can be terribly dangerous. I've never done that. I told one of our producers, Dick Barr, that I'd like to have Gielgud, and he sent him a script, and then called and asked if he was interested. Gielgud took two days, and then he said yes. He's a wonderful actor, of course. He still keeps insisting that he doesn't know what the play is about. I told him I'm not sure what it's about, either. It's a mystery play, in both senses. And it's also a morality play. I wish that when the critics write about a play, they'd preserve the element of surprise, and not tell all that they like to tell of what a play is about."

Looking rather happy, Mr. Albee gently wove his way through the line of ticket buyers in front of the Billy Rose, many of whom hastily spoke words of admiration and anticipation, and we followed him into the darkened theatre. The stage manager was calling for props. The director was measuring Sir John against an enormous fireplace at stage right. Other members of the cast were taking their places, also at stage right. Mr. Barr, the co-producer, came over to Mr. Albee and said in a loud whisper, "Beckett wrote that Woolf is a big hit in Paris."

A lighting man began trying out various spots.

"It's a lot of fun, trying to pull all the elements of a play together," Mr. Albee told us, unwrapping his package of rug samples.

🌺 MOSTEL REVISITED

IT'S ALWAYS such a pleasure to see Zero Mostel, onstage or off, that we easily found two very good reasons for seeing him the other day. One was that we hadn't had a talk with him in three years. The other was that since he opened in *Fiddler on the Roof*, in which he plays the role of Sholom Aleichem's harassed dairyman, Tevye, he has become even more famous than he became in *A Funny Thing Happened on the Way to the Forum*, which had made him more famous than he had been the year before *that*, in *Rhinoceros*, which had made him more famous than he had been when he played the part of Bloom in *Ulysses in Nighttown*, Off Broadway, back in 1958. *Newsweek* recently called Mr. Mostel "the greatest performer (it is an inadequate word) on the American stage today," and the *Times* called his portrayal of Tevye "one of the most glowing creations in the history of the musical theater." In fact, Zero Mostel is now popular as well as famous—a situation that, inevitably, has set off a small shower of indignant articles written by sour apples who think that he is a genius and should therefore be enjoyed by as few people as possible. We saw Mr. Mostel in his home, a large, old-fashioned apartment on the West Side, where he has lived for the past dozen years, with his wife, Kathryn; his sons, Joshua and Tobias; and his possessions, which consist mainly of antique furniture, two Steinways, some of his own paintings, a lot of other people's paintings (including a big one, in his living room, by Israel Litwak, who started painting when he was seventy and is still painting at the age of a hundred and three), and a large collection of pre-Columbian art—Mayan sculpture, Mexican and Peruvian painted cloths, and so on. "If you think *this* is a lot of stuff, you should see the stuff I've got hidden in all the closets," Mr. Mostel told us. "When the apartment gets painted, I always find some excuse to leave town, so I don't have to take the stuff down and put it back up. Or I bribe Joshua to do it. I buy him a piano."

We congratulated Mr. Mostel on all the acclaim he has received for his performance in *Fiddler on the Roof*, and he gave us a slight, Tevye-like motion of a third of his hand. "I'm getting it calmed down a bit," he said. "They say I'm the greatest thing since 7-Up, but when I played Bloom it was just as satisfying to me. This show was on the road for so long—three whole months—that it began to feel as though we were doing seven matinées, in addition to seven night performances, a week. I now know why Rex Harrison, after *My Fair Lady*, said 'Never again.' It got so he had to stay in bed till curtain time. After I opened in *Forum*, it was a couple of months before I regained my full energy. I'm just beginning to write letters again, and I'm doing a lot of reading and a little drawing. One thing that bothers me is I still can't make it down to my studio, because I need to rest my leg, which was injured about five years ago in a traffic accident. My studio is in the West Twenties. Before long, I'll be able to get to it and paint. Every afternoon, I'll paint. Then down three flights to supper at the Parnes Dairy Restaurant, which I love, and over to the theatre at eight. I grew my own beard for the Tevye part, and I use no makeup, so it takes me only five minutes to dress."

"Well, how's it going?" we asked. "Do you like it?"

"Of course I like it," Mr. Mostel said. "As soon as I start painting again, I'll like it even more. You just can't beat our audiences. They get right into the show with us. I'm especially fond of the matinées. We call them 'the shopping bags,' because all the ladies come to the theatre from their shopping carrying those big paper bags. Every night, we're mobbed backstage—by Jews and non-Jews, by readers of Sholom Aleichem and nonreaders of Sholom Aleichem. A lot of the people have some previous knowledge of the way of life written about by Sholom Aleichem; a lot of others had parents who knew, but they themselves, born here, never heard about the old country from their parents. However, whether they know or don't know, when they come backstage they're *all* overwhelmed by feeling. One man came back and immediately broke down. I had to give him a drink."

"You enjoy playing Tevye?" we asked.

"Of course," Mr. Mostel said. "Tevye is as classic as any part could be. It's as broad, as full, and as active as Lear, and it's broader and better than Sir Toby Belch. I'd always wanted to play Tevye. I read the original Tevye stories in Yiddish—that is, my father read them to me—when I was a little kid, and I never forgot them. When I first heard about the show, I didn't even want to read its book. All I heard and all I needed to hear was 'Tevye.' That was enough. I knew I would have something to say about the way the show was shaped."

"Did you?" we asked.

"Of course I did," Mr. Mostel said. "All of us worked together to keep the feeling and spirit and characters of the Tevye stories intact, and the show is all of a piece—the book, the music, the lyrics, the choreography, the characters, the acting. All of it is Sholom Aleichem. There has never been a musical like this one. The songs are never gratuitous; they're always part of the show. On the whole, if I do say so myself, it's great. A few self-elected Sholom Aleichem experts want to give you this little twist of the arm, so they say the show is 'too Broadway.' What does that mean? Nothing. Off Broadway, things are the same, except that shows make less money and the actors are exploited. Or the guardians of culture describe some little thing I do as 'a Broadway gesture.' What the hell is a Broadway gesture? I goggle my eyes, they say. I've been in the business for twenty-two years, and for twenty-two years I've goggled my eyes, but now it's described as a Broadway gesture!"

Mr. Mostel laughed, and demonstrated goggling of the eyes. "This show is one of the best things done on Broadway in years, and it's the best dramatization of the Tevye stories ever done in history, anywhere in the world," he went on. "In addition to being a musical, it's a play. It's a show that's a cut above anything else ever attempted. What do those experts want? Something for the invisible, nonexistent theatre? Importing English casts for the theatre is another example of snobbery. English actors say 'cahst' instead of 'cast,' and you're supposed to fall over. In England, they act Shakespeare the worst in the world; they approach Shakespeare with great fear. Or you should see what they did to Tevye in the Russian theatre. Junk! Or go to the Polish theatre and see Tevye. They made a big propaganda play out of it. Or the Yiddish Theatre. I saw Maurice Schwartz do Tevye, and I can tell you that it was sentimental and maudlin, and not Sholom Aleichem. Our show is an honest piece of work. The audience responds the way an audience should. If theatre is not what the audience gets from the stage, what is it? It should enlighten, make you identify, make you feel better—all those things—and our show does that. We could have thirty curtain calls every night if we wanted them. The people don't want to let go. What more could you ask for? I'm getting a lot of unsolicited advice these days. One critic said I shouldn't play in this play, I should play in some other play, but, unfortunately, he said, 'Zero has sold out to the ladies from the Hadassah.' What I want to know is: What's wrong with them? They're all nice ladies who collect money for Israel and do good work. What's wrong with that?"

"Well, do you pay any attention to what critics say?" we asked.

"Of course not," Mr. Mostel replied. "I've never read a single review through to the end. On opening nights, all I want is to take a drink and talk to my friends, and I just don't read the reviews, and by the next day I'm no longer interested. The critics never have any real effect—not on actors, not on writers, not on painters. If you had entered the mind of Cézanne when the critics told him to stop painting his way and to paint the way they wanted him to paint, you would have found he didn't care what the critics said; he just painted the way he wanted to paint."

Mr. Mostel, behind his Tevye whiskers, looked wise, and he said he thought he was just about ready now to get back to his painting. "Painters are the most admirable people around," he said. "They're the only people who do what they want to do. I have a friend, a painter named Joe De Martini, who lives alone, happy as a lark. He cooks for himself. He refuses to teach. He wants to paint, only to paint. He lives with great dignity. He goes to Europe more times than Otto H. Kahn. In Europe, he looks at paintings. Then he comes home and paints. Painters live longer than anybody else. Matisse, Bonnard, and Braque all lived into their eighties. And there's Litwak, too. Titian died at eight-six—though he lied and said he was ninety-nine, because he wanted to put himself on record as the first colorist, before Giorgione. Chagall is seventy-seven, and Picasso is in his eighties. Painters are marvellous. Painters and actors."

REASONS OF THE EYE

OUR MAN Stanley rushed into the office, a sixteen-millimetre Arriflex on one shoulder and a Nagra synchronized sound recorder under his left arm, and declared that he had just finished shooting a movie—fifteen thousand feet of film—featuring his typewriter, uncovered and motionless, without him at it. He informed us that it was a highly charged portrait of The Writer, 1965, and assured us that although he would have to stay with his Moviola for a while, he had no intention of abandoning the written word. To prove it, he presented us with the following notes:

"Enrolled in course called 'The Visual Nature of the Film Medium,' given by Slavko Vorkapich, Mondays at 8 P.M. at Museum of Modern Art. Forty dollars for ten lecture-seminars. Real bargain. About same price as twelve hundred feet of black-and-white raw stock. Getting Vorkapich as teacher almost like getting Eisenstein. With-It people know Vorkapich born in Yugoslavia, March 17, 1895; studied painting in Paris; emigrated to New York in 1920; emigrated to Hollywood in 1921; made experimental film *The Life and Death of a Hollywood Extra*, with miniatures, on kitchen table, in 1928; created montage sequences for *Crime Without Passion* (1934), *Viva Villa!* (1934), *David Copperfield* (1935), *A Tale of Two Cities* (1935), *The Good Earth* (1937), *Test Pilot* (1938), etc. First lecture listed in syllabus as 'Introduction: The Eye Has Its Reasons.' At Museum, few minutes before eight, found big mob of fellow-students pushing into auditorium in basement. Latched onto seat in rear, practically last of four hundred eighty seats in auditorium, beside eager, studious-looking young man wearing steel-rimmed spectacles. Young man introduced himself as Hamilton. 'Oversubscribed!' he said, and pursed lips. Heard crowd outside clamoring to get in.

"Next to Hamilton, attractive young woman with big eyes, hair wound around head in braid, said, 'Andy Warhol got in. Herman Weinberg got in. His daughter Gretchen Weinberg got in.'

" 'Meet Miss Ataner,' Hamilton said, nodding at young lady. 'Miss Ataner played in Scorpio Rising.'

" 'A bit part,' Miss Ataner said. 'I sat on a hot stove.'

" 'Meet Mr. Rozam,' Hamilton said, indicating dark, brooding young man on other side of Miss Ataner. 'And let me study the syllabus.'

" 'I'm probably the only one here who doesn't even want to make a movie,' Mr. Rozam said.

" 'E. G. Marshall is sitting in the front row,' Miss Ataner said.

"Looked audience over. Very young. Average age of members somewhere in twenties. Most dressed same way they dressed in college. Many girls wearing black boots, black stockings. Many young men wearing pullover sweaters over white shirts open at collar. A few stony-faced, bearded disciples of Jonas Mekas, cinematic avant-avant-gardist. Looked over Hamilton's shoulder at syllabus. Read, under heading 'Lecture 1,' 'Unawareness of the visual-dynamic forces at work within every shot and every sequence of shots often leads to undesirable effects, unintentional ambiguities, absurdities. . . . Knowledge and mastery of visual-dynamic principles leads to greater clarity and force of presentation, and eventually to the development of the film as a truly independent form of art.'

"Up front, as screen was adjusted, Richard Griffith, curator of Museum's film library, came forward, looking distraught. Outsiders still protesting. Griffith introduced Vorkapich quickly (said Vorkapich would reëxamine visual nature of film in this first lecture), then disappeared. Vorkapich looked like Mr. Chips. Nice. Mild, undramatic voice. Like good movie, lost no time getting going. Said he would start by telling anecdote about himself at beginning of film career—around time sound came in. Told how producer of film about chorus girl asked him to shoot scene of her walking and dreaming of seeing her name in bright lights. Shot took long time to set up, lot of work, lot of money. Had to build track for dolly, so that camera could follow girl walking. 'And the cameraman wanted good lighting on her face, because she was a star in real life,' Vorkapich said. Lot of laughs in audience. Laughs knowledgeable. Vorkapich told how shot was failure. 'That beautifully lighted face was bobbing up and down, swaying from side to side, but the way the shot came out, the girl did not seem to be *walking*,' he said. 'My shot was a failure. When I think of all that work, all that time for the dolly! But I did not understand the principle of induced motion: If a stationary object is shown against a moving background, the object appears to be moving and the background seems to be stationary. In most dolly shots, the distance between the moving camera and a moving object is kept constant; if the object moves against a homogeneous background, the movement of the object is cancelled by the movement of the camera.'

"Overheard shaggy-mustached fellow in row behind me say, 'About time somebody gave it to them!' Asked Hamilton, Miss Ataner, Mr. Rozam for explanation. In row in front of ours, young girl in Mod getup turned around, said sternly, 'Rift between underground know-nothings and people who want to make *movies!*' Hamilton admonished Miss Ataner, Mr. Rozam, me to take notes.

"Onstage, Vorkapich took drink of water, said he would now show examples of cancelled motions, including weak spots in work of masters. 'Don't think I'm condemning the whole film, though,' he said. 'I just want to show you some things about the film language. It's like learning the English language—the right and wrong ways to construct a sentence. Our language is a *recent* language, whereas the English language has been around for a long time.' Examples of lack of complete mastery of visual language then shown on screen: Gary Cooper in *High Noon*, filmed against a clear sky; Gary Cooper supposed to be walking, but only bobbing up and down. Then he showed scene of Gary Cooper walking on street, passing houses close by. Not bobbing. *Walking*. Then scene of Paul Muni walking in fields, frame showing ground under Paul Muni's feet. Not bobbing. *Walking*. Then same shot blown up so that only enlarged closeup of Paul Muni shown, without ground, against distant hill. 'Distant background will not help,' Vorkapich said. Now Paul Muni bobbing, *not* walking. 'See how we get the essence of a thing,' Vorkapich said. 'The essence of walking is progression. Now watch carefully.' On screen, enlarged Paul Muni without ground seen bobbing up and down, same as previous bobbing. Shot was then zoomed away, revealing Muni walking backward, film running backward. Audience applauded. 'Applause!' Mr. Rozam said. 'I thought these people were supposed to be *cool!*' Miss Ataner said, 'My God, he's making Andy Warhol sit still!'

"Vorkapich now saying he would take up most elementary level of film-making—treatment of static shots. Said he would read from Wolfgang Köhler's book *Gestalt Psychology*. Read, 'Under appropriate conditions successive presentation of two lights at two points not too distant from each other results in experience of movement.' Assistant hung rope down middle of screen, marked areas it divided A and B. On mobile blackboard, Vorkapich wrote 'PHI.' Then he explained that perceptual phenomenon known as Phi phenomenon creates illusion of motion. Said, 'When you deal with a film, you deal with a world of illusion of reality and illusion of magic reality.' On screen, projected roll of paper towelling, first in Area A, then in Area B. Ran A-B-A-B quickly, giving illusion of roll jumping back and forth. Hamilton, Miss Ataner, Mr. Rozam, and Mod girl looked impressed. Vorkapich read from another book, *Principles of Gestalt Psychology*, by K. Koffka: 'In stroboscopic motion, one process fuses with another process, and that even when the two processes are different in respect of color, size, and shape.' Then he showed more examples from movies: Monica Vitti and another girl in *L'Avventura* shown talking from front. Monica Vitti in Area B, looking to her left. Cut to shot from back. Monica Vitti in wrong place, looking to her right. 'Disorienting,' Vorkapich said. 'The perception to the innocent eye is a moment of confusion. The lesson is don't try to make beautiful compositions alone without thinking how they will combine with the preceding and succeeding shots. It's like using a word in a poem. We have taken the liberty of reversing the shot so that the girl would remain in the proper place and facing in the proper direction. Watch.' Showed reversal. 'Is it convincing, do you think?' he asked. More applause from audience. Miss Ataner said, 'Andy Warhol is leaving. The Weinbergs are staying.' Vorkapich showed example—this one from *Breathless*—of people getting out of position because of angle change. Then scene cut to Belmondo laughing, as if laughing at Godard's mistake. Audience dug joke. Laughed. 'When in this kind of an angle-change trouble, use the Western principle,' Vorkapich said. 'Cut away to the horse.' Hamilton, Miss Ataner, Mr. Rozam, Mod girl taking notes.

"Griffith reappeared onstage, said now there would be a question period. 'We did not expect so large a group,' he added. 'Any questions?' Girl rose. Asked if showing movie examples of faults out of context distorted film. Vorkapich said no—faults were still there. 'It's like getting the language wrong,' he said. 'It's like constructing a sentence that reads, "Walking briskly, she stood in the middle of the road."'

"Lecture-seminar continued with more scenes from famous movies—faulty scenes, also great scenes, illustrating how to put Phi phenomenon to creative use. Vorkapich showed a sequence from *High Noon*—series of shots, all stationary, all same length: Cooper watching clock, bad men waiting, Grace Kelly worrying. Series of cuts effectively created feeling of waiting, of tension. Clarity helps a film to become art, Vorkapich explained. 'We're just at the beginning,' he said. 'There's much to be done.'

"At end of session, conferred with fellow-students. Formed film company called HARS—for Hamilton, Ataner, Rozam & Stanley. Much to be done."

❦ PITCHING FOR HOLMES

WE CAN'T KEEP our man Stanley away from show business. Who but Stanley was hanging around with Alexander H. Cohen, the Broadway producer, last week on the eve of the first New York preview of his new musical, *Baker Street*, at the Broadway Theatre? Here is Stanley's report:

"One more hot ticket coming up! *Variety* says 'SEE $1-MIL SALE ON "BAKER STREET."' Mail orders, theatre parties, Play-of-the-Month, Macy's Club, other subscriptions piling in. Show biz! Show biz! *Baker Street*, based on Conan Doyle's stories about Sherlock Holmes, just sold to Metro at million-dollar ceiling, with Alexander H. Cohen, show's producer, producing movie, too, and he and his backers getting fifty per cent of movie profits. Stage tuner capitalized at $630,000; Metro biggest of a hundred and eighty-one backers, with $225,000 stake. Big-time stuff! Approaching this-is-it day, Cohen exhilarated, confident, not worried, laughing, eating five meals in nineteen-hour day, eating twelve candy bars—Hershey's with almonds, Mounds, Baby Ruths—in between meals, stopping for pre-cocktail hot-dog snack at Grant's Forty-second Street hot-dog stand, riding hundred miles from home in Pound Ridge to city and back in chauffeured Lincoln Continental with two telephones, talking, talking, keeping mobile-service telephone channels hopping, thinking up promotion ideas for show, living it up. How come, when show not even open yet? Hooked up with Cohen finishing lunch at Dinty Moore's, on West Forty-sixth Street. Cohen dark-haired, dark-suited, good-natured, well-organized, alert man of forty-four. Easy laugher. Easy come, easy go. Man of action. Told me he was on way to Broadway Theatre. Offered me lift in two-telephone Lincoln. Then it turned out his wife, Hildy Parks, had Lincoln, so quickly hopped cab. En route to theatre, Cohen explained why wife had car:

'Hildy is, A, a mother; B, an actress; C, my assistant and associate; D, studying for her Master's in education at Danbury State College; and, E, teaching first grade, 8:30 A.M. to 3 P.M., at Royle School in Darien, twenty miles from our farm. We have two children, two goats, five dogs. Hildy's teaching schedule usually dovetails beautifully with everything. Maybe, with the preview tonight, we're getting thrown off a little bit. The car has gone to call for Hildy after school. Hildy decorated the stars' dressing rooms at the theatre. Hildy designed the deerstalker hats that our lobby hostesses wear while serving coffee and cake to people waiting in line to buy tickets to the show. Everybody likes Hildy. The car's supposed to rush her down to the theatre.'

"Cohen took two Baby Ruths from pocket, offered me one. Thanked Cohen, who said to call him Alex. 'Everybody calls me Alex,' said Alex, calmly eating. Asked Alex how come he wasn't nervous about *Baker Street*, how come he had achieved whole business anyway? 'I do everything on instinct,' Alex said. 'After *Baker Street* opened in Boston, I said, "Gee, I think I know how to sell this show." So I got on the shuttle plane to New York and I worked on some ad copy. I do my best work on planes. No telephones on planes, and the fellow next to you doesn't know you. We opened the show in Boston on December 28th, and the notices in Boston were three to two against it, but *Variety* had given us a rave that began "Splendid is the word for *Baker Street*, a big rousing musical success." So I became the old pitchman. I wrote an ad, headlined it "You Can Have All the Tickets You Want! But You Are Advised to Order Them Now!," and reprinted the *Variety* review—the whole review—word for word. Nobody had ever done that before. It was like breaking an unwritten law. On January 20th, we opened in Toronto. The notices there were two great, one bad. We had already run full-page ads for the show in the Sunday *Times* and *Tribune*, making it clear that we would give the public service on *Baker Street*. We ran more ads about our *service*.'

"Asked Alex for opinion of Sherlock Holmes. Alex said Sherlock Holmes one reason he could think up so many good ideas to promote show. Said, 'On a sign I'm putting up above our marquee, I say, "Sherlock Holmes Taught James Bond Everything He Knows."' Said sign would be five feet high. Said, 'If I have a success with *Baker Street*, it will be because Sherlock Holmes was a man who solved problems with his mind. Sherlock Holmes used powers of the *intellect*. What I'd love to say to all kids today is "Turn in your guns and your brass knuckles and use your *intellect*." ' Laughing, Alex said Sherlock Holmes great character for stage, because Sherlock Holmes has his roots in literature. Asked Alex for fast run-down of his experience both as producer and as pitchman. Alex said he co-produced *Angel Street* in 1941, went into Army for a year, became press agent for Bulova watches at two hundred dollars a week, two years later became vice-president in charge of advertising at Bulova. Then he told A. B.—what everybody called Arde Bulova, who was the last of the big-time spenders, and he'd learned lot from A. B.—that he wanted time to produce at least one play a year, but A. B. said no, so Alex took off on his own. 'I've always been good at handling talent and I've always been a very good press agent, so I was well equipped,' Alex said. 'Besides, I think I've got good taste, and although I've had a string of flops as well as successes, I've had flops, such as *King Lear*, with Louis Calhern, that were very distinguished. The last ten years, I've had mostly hits—the Nine O'Clock Theatre productions of *At the Drop of a Hat* and *An Evening with Mike Nichols and Elaine May* and *Beyond the Fringe*, along with Richard Burton's *Hamlet* and the revival of John Gielgud's *Ages of Man*. Here's the Broadway. Stick close, because I move fast.'

"Stuck close to Alex as Alex looked up at Broadway Theatre marquee, crawling with painters and workmen, then took off and ran across Broadway, followed by me, to position under marquee of Riviera Terrace, formerly Arcadia Ballroom. Alex pointed out two magnifying glasses, each looking as long as a Boeing 707 wing, that had been put up on either side of Broadway marquee. Marquee also had mystery-blue-painted sign saying 'Baker Street' and giving names of stars—Fritz Weaver, Inga Swenson, Martin Gabel. Workmen working at windows of building above marquee, on building between two magnifying glasses on marquee. Signs advertising *Baker Street* on sides of neighboring buildings, also on sides of building two blocks away. Alex noticed Riviera Terrace not in use. Said he would move in quickly to set up auxiliary box office for *Baker Street*. Said magnifying glasses on Broadway marquee would magnify series of color slides of scenes from show. Building windows overhead would have animated-dummy people standing in them. Building's walls would have dummies of knife-carrying men climbing up ladders, being pushed away by figures of Mrs. Hudson and other friends of Sherlock Holmes in windows. Marquee-and-façade improvements to cost forty thousand dollars, Alex said, laughing. Alex said crowd would stand under marquee of Riviera, watch dummies, watch colored slides, then duck into Riviera Terrace auxiliary box office for tickets. Congratulated Alex on pitchmanship. Stuck close as Alex ran back across street, entered theatre. 'Let me show you the original manuscript of "A Scandal in Bohemia,"' Alex said, and showed me glass-enclosed display case in lobby containing Sherlock Holmesiana. Man rushed out of box office saying 'Alex, you've done it again!' and rushed away. Followed Alex into box office. Under cubbyholes for tickets saw several bottles of pills with labels reading 'One Tablet Every Four Hours.' 'How's business?' Alex asked lady in box office. 'Steady all day, Alex,' box-office lady said. Followed Alex back to lobby. Alex pointed to standing sign advertising Baker Street, called for somebody to take sign to some other Shubert theatre, because no need to advertise Baker Street in place where people already sold on Baker Street. Man took sign away. Young fellow, distraught, unshaven, in shirtsleeves, wrinkled pants, ran over to Alex carrying books by Conan Doyle, was introduced as Jerry Coopersmith, writer of book for show. 'Howard Taubman wants to see the books we used for the adaptation, but what we did isn't an adaptation!' Coopersmith said. Alex said to keep calm, of course not an adaptation, not an adaptation of anything. Coopersmith ducked into darkened theatre.

"Still sticking to Alex, followed him down to basement, found six ladies sitting at desks filling mail orders. Met a Miss Benjamin. Met other ladies. Everybody working. 'Look, Alex!' Miss Benjamin said, showing Alex big box of orders. 'This is all to be filled.' 'And this is just the To May 22nd Room,' Alex told me. 'I've got a To July 3rd Room somewhere else.' Alex laughed, headed back upstairs, went backstage. Visited Inga Swenson's dressing room, all in baby blue, decorated by Hildy. Inga Swenson told Alex she was writing Hildy letter about wonderful blue room, which even had blue towels. Alex showed Inga Swenson little love seat. 'This opens up into a bed, so you can nap on Wednesdays and Saturdays between shows. Did you know that?' Alex said to Inga. 'Marvellous!' Inga said. Upstairs to Martin Gabel's dressing room. Alex said, 'Marty, be sure to ask for the key to the telephone,' and 'Marty, be sure to cover the number on the telephone, so the newspapers won't get it.' Marty this, Marty that. Down again to stage. Hal Prince, *Baker Street* director, nabbed Alex, told him Howard Taubman wanted books they'd based show on. 'The hell with it,' Alex said. 'The purist! This show is freely adapted.' 'Very freely,' Hal Prince said. Alex said not to worry about it, said, 'I happen to believe that Taubman is a positive force in the theatre.'

"Outside theatre again, Alex dropped in on little shop next door, dealing in paintings, whose proprietor was preparing, at Alex's urging, to convert it into The Sherlock Holmes Shop. Alex informed man that he'd be transformed into one of best-dressed Victorian figures of all time, also that he'd receive new shop sign in few days, explained shop would sell deerstalker hats designed by Hildy, Conan Doyle books in paperback and hard cover, show records, Sherlock Holmes statues, footprints of 'Hound of the Baskervilles' in cement. Alex laughed, said, 'Everybody will have fun.' "

❧ PACKAGE

WHAT ELSE that's happening, Baby, these frenzied days, is the appearance of an instant, or do-it-yourself, or packaged, discothèque, which is the invention, or promotion, of the Seeburg Corporation, a Chicago-based outfit that is the world's largest manufacturer of coin-operated vending machines, and last week was New York's turn to watch a bunch of energetic Seeburg salesmen on the national demonstration circuit deliver the package to the people. We were invited, and we ran. The place: The Oriental Room, on the twenty-sixth floor of the Park Sheraton Hotel. The time: Two days. The scene: Seeburg's own instant night club, a three-thousand-dollar package called the Seeburg Discothèque and consisting of a lovely jukebox, with places for dimes, quarters, half dollars, and eighty Rec-O-Dance records (six dance numbers to a record); lovely wall panels bearing drawings of dancing couples entitled "The Watusi," "The Frug," "The Frankenstein," "The Monkey," "The Swim," "The Etc.;" lovely paper napkins with same and coasters with same; lovely extras, like a dance floor that is thrown in for only seventy dollars a square yard; a lovely list of Seeburg Discothèque locations (including such establishments as the Willow Brook Country Club, in Huntsville, Alabama; the Surf Rider, in Santa Monica, California; Sid King's Crazy Horse, in Denver, Colorado; the Lamplight, in Lebanon, Illinois; the Club Hawaii, in Gary, Indiana; and the Top Hat, in Missoula, Montana, not to mention the A-Go-Go, the Whiskey A-Go-Go, the Bucket A-Go-Go, the Frisky A-Go-Go, the Champagne A-Go-Go, and the Blue-Note A-Go-Go, which are in Aspen, Colorado; New Orleans, Louisiana; Park City, Uath; San Antonio, Texas; Madison, Wisconsin; and Whitesboro, New York, respectively); press releases ("The deluge of orders is dramatic evidence of America's enthusiasm for discothèque dancing in general and the

Seeburg Discothèque in particular"); sales brochures ("Say 'Dis-ko-tek' . . . Great new money-making MUSIC-DANCE Entertainment . . . DRAWS to your place of business the tremendously profitable EVENING DANCE and REFRESHMENT TRAFFIC! . . . LP CONSOLE/480 pours out a thrilling cascade of stereo BIG SOUND through the new RHYTHM TWINS—sensational new floor-level remote multi-channel stereo speakers"); and live dancers, including Arthur Murray teachers named Pat Traymore and Terry Leone and one of the first discothèque operators in history, a twenty-seven-year-old dancing Frenchman named Joseph Panarinfo, who started a discothèque in Cannes when he was seventeen. Pat Traymore, Terry Leone, and Joseph Panarinfo were all sloe-eyed tango types. Also, they all had the flu. The Seeburg people—there were forty-two of them, by our count—looked prosperous, ambitious, and satisfied, but they all had the flu, too. When we arrived, the instant Discothèque was smoky and dark, with flaming wax candles on the tables, and everybody was coughing, on the dance floor and off.

On the dance floor—about twenty-five square yards', or seventeen hundred and fifty dollars', worth—to a thundering rendition of "Chug-a-Lug," the dancers were doing the Hully-Gully. Off to one side, we sat with a coughing Seeburg vice-president named Frank Finneran and a coughing Seeburg promotion manager named Arnold Silverman. They spoke tenderly and humbly of Joseph Panarinfo.

"Our European representative stumbled on Joe in Geneva," Finneran said. "Joe and his brother Michel were running Club 58—a discothèque with three thousand members, each member paying sixty dollars a year. Victor Emmanuel is a member! Yul Brynner is a member! And many others."

"We flew Joe over here on December 1st," Silverman said. "I met him in Chicago, and the next day we were unveiling our Discothèque at the Butterscotch Lounge in St. Louis. I've travelled with Joe to eighteen unveilings of the package in twelve states, including places like Chickasha, Oklahoma. Tomorrow we're going to Detroit."

"I've been in the coin-operated business all my life," Finneran said. "Not only jukeboxes but vending machines for coffee, soft drinks, cigarettes, milk—things like that. The impact of our

Discothèques on the market has been the most sensational I've ever seen in the coin-operated industry."

"Our concept is to get Americans dancing again, as they did in the thirties," Silverman said. "My interpretation of the significance of it is that getting Americans dancing again is doing a constructive serv- ice for society as a whole. What's wrong with that?"

"Nothing," we said. "What happened to Joe's brother Michel?"

"He's still in Geneva, managing Club 58," Silverman said. "As our consultant, Joe helps us program our music. All the planning. All the thinking. Figuring out what number should come after what on the records."

"Joe was playing records in Europe by hand," Finneran said. "We took the concept and automated it. Say we start with a slow number— 'Danke Schoen,' a fox trot. Then, without losing a beat, we go into another fox trot—'I Left My Heart in San Francisco.' Then, without losing a beat, we go into a Frug—'If I Had a Hammer.' Then we go into 'The Girl from Ipanema,' which is a Bossa Nova. And we wind up with a 'Tea for Two' cha-cha. The secret is nonin- terrupted music."

"We do all our own recording, all our own editing, all our own mixing on our own records. And what Joe does—Joe shows us how to build the Seeburg tempo," Silverman said.

Joe came over from the dance floor with Pat Traymore, and Sil- verman introduced them to us.

"Joe is showing me the Parisian version of the Hully-Gully," Pat Traymore said, in tones of laryngitis. "Let's go, Joe." Back to the dance floor.

Another Seeburg man—an executive vice-president, named Wil- liam F. Adair, Jr.—joined us, and told us more about Seeburg's con- cept of the instant night club. "It's designed for Mike's Bar & Grill," he said. "We want to bring dancing back to the local tavern, where everybody used to dance in the thirties. After the war, people started staying home and looking at television, regardless of what it was. Now the wife or the girl friend wants to go out. We give the corner tavern a night club the working man can afford. Five or six beers with the wife. And the fox trot. Or the Frug."

"Every discothèque has a nucleus of youngsters at the center," Silverman said. "They love it when the older folks show up and dance the Frug. They *love* it. 'Look!' they say. 'My *grandmother* can do it!' "

"Look!" Adair said, nodding toward the dance floor. "Now they're doing a new one. The Cat. Listen!"

We looked at the Cat and listened as it wound up with the dancers going "Miaow! Miaow!"

Then Joe and the other dancers came over to us, still going "Miaow!"

"How was the Parisian version of the Hully-Gully?" we asked Pat Traymore.

"Joe and I agree the base is the same, but over here we do it a little broader," Pat Traymore said. "Over there, they do it a little tighter, with more feeling. But here we're more individual—everybody tries to outdo everybody else. Over there, one person sets a style and other people tend to follow."

"Any night of the week, in Europe, you can't get on the dance floor, it's so crowded in the discothèques," Executive Vice-President Adair said, getting back to the subject of the market. "Over here, the American public is hungry for them."

Finneran and Silverman coughed and looked proud.

❧ SEMINAR

"Tin-Lizzie Thinking Doesn't Belong in the Clothing Business!" That is just one of the axioms we picked up the other day while attending the Petrocelli Clothes Seminar on Selling Showpoints, which was held in tribute to Clothing Market Action—a two-week jamboree that brought about four thousand buyers into town from all over the country.

Les Dember, the Petrocelli-clad Petrocelli man who invited us to the Seminar, instructed us to meet him in the Schenley Industries' Hospitality Suite, on the eleventh floor of 1290 Sixth Avenue, because that was where the Seminar was going to be held. "We're featuring burgundy and bottle green in our new shaped-suit Petrocelli suits, and—lo and behold!—we're giving gift packages of Schenley's newly acquired Stock liqueurs to all who attend the Seminar," Mr. Dember announced to us as we arrived in the Hospitality Suite. "And—lo and behold!—the colors of the liqueurs just naturally happen to correspond exactly with the hues of Petrocelli's burgundy and Petrocelli's own muted bottle green, not to mention the hues of some of our new linings. Of course, we have to strain a little bit." Mr. Dember led us to a two-window display consisting of a Petrocelli burgundy shaped suit in one window and a Petrocelli bottle-green shaped suit in the other. "Lo! Behold! There's Tony," Mr. Dember said, planting us alongside a glum-faced, Petrocelli-suited man who was staring, transfixed, at the burgundy and green, and paying no attention to Mr. Dember or to us.

"Tony who?" we asked.

"Tony Petrocelli," Mr. Dember said indulgently. "Tony and Sam Eisenberg and Oscar Somerfeld are partners. Big Sam is our president and our idea man. Who thought of using Cesar Romero as our image? Big Sam. Big Sam is going to give one of the lectures at the

Seminar. You'll hear Big Sam on 'How Lapel Treatment Intrigues the Consumer.' You'll hear Big Sam on 'The Hipper Retailer Knows Doing Interesting Things with Linings Will Interest the Buyer.' You'll hear Big Sam on pockets—on everything. This Seminar will, I promise you, be historic."

"Why Cesar Romero for your image?" we asked.

"Surely you must be jesting," Mr. Dember said. "Cesar Romero has been our image for nine years. One of the world's best-dressed men, along with Cary Grant and the late Adolphe Menjou. Adolphe Menjou, that is, *prior* to that historic *Tonight* show when Jackie Leonard pointed out that Adolphe Menjou—both were appearing on the show—was wearing brown shoes with a blue suit, and Jackie Leonard spoke those never-to-be-forgotten words 'He dresses like a Pierce-Arrow!' "

After laying a friendly hand on the back of Tony Petrocelli, who nevertheless continued to gaze at his suits, Mr. Dember guided us toward the Seminar room, which was filling up with about two hundred men wearing shaped suits. "Big Sam invited all his competitors —other manufacturers—to come, and I see they're here," Mr. Dember said, looking around with satisfaction. "Phoenix is here. Hammonton Park is here. Botany Industries. Everybody! And all the retailers."

"Brooks Brothers?" we asked.

"Brooks Brothers wouldn't be caught dead west of Fifth Avenue," Mr. Dember said. "What a business! All those slopy shoulders! Even though some of their suit materials are handsome. But that's for people who want what they think is the Ivy League look. The Petrocelli man is in a different category. The Petrocelli man is in the ten-per-cent group of men who are fashion-conscious, who want to look different, who want to be status-symbolized. Johnny Carson belongs in that group. He's dressing much better lately, since he started wearing Petrocelli suits. Jack Carter wears them. Jackie Mason. Jackie Kannon. All the Johns and Jackies."

"Jackie Leonard?" we asked.

"Not Jackie Leonard," Mr. Dember said.

"Any Bobs or Bobbies?" we asked.

"It just happens that Robert Redford is the winner of the first Petrocelli Platinum Needle Award, something we started giving—a real needle-size platinum needle mounted on a plaque—last year to somebody who made a public impression in dress," Mr. Dember said. "He happens to wear Petrocelli suits, but we almost gave it to somebody else. Bob deserved it, though. He started out, when he first appeared in *Barefoot in the Park*, wearing a Brooks Brothers suit in gray—a *battleship* gray. He sweated through it after five minutes onstage. So we made him a nice lightweight. In gray, but a lovely, muted gray. He looked very nice. Lo!" Mr. Dember and another cheerful man wearing a you-know-what hugged each other, each laying a flat palm at the back of the other's neck, and Mr. Dember introduced us to the third Petrocelli partner, Oscar Somerfeld, who asked us if we had heard what Big Sam said in reply to a certain suit manufacturer who had attacked the shaped suit, calling it "feminine."

"Big Sam posed a couple of questions," Mr. Somerfeld said. "Did this certain manufacturer think that the definitely contoured waists of the West Point cadet uniforms were feminine? Oh, Big Sam took him to task! The New York police have sharply defined waists, he pointed out. Would you call the New York police feminine?"

We sat down. On our right was a man wearing a very shapely shaped suit and Italian-style shoes, and we asked him if his suit was a Petrocelli.

"A De Rogatis," he said. "The most expensive ready-made. Retails for two hundred and seventy-five dollars. Here." He handed us a booklet about Clothing Market Action. Opening it, we read, "Look for Shape to Lead the Way . . ."

We asked how he was finding Clothing Market Action.

"It isn't a Good-Time Charlie affair," he said dogmatically.

Up front, the Seminar was being called to order. The speakers sat lined up before a backdrop decoratively encircling such Selling Showpoints as "Shape Traced Waists," "Living Comfort Construction," and "Tailoring Extras to Make Money for You." The m.c. was Bert Bacharach, the *Journal-American* clothing columnist. He was forthright. "Why is Petrocelli doing this?" he said. "This is not a commercial stunt. I went to Las Vegas with Big Sam last December. We put on a fashion show for a thousand of the international press. It was a fantastic success. I don't know if it sold a single Petrocelli suit, but it sold *clothing*. Why am *I* doing this? Because anything that's good for the industry is good for me. Now, I'm going to keep close tabs on the speakers. First, a fellow who needs no introduction—the head of Petrocelli, Big Sam Eisenberg. Sam?"

Big Sam was big (six feet four inches) and very benevolent-looking. "This industry is too staid, too stick-in-the-mud for its own good," he said, smiling at his audience as if he loved everybody in the room. "We think it's high time for the clothing business to take a leaf from the automotive industry. Makers of automobiles offer the consumer a wealth of options. We believe in giving the consumer the opportunity to express his individuality. Our tendency in the past has been to sell suits mainly as *replacement* items. We believe in offering one irresistible feature after another. Creative-color linings. More personalized lapels. These Selling Showpoints are the sum total of individual fashion details over and above the basic suit of clothing. It's like buying the basic car and then ordering special color or style features to your individual taste and liking. I'd like to repeat that. As a matter of fact, I *will* repeat that. These Selling Showpoints are the sum total of individual fashion details over and above the basic suit of clothing. It's like buying the basic car and then ordering special color or style features to your individual taste and liking." Mr. Eisenberg gave a rapid outline of the Showpoints: The slightly contoured waist. The shape that fits. It's safe. It's sane. Jacket linings in colors. Red. Blue. Yellow. "It *can* be done," Mr. Eisenberg said. "You pay for it. You make a profit on it. For every thirty cents you invest, we give you a seventy-per-cent return. *Better* than the stock market." Style emphasis, Mr. Eisenberg explained, gives men *reasons* to buy. "Get something *new* into your store. New! New!" he said. "Get something new on the backs of your customers. We've sold iceboxes in Greenland. We can certainly sell a suit with a half-inch besom on the breast pocket."

The next speaker in the Seminar was Oscar I. Dodek, of the D. J. Kaufman store, in Washington, D.C. He was introduced as "the man who will speak for the retailers."

"This is not a speech," Mr. Dodek told the Seminar. "This is not one of the demagogic panel talks we all dislike. I like to participate in something like this because it is a dip into the future." Mr. Dodek asked the seminarians to recall how dramatically the shaped suit had been presented last September. "When the garments were delivered, we were ready for fashion leadership. We sold over eighty-five per cent of our purchases. Why? Because we had something new and different in men's clothing to shout about. Your clientele is always ready for the new, and you'd better have it. Sam—" Mr. Dodek turned to Mr. Eisenberg and congratulated him on everything he was trying to do with pockets, concluding, "Sam, I salute you!"

At this, Mr. Eisenberg, who had been smiling with pleasure, looked serious.

Mr. Bacharach urged Mr. Dodek to finish his speech, and Mr. Dodek said he would like to close by paraphrasing Gertrude Stein. "A black suit is not a black suit is not a black suit is not a black suit when the details are different," he said. The seminarians nodded in agreement. Mr. Dodek then likened Petrocelli's efforts to the United States Missile Project. "Each new feature we introduce is a more powerful thrust, so that each new phase begins from a new plane," he said, and, to applause, he sat down.

❧ RESURGENCE

FOR THE seventy-ninth consecutive spring, the circus has come to Madison Square Garden, and last week, on the eve of the opening, and two days after the Torres-Pastrano fight, we called on the man in charge, Henry Ringling North, vice-president of Ringling Brothers and Barnum & Bailey—the Greatest Show on Earth—and younger brother of John Ringling North, its president, who is in Europe. We saw Mr. North in his suite in the New York Hilton, and, to give us a hand in the interview, we took along an eleven-year-old assistant named Amy, who has been a circus buff for the past two years, and who was wearing, fortuitously, a new circus-red wool suit, along with short white socks, black patent-leather Mary Janes, and white gloves, and was carrying a wheat-colored straw purse—stuffed, we happened to know, with a long list of interview questions.

Mr. North, a tall, elegant, distinction-gray-haired, Old World-style man of fifty-five, received us wearing a Paisley silk dressing gown and Peal slippers, and apologized for having a cold, which he said he had got while shopping in a discount house with his Italian-born wife, Gloria, for a toaster-oven, a percolator, and other appliances to go in their Hilton cook-if-you-want-to kitchen. "Gloria makes wonderful breakfasts and *mousse au chocolat*," Mr. North informed us. "We bought a toaster-oven when we were here last spring, but we sent it to Italy—to Rome, where we live. I've had an apartment there, on the Via Gramsci, since 1951. My big brother John keeps an apartment in Zurich. Strangely, neither of us has ever had a home of his own in this country. We lived with our mother in Sarasota until she died, in 1950. We used to pile in with her, along with our wives—everybody. Most of the circus acts come from Europe, and now it's once more possible to get acts from behind the Iron Curtain. Brother John is busy rounding acts up all over Europe for next year's circus while I take the show on tour here. The trouble with the circus is that I've been able to spend only three days in Rome in the past year and a half, and hardly more than that at Northbrook, our farm in County Galway, Ireland, where our grandfather, Samuel Wade North, was born. Brother John has no children. I have a son, John Ringling North II, who will be twenty-five on July 29th, and a grandson, John Ringling North III, who is two and a half. They're both at Northbrook, minding the farm, as it were—we hope to turn it into one of those model farms—but my son can't wait to get to work with the circus, his real love."

Amy opened her purse and took out her list of questions. "When you were a little boy, what did you want to be?" she asked Mr. North.

"Darling, I always wanted to be with the circus," Mr. North said. "I was born with the circus. I had seven uncles with the circus; five of them were the original Ringling brothers. I had sawdust in my shoes before I started to walk."

"But what did you want to be, in the circus?" Amy asked.

"Just the boss," Mr. North said. "My big brother and I always knew that someday we'd both be running the circus, just as my son knows that he'll be continuing the circus. When I was still in school, I used to spend my summers working for the circus, and I went to work for it full-time in 1933, as soon as I graduated from Yale. We have no intention of giving it up. My oldest friend is Pat Valdo, general director of the circus, who is now in his eighties. He's been with the circus since 1902. He always says, 'As long as there's a child and a horse, there will always be a circus.' The circus is still unique. It's alive. And the public still seems to want the circus. As a matter of fact, there's been a resurgence of interest in the circus. For a time, in the early fifties, when television made its first impact, it seemed that children might be more interested in television than in an annual visit to the circus."

"Oh, no!" Amy said, apparently forgetting her role as a detached reporter.

"You're so right, darling," Mr. North said to Amy. "Now the enthusiasm we get from the kiddies is like the good old days. Television lost that first, compelling glamour. Furthermore, television actually helps promote the circus, with all those circus acts on television working as teasers to see the real thing. You can't catch the circus on a twenty-three-inch screen."

"I love the lion act. It's scary but good," Amy said.

"I love the bareback riders and the flying acts," Mr. North said. He fixed a cigarette in a long holder and lit up.

"My little sister Ellen loves the clowns," Amy said, talking fast.

"I love all the beauty and the great skill," Mr. North said. "I love the giraffes, even though they kick. I love the way elephants smell. I've smelled it all my life. We used to carry a menagerie on tour, but now every town we play in has its own zoo. However, we still carry the animals used in the show—camels, zebras, llamas, twenty elephants, nine tremendous tigers, lions, chimps, monkeys, bears, and three hundred dogs."

"Are any of them your own personal pets?" Amy asked.

"Bimbo, the chimp, likes to light my cigarettes for me," Mr. North said. "And Mme. Toto, the lady gorilla, who used to be married to Gargantua I—we now have Gargantua II—is very fond of me."

We asked Mr. North to give us some idea of business conditions.

He said that during that bad period about ten years ago he and his brother had thought they might not be able to keep the circus going. "And it seemed like the end of the world," he went on. "But last year we had a good season—well in the black. This season, we've been nicely ahead of last year. Our two weeks in Washington, D.C., broke all previous records."

"Why does the circus have three rings?" Amy asked, consulting her notes.

"Because that's the way people in this country want it," Mr. North said. "Brother John took the three-ring circus to Europe, but they didn't go for it. They're not used to it. But if we tried to have one ring here, the way they do, everybody would say, 'What happened to the Greatest Show on Earth?'"

We asked Mr. North how the circus had changed from the old days.

"It isn't the tricky thing it used to be," Mr. North said. "We now play in big, air-conditioned auditoriums. We've had to give up that glamorous old impossible routine with all the different tops—setting up the tops in a town, playing two performances, then moving and setting everything up for the next day in another town. On a fine day, it was a wonderful sight. All the tents, Amy, darling, were called tops in those days, except the dining tent, which was called the cookhouse. We had a menagerie top, a horse top, a baggage top, a ring top, a sideshow top, a candy top, a blacksmith top, a wardrobe top, a band top, a Wild West top, and a bull top, for the elephants."

"Did you have doctors travelling with you?" Amy asked.

"Of course—the doctors' top," Mr. North said.

"Doctors for the people?" Amy asked.

"For the animals," Mr. North said. "You could always get the other kind in the towns."

"Did they sell that cotton candy in the candy top?" we asked.

"The concessionaires used to make it for you right in front of your eyes in the candy top," Mr. North said. "Now they do hundreds in advance, and wrap it up in plastic."

"Do you eat it?" we asked.

"I should say not," Mr. North said. "I have always had a dreadful fear of sitting down in it."

"They made it right in front of your eyes?" Amy asked.

Mr. North took his cigarette holder out of his mouth. "But, Amy, darling, it's all so much more comfortable now," he said. "And, besides, darling, you can't miss what you didn't know."

"Would you say the circus has excitement on a par with the James Bond movies?" we asked Mr. North. "Amy's favorite television program is *The Man from U.N.C.L.E.*, and she and all the children she knows are crazy about *Goldfinger*. Can the circus compete with all that?"

"I love *The Man from U.N.C.L.E.*," Mr. North said. "I can never follow what's going on."

"I love *The Man from U.N.C.L.E.*, but not as much as the circus," Amy said.

"If you had to choose between seeing *Goldfinger* and seeing the circus, which would you choose?" we asked Amy.

"The circus," Amy said.

"Why, God bless you!" said Mr. North.

❦ MOLTO, MOLTO, MOLTO

WE HAVE MET Angelo Rizzoli, who was just here from Milan, his headquarters, to visit his Rizzoli International Bookstore, on Fifth Avenue; to be presented by the City of New York with "a declaration of commendation for his active participation in New York City's 'diverse and expanding economy;' " and to preside over festivities honoring *White Voices*, a movie produced by Signor Rizzoli and released by Rizzoli Film Distributors.

Signor Rizzoli, who is seventy-five years old, looks like Julius Caesar, and keeps a cigarette almost constantly dangling, Roman style, from his mouth, has the complexion of a baby, the build of a soccer player, an expansive sense of humor, a knowing smile, and an air of deep calm. Signor Rizzoli's bookstore has, in addition to books (including quite a number published by Rizzoli Editore, one of the largest publishing houses in Europe) and magazines (including over a dozen published by Signor Rizzoli, one of which, *Oggi*, has a circulation of a million, the highest weekly-magazine circulation in Italy), upstairs offices for the many Rizzoli enterprises, including the Film Distributors, which has distributed such Rizzoli-produced films as *La Dolce Vita*, *8½*, and *Red Desert*, and a catchall classified as Tourism, which embraces, among other things, a Rizzoli hotel complex on Ischia, where Signor Rizzoli also has one of his homes. The bookstore and offices have such embellishments as a large Renaissance chandelier imported from a cathedral in Zagreb; walls panelled with eighteenth-century *boiserie* imported from France; further wall decoration in the form of hand-carved wooden replicas of Roman coins; a recessed entrance of white Carrara marble; floors of Vicenza marble; antique Venetian cabinets; a Louis Quinze desk; and some silk-upholstered sofas and chairs. We sat on a silk-upholstered sofa in an upstairs reception room and talked with Signor Rizzoli. Nearby, to help in the interview, because Signor Rizzoli speaks only Italian, sat three interpreters: No. 1, an anxious-looking publicity man wearing Mastroianni-style sunglasses; No. 2, an attractive, stylish young woman, who helps manage the bookstore; No. 3, a worldly executive vice-president representing the Rizzoli Corporation as a whole in this country.

We quickly picked up some basic facts about Signor Rizzoli. He was born in Milan to an impoverished widow, who died when he was three; he spent his childhood in an orphanage; he started working as an apprentice printer at the age of twelve; in 1909, when he was twenty, he bought a printing press (now on display in the lobby of the Rizzoli printing plant in Milan) and started a printing business; he was the first Italian to import a rotary printing press from Germany; one of the magazines he then began publishing, *Il Bertoldo*, was satirically anti-Fascist before the Second World War; in 1933 he produced the first of a hundred and fifty movies, *La Signora di Tutti*, which was directed by Max Ophuls; he has a son, Andrea, and a grandson, Angelo, who work with him in the Rizzoli enterprises; and the grandfather has more stamina than the son and the grandson put together.

"Why did you want to open this international bookstore in New York?" we asked.

Signor Rizzoli smiled, twinkled, shrugged, puffed on his cigarette, and said (according to one or another of the interpreters, speaking separately or en masse), "It is very difficult to be modest when one is asked about the good things one has the duty to do when one is in a financial position to do them. I am an industrialist who has had the good luck to be very successful, and I feel I have the duty to do good. Although I was born poor, I never bowed to any powers. I am the person who pays the most taxes—un'onore—of anyone in Italy. I personally pay two million dollars a year, and for my son, my grandson, and several nephews—for the *famiglia gruppo*—I pay an additional half-million dollars a year. I was given the biggest honor in Italy, the Cavaliere del Lavoro, when I was forty. I am very proud of

Italy. I am very proud of being an Italian. I must tell about myself in this way so that you will understand why I do what I do."

Signor Rizzoli held up a forefinger, smiled, puffed on his cigarette, and continued, "Three years ago, I was walking on Fifth Avenue with the Italian Consul-General. He was talking about feeling ashamed of the Italians because they had nothing in this country to show of themselves, of their work, of their inventions. Together we said what a shame it was that there was not one single bookstore in the United States of America in which one could find the beautiful books published in Italy. We were just then passing by No. 712 Fifth Avenue—the site of the old building that we have now, as you see, remodelled." Signor Rizzoli looked with obvious pleasure at the Venetian cabinets along the panelled walls. The three interpreters smiled at the cabinets and at the walls and at Signor Rizzoli and at us, and we smiled back at one and all. Signor Rizzoli shook his finger at us paternally and said, "And so I decided to build a bookstore that would be the most beautiful bookstore in the biggest city in the most important country in the world."

"What Mr. Rizzoli decides to do, he does," Interpreter No. 3 said, and repeated it in Italian, and everybody, led by Signor Rizzoli, laughed.

"*Molto, molto, molto bello,*" Signor Rizzoli said, looking around with satisfaction.

We asked Signor Rizzoli to tell us about his daily work schedule in Milan.

He said he has breakfast at eight every morning, arrives at his office promptly at nine-thirty, goes home at one-thirty for lunch, returns to his office at two-thirty, and stays at his desk until eight-thirty at night.

"With these hours, you can see how happy everybody is working with Mr. Rizzoli," Interpreter No. 3 said, and laughed all by himself.

"Since I was twelve years old, I have never had ten days' vacation," Signor Rizzoli said. "I find my vacations at night, when I leave the office. I go to dinner and then to the theatre or to a movie."

"Mr. Rizzoli doesn't like to go to dinner with a great many people," Interpreter No. 2 said. "He never takes more than twenty people to dinner with him. He does not like to be with crowds."

Signor Rizzoli told us that for his publishing enterprises, which represent sixty-five per cent of his industrial activities, he owns an ink factory; two printing plants; a large forest, for pulp; and a paper mill, at Marzabotto, which produces twenty-five per cent of all the newsprint manufactured in Italy.

Interpreter No. 1 added that Signor Rizzoli's company uses fifty-four hundred miles of paper each week for his magazines and books.

We asked Signor Rizzoli what he had read lately that he liked.

"With sorrow, *sinceramente*, I must tell the truth and say I do not read any of my books or magazines," he said. "I do not have time to read." He shrugged, and threw us a smile.

We asked Signor Rizzoli what he likes about being a producer of movies.

"*Molto semplice*," he said. "Producing movies gives me an opportunity to be with men of talent and with women of beauty."

Signor Rizzoli looked as though he thought he had given us a complete answer, but we urged him to tell us a little more. He shrugged indulgently, and continued, "I like to become older as slowly as possible. Imagine being with serious old bankers, talking and listening only to talk of stocks and of bonds. As a producer, I can be with all the first-class directors in Italy—with Fellini, Antonioni, Rosi, De Sica, Rossellini. When I am with Fellini, you may be sure that I do not talk about boring subjects like stocks and bonds. With Fellini, I talk about everything in life—everything. He is interesting. Most industrialists are not interesting. They are very boring. Fellini is a man of great talent, of good taste, not like somebody on the Stock Exchange. With these men of talent, I am able to forget, at times, the sides of life that are not beautiful."

While Signor Rizzoli took a breather, Interpreter No. 3 told us, "In Mr. Rizzoli, the very straight human factor shines through in a jolly way and in a straight business way."

Interpreter No. 1 said, "Mr. Rizzoli is the most important man in the Italian cinema today. He has twenty-eight writers under contract."

Interpreter No. 2 said, "All people love Mr. Rizzoli."

We asked Signor Rizzoli how he had happened to meet Fellini.

and he said that their meeting occurred at a time when Fellini was trying to make *La Dolce Vita* but wasn't getting along with the producer he was then working with on the movie.

"Without even knowing the story of *La Dolce Vita*, I immediately said that I would produce it," Signor Rizzoli told us. "I figured that my maximum loss would be only fifty million lire—only a hundred thousand dollars. But I took the initiative to lose money just for the pleasure and satisfaction of making a film with Fellini. Of course, the film turned out to cost a million dollars, and I have already made a clear profit of two and a half million dollars. A Fellini movie that we have just finished, *Juliet of the Spirits*, may be shown at the Venice Film Festival at the end of the summer and will have its world première in New York in the fall. It is the most beautiful Fellini film of them all."

"Do you give Fellini a free hand while he is making a movie, or does he tell you what he is doing?" we asked Signor Rizzoli.

Signor Rizzoli shrugged again and gave us a knowing smile. "Our relationship is very friendly," he said. "But these talented directors, these geniuses, are very difficult about their artistic endeavors. I ask them questions about their movies, and I always get zero per cent in answers. But always with a great deal of cordiality." Signor Rizzoli beamed, and everybody around him laughed.

❦ THE RETURN

ON A WARM, humid afternoon last week, eight days after Vladimir Horowitz made his triumphant reappearance on the concert stage following a twelve-year lapse, Goddard Lieberson, president of Columbia Records, which is bringing out a two-record album of the concert, went to see the Maestro at his town house, on East Ninety-fourth Street. A butler, who was smiling exuberantly, took Mr. Lieberson upstairs to the living room, facing a garden in the rear, and left him with two poodles—one black, one white—who were chasing each other around the room. It was dark and cool in the room, with lamps unlit, with an air conditioner humming gently at the base of a large window, with a large circular sofa and easy chairs freshly plumped and protected by summery floral-print slipcovers, with paintings by Manet, Degas, Rouault, and Picasso on the walls, with dozens of vases of fresh flowers placed all around, with a Steinway grand—on which stood a metronome, a framed photograph of Arturo Toscanini (the late father of Mme. Horowitz), and an open book of Schubert sonatas—and with, on either side of a large wood-burning fireplace, conventional rectangular stereo-system speakers. Mr. Lieberson looked appreciatively at the Picasso—a painting of a circus acrobat—and then wandered over to the piano, where he peered at the book of Schubert sonatas. Still standing at the piano, he gave a sigh and quickly played a few bars of a sonata, and then, as Mme. Horowitz entered the room, he took his hands from the piano and embraced her. She was smiling as happily as the butler, and for a moment she and Mr. Lieberson smiled knowingly at each other without saying anything. Then they sat down, Mme. Horowitz on the sofa under the Picasso, and Mr. Lieberson on a chair with his back to the piano.

"So. How's life?" Mr. Lieberson said, apparently making an effort to sound calm.

"Flowers are still coming every day, and more and more flowers," Mme. Horowitz said. "And more telegrams and letters. Between me and Volodya, we had fifteen letters today. One letter, from a manager in South Africa, asking him to play there, offered him a safari through lion country in return."

"Lions!" Mr. Lieberson said.

"But he *likes* that!" Mme. Horowitz said.

"Except that he won't fly in a jet," Mr. Lieberson said. "He won't fly in a jet, but he flies in a two-engine DC-3 to Maine!" He sighed indulgently.

Mme. Horowitz studied him. "You look much better," she said. "At the concert, when I saw you during intermission, my God, you looked terrible!"

"By the time the concert started, I was so involved with him I had a stomach ache," Mr. Lieberson said. "It was like a prizefight. Not that there was ever a doubt in my mind for one moment that he would play once he *said* he would play."

"Since he played the concert, he's gained two pounds," Mme. Horowitz said.

As she and Mr. Lieberson sat smiling at each other, the living-room door opened and in strode the Maestro himself, bouncy and ebullient, wearing tortoise-shell-rimmed glasses and decked out in well-creased slacks, a hound's-tooth sports jacket with a white handkerchief in the breast pocket, and a blue-and-white polka-dot bow tie. He entered laughing, shook hands with and hugged Mr. Lieberson, and sat down on the sofa, putting his legs up and crossing them.

"You look wonderful!" Mr. Lieberson said.

"It agrees with me!" Mr. Horowitz said, laughing again, and the others laughed, too. Mr. Horowitz waved a hand at the air conditioner. "It's not too cold in here? We have since yesterday a new machine. It is wonderful."

Everybody laughed some more about *that*. Then Mr. Lieberson mentioned the tremendous applause that had greeted Mr. Horowitz when he first appeared on the stage. "You could have left right then and there," Mr. Lieberson said. "What applause!"

"I should have bowed and gone out," Mr. Horowitz said.

"There was a German, long ago, who actually did that," Mr. Lieberson said.

"Reisenauer," Mr. Horowitz said. "He was drunk."

More laughter. "I was more nervous than you," Mr. Lieberson said.

"Next time, I will be more free from tension," Mr. Horowitz said. "It was sometimes worse when I was making recordings. For invisible people. The printed music is like the law, and I was presenting my case to the studio walls. So I was anxious; I wanted that my words through the piano would get to the people. I had been rehearsing in an empty hall. The afternoon of the concert, when I arrived, I was very nervous, and my hands were very cold. I saw the ushers—the young students who work as ushers—and I went over to a tall young usher, and I said to him, 'You are a young man; you have warm blood. My fingers are ice cold. Please take my hands in yours and warm them.' So he did, and"—Mr. Horowitz paused and laughed again—"his hands were colder than mine!"

"Everybody was more nervous than you," Mme. Horowitz said. "The way everybody cared. The reviews! The telegrams!"

"I'm like a little baby about the publicity," Mr. Horowitz said. "I never wanted publicity before. I would never let *Life* take my picture. Now I love it. I want people to know I came back. Yesterday, I took the dogs for a walk, and a strange man comes over to me and he shouts 'Bravo!' and he hits me on the back! And you can't imagine how many people—and the kind of people—sent letters and wires. Clergymen. Judges. These are real. And all the colleagues—Richter, Rubinstein, Stern. A beautiful letter from Stokowski. In a way, that's nice, because some of them are professional enemies. It is very nice. I love it."

"Tell him about the people who stood in line the whole night to get standing room," Mme. Horowitz said. "It was late at night, and we got a telephone call telling us they were standing there. So Volodya said, 'Go down and send them coffee.' So I went down to the drugstore near Carnegie Hall and had them send these young people the coffee."

"They were *genuine*," Mr. Horowitz said. "That is why, at the end of the concert, I was doing this—pointing and waving to them in the gallery." Mr. Horowitz stood up and waved a pointing finger at an imaginary gallery. Then he sat down again and said to Mr. Lieberson, "And the next time it will be better. You will see."

"That humidity!" Mr. Lieberson said.

"The perspiration was coming here," Mr. Horowitz said, indicating his eyes. "It literally closed my eyes twice. I didn't see the keyboard. When you have that kind of wetness, you have to hit the keys differently, and when the perspiration got into my eyes, I hit some wrong notes. But the recording will come out with everything as it was. A performance is a performance."

"You know what Zero Mostel told you when I brought him to see you backstage," Mr. Lieberson said. "Zero said, 'I'd rather hear you play wet than hear anybody else play dry.' "

"He told me he is in some kind of show on Broadway, and he promised to get me tickets," Mr. Horowitz said. "He *promised* me." He looked worried, but Mr. Lieberson assured him that Mr. Mostel would get him the tickets, and when Mr. Horowitz smiled again, Mr. Lieberson asked him if he liked the test pressing of the records of the concert. Mr. Horowitz said that the sound level was just right. He stood up and went into a small side room containing a record-player, and put on a test pressing. He put the needle on in the middle of the record, and it slipped, sending a scratching sound over the speaker system in the living room.

"Volodya! You're spoiling the needle!" Mme. Horowitz called out.

Mr. Horowitz let the needle stay where it was, and returned to the sofa as his playing of the Schumann Fantasy in C Major came over the speakers. Mr. Horowitz took off his glasses and moved his fingers in the air along with the playing.

Mr. Lieberson said it sounded beautiful. "I've never seen an audience sit so quiet and spellbound for this piece," he said. "It was flabbergasting. It's such a profound and difficult piece for an audience. It's curiously abstract in its romanticism. It's not like playing the Tchaikovsky Piano Concerto at a concert. It's not for the usual public."

"It's *against* the public," Mr. Horowitz said.

"It's like reading Goethe aloud to an audience," Mr. Lieberson said. "The way you played it."

"It was dedicated to Franz Liszt, but Liszt wrote to Schumann,

'It's one of the greatest, but I will not play it for the public, because it is so difficult to digest.' "

"So you had to choose it," Mme. Horowitz said.

"Even Scriabin is easier," Mr. Horowitz said, with satisfaction. "You know," he added to Mr. Lieberson, "I played for Scriabin in Kiev, before one of his concerts, when I was a boy of ten. Just three months before he died, at the age of forty-three. My uncle, the brother of my papa, was an accomplished pianist and musicologist, a music critic, and the greatest friend of Scriabin, so when he told Scriabin he had a very talented nephew, Scriabin probably hated to do it, to listen to me play, *just before his own concert!* But he probably said to himself, 'I *have* to do it.' So my parents took me, and I played some Chopin, some Paderewski, some other things, and he told my parents, 'Don't make of him a sectarian pianist; make him a cultured musician.' " Mr. Horowitz put his glasses on, rose quickly, and went into the side room as the bravos and applause came over the speakers in stereo. He changed the record.

As Mr. Horowitz, on the record, played the first encore—Debussy's "Doll's Serenade"—Mr. Lieberson said that it had come out sounding good. "Debussy was making fun of Wagner," he said.

"Tongue in the cheek," Mr. Horowitz said.

"Wonderful!" Mr. Lieberson said.

"If I played it in the studio, I would never do it like this," Mr. Horowitz said. "In the studio, it is a dry studio, and that's what you are hearing. In a performance, everything should be warmer. In a concert, the artist takes chances. In a studio, he is just sitting there. With real people listening to you, it is a show. It is emotional and aesthetic, but it is still a show. It is the brilliant lawyer presenting the case. I do my best you should get it. Listen to this!"

The record was playing Moszkowski's Étude in A Flat Major, and Mr. Horowitz laughed as he ran his fingers rapidly along in the air to the music.

"That's marvellous," Mr. Lieberson said.

"It is the postcard, this record," Mr. Horowitz said. "It is what you send after you visit a beautiful canyon, and you decide to send a postcard of the panorama you have seen. When I play, I listen to myself, and I hear it much better than I hear it on the record."

"Nobody else hears it the way you do," Mr. Lieberson said. "It's always unique for the pianist."

On the record, Mr. Horowitz was playing the last of his encores—Schumann's "Träumerei." The Maestro cocked his head to one side, listening. Smiling at Mr. Lieberson, he said, "I chose 'Träumerei' to play because I wanted to finish the concert like a dream—it never really happened; it's not true. But after it was all over, when we were driving back from the concert, we asked the driver to let us out at Eighty-sixth Street, on Fifth Avenue, and we went to sit on a bench in the Park. Then we walked the rest of the way home, and there, in front of our house, we found five young people waiting. I loved it. For twelve years, I was living just a normal life, not being recognized. Then I saw these young people, and I said to myself, 'I really did play my concert. It really happened.'"

❦ GODARD EST GODARD

Extérieur: Philharmonic Hall. End-of-summer twilight. Long shot reveals people hurrying toward Hall, across open plaza with fountain—singles and couples. Closeup of poster near fountain reading, "3RD NEW YORK FILM FESTIVAL." Closeups of singles and couples hanging around fountain, eying each other carefully, nervously, grimly. Many girls alone, wearing tight-fitting pants. Many young men alone, wearing tight-fitting pants. Some sloppy, intellectual-looking types regarding everybody else with hatred. Some Festival-goers greeting each other with exaggerated exuberance, false friendliness, and making references to Cannes, Berlin, and Venice. Twilight deepens. Taxi draws up to curb. Slightly built man in his mid-thirties gets out of taxi in leisurely way and pays driver, taking a loose bill from his pocket. He is wearing a dark suit, white shirt, knit tie, moccasins, and horn-rimmed glasses with slightly tinted lenses. His face is completely immobile as he calmly takes his time about examining change he gets from taxi-driver. His face in closeup reveals eyes, behind glasses, likewise devoid of expression. Hand-held camera follows young man as he moves away from curb, walking toward Philharmonic Hall, paying no attention to other Festivalgoers, many of whom stare at him and start talking, in an effort to be overheard by him: "Jean-Luc Godard . . . Jean-Luc Godard . . . Jean-Luc Godard . . . *Breathless* . . . Brilliant technique . . . *Vivre Sa Vie* . . . Genius . . . Golden Bear Award . . . Innovator . . . Sexual liberation . . . *Une Femme Est une Femme* . . . Anna Karina . . . Jean-Paul Belmondo . . . *Cahiers du Cinéma* . . . *The Married Woman* . . . Jean-Luc Godard . . . Jean-Luc Godard . . . Jean-Luc Godard."

Intérieur: The lobby of Philharmonic Hall. Hand-held camera goes through revolving door with young man. We see his image multiplied by glass in revolving door. Camera plays for a while with other images seen in glass of revolving door, then reveals distorted image, in glass of revolving door, that emerges as a derby-hatted dwarf clutching copy of *Cahiers du Cinéma*. Camera plays a while longer with revolving door, now seen upside down. Festivalgoers seen upside down. Finally, hand-held camera hurries to catch up to young man, showing him from rear. Camera somewhat shaky, but no matter. All part of technique. Camera shows Festivalgoers pawing over movie-literature table set up in lobby. Copies of *Films in Review*, *Films & Filming*, *Film Quarterly*. Derby-hatted dwarf reading *Films in Review*. Ready now for inside jokes. Closeup of montage of scenes from *Breathless*, *My Life to Live*, *The Married Woman*, and *Contempt*. Cut to closeup of the married woman's nude back from *The Married Woman*. Cut to closeup of a woman's hand, rings on fingers, paging through *Films in Review* on lobby table. Closeup of woman's forefinger and thumb turning page showing sexy scene from *My Life to Live* to reveal page showing sexy scene from *Breathless*. Camera shows literature-examiners quickly turning from literature and following young man. Dwarf runs after him, *his* face immobile, too. Hand-held camera accompanies young man up escalator, focusses on his face, still immobile, his eyes showing nothing, nothing at all, in the way of reaction to what is around him. Camera shoots young man on escalator from a few steps above him, showing faces of young men and women below him regarding him with adoration. Then camera shoots from a few steps below him on escalator, showing heads turned down toward him, regarding him with what looks from this angle like even more profound adoration. Camera zooms in on metal steps of escalator, showing feet of Festivalgoers. Lots of sandals. Black boots. Courrèges-type white boots. Space shoes. A woman's bare feet. The young man's moccasins. The woman's bare feet move in on the moccasins. One bare foot brushes one moccasin. Cut to young man's face. Immobile. Still cool. Sound now gets louder and louder. The click-click-click of the escalator, which had started as barely audible, now becomes louder and more insistent. Very metallic.

Intérieur: The seats in the Hall. Young man is not to be seen. Camera, still hand-held, moves jumpily along rows of seats. Faces upturned. Very little buzzing. Several middle-aged and elderly ladies in each row, among grim-faced pants-wearers. Some obvious celebrities in audience. One young woman wearing transparent black lace tights and matching top, escorted by foppish young man. All they do is look, look, look. Many young men in audience wearing sweaters instead of shirts and jackets.

Intérieur: The stage. The Hall becomes dark. Long shot from rear of Hall shows darkness blacking out backs of heads of audience. Now shown as black silhouettes—all the same—looking up at stage, at rectangular white screen. Then total blackness. Spotlight on stage. Man walks into spotlight, announces the opening of the Third New York Film Festival, says he is happy that the Festival will open with the showing of *Alphaville,* directed by Jean-Luc Godard. Man says that Jean-Luc Godard is with them tonight in person. "Jean-Luc . . . Godard!" he announces. Young man whom hand-held camera has been following steps into spotlight. Big ovation from audience. Prolonged. Devoted. Strong.

Godard's *Alphaville* is projected on screen, and as it starts, camera zooms back from stage. Over blurring heads of audience, still applauding enthusiastically, we at last see title of *this* movie:

GODARD EST GODARD

Now, after credits, movie finally gets going.

Intérieur: Godard's hotel room. The young director, wearing same suit and tie but this time a shirt with stripes, is sitting on sofa, sipping tea with cream and eating buttered toast. He is wearing the moccasins. He is wearing the tinted glasses. He is watching a television set, which is turned on with picture but without sound. The picture is one of those afternoon game shows ceremoniously conducted by an overly cheerful m.c. Closeup of Godard's face; the upper half, over the rim of the teacup, reveals absolutely no expression in the eyes behind the glasses as he watches the m.c. Seated on a straight-backed chair, her back to the window, and facing Godard, is a very serious-looking woman, a French Film Office aide, dressed seriously in a black dress. She converses with Godard in English.

WOMAN: This evening you are scheduled to participate in a panel discussion at the Film Festival.

GODARD (*without changing his expression or looking away from the television screen*): Yes. (*He speaks in a soft voice, without expression.*)

WOMAN: The panel discussions are called "Film '65." Some of the topics are "Do We Need a New Film Criticism?," "Style, Content, and the Plotless Film," "Film and the Good Society." They are being held in a new auditorium near Philharmonic Hall, at Lincoln Center. There will be film critics seated with you on the panel. Perhaps you have heard of these film critics? Parker Tyler? Pauline Kael? Andrew Sarris? Hollis Alpert? (*She pauses after each name, and during each pause Godard nods affirmatively at the television set.*) There will be a young American director, James Ivory, on the panel, and the moderator will be Arthur Knight. He used to be a full-time film critic, but now he has graduated to a job as a kind of professor in California.

GODARD: I have heard there are many professors of films in California now. Why do they not make Adolfas Mekas a professor of films in California? I saw his picture *Hallelujah the Hills*. It is a marvellous picture.

WOMAN: Yes, it would be nice if they made Adolfas Mekas a professor, the way Arthur Knight is a professor. (*Her face goes as blank as Godard's.*) You do not mind appearing in a panel discussion with our film critics?

GODARD: I am used to doing it. There is a television program in France called *The Mask and the Pen*. It is taped, in the afternoon, in a theatre. Mostly old ladies are in the audience. We discuss Eisenstein. Or they ask me questions about my movies. On the panel are the French critics: Georges Sadoul; Claude Mauriac, of *Figaro Littéraire*; Pierre Marcabru and Jean-Louis Bory, of *Arts*. The critics like to talk about the meaning of my movies. I go each time I make a movie. The more I'm getting older, the more I'm getting interested in what people have to say about my movies. Also, it makes publicity for each new movie. Of the ten movies I have made these past seven years, only three made money—*Breathless, My Life to Live*, and *The Married Woman*.

WOMAN: Yesterday, at the Festival, do you remember the young man who was wearing blue jeans who asked you for your autograph? I forgot to tell you he is a student at the University of

Minnesota. He told me your autograph brings ten dollars there.

GODARD: Yes. I have heard the kids in America say about *Breathless* that it was for the first time they are seeing their own life in a picture. It is of their own kind.

WOMAN: But do you really want to know what people in the audiences say about your pictures?

GODARD (*coolly and tonelessly, after taking a sip of tea*): In my pictures now, I am more and more improvising, and so I don't always know what I have done in the picture. But if I shot a tree, and if people are telling me it's a tree, then I know it's a tree. My new picture, *Pierrot le Fou*, got rather bad reviews at the Venice Film Festival. Afterward, I showed the picture to François Truffaut.

WOMAN: Your closest friend. From your *Cahiers du Cinéma* days.

GODARD (*with a small smile*): I don't know if we're friends, but we're very close. He said it's a startling film, and he said, "I hope everyone doesn't start to make movies like this, because then I'll have to give up making movies."

WOMAN: But Truffaut wrote me that the picture was superb. He said it reaches new heights of improvisation.

GODARD: I'm not sure. I might have gone too far in working by instinct. I'm happy I'm still a critic. I still write for *Cahiers du Cinéma*. I will always be a critic. I will never stop being a critic. Next month, I go to Sweden to prepare my next picture, based on two de Maupassant short stories—"Paul's Mistress" and "The Signal." I'm doing the adaptations myself. The picture will be produced by the Svensk Film Industri, which has produced all the Ingmar Bergman pictures since 1957. While I am in Sweden, I will interview Ingmar Bergman for *Cahiers du Cinéma*.

WOMAN: How do you feel about making a new picture?

GODARD: I feel in danger each time when I am going to make a picture. I never feel safe while making the picture. When I get into the editing room to edit my picture, then I feel safe at last. I always feel safe there.

WOMAN: Do you see many movies?

GODARD: I go to the movies at least ten times a week. I like to go to movies. I like to see people move. (*Camera has been cutting back and forth in closeup from Godard's face to the woman's. Now it pans briefly to the television screen, which is still silent. Over the picture of contestants on the television screen we hear Godard's voice continuing.*) I saw *Darling* last night. It is a very bad picture. It is a Vicki Baum story, a Daphne du Maurier story, a very bad picture. If a picture is a bad picture, I go to sleep watching it. There are three types of bad pictures: one, pictures like *Darling*, which don't affect me at all; two, like *Zorba the Greek*, which exasperate me; and, three, like many French films that depress me so much I don't feel like making films anymore. These are mostly French films, because I still go to see American films like a tourist. Although I must include *What's New Pussycat?* among the films in the third category. It is a bad picture. It is like such a bad picture that one wonders if it is not good.

WOMAN: How many categories do you have for good pictures? (*Camera zooms in for closeup of Godard.*)

GODARD: Each good picture has its own category. (*He puts down his teacup, takes a box of cigars from the table, puts a cigar in his mouth, and lights it. The cigar is small and has a pale-yellow covering. He puffs at the cigar and then takes it from his mouth. He blows out the smoke without putting effort into it.*)

Intérieur: The auditorium. Godard is seated onstage, behind a table. To his right are Pauline Kael and Parker Tyler. To his left are Arthur Knight, James Ivory, Andrew Sarris, and Hollis Alpert. The atmosphere of a college talkfest. No sound at all. We see the mouths moving in what looks like serious, grim, pedantic discussion. Mouths in closeup. Pan from one mouth to the next. Get all the mouths confused with each other. A couple of tongues. A few sets of teeth. There is a burst of sound suddenly—Donald Duck, playing-the-tape-backward gabble. Then silence again. Fast cuts—closeup of Godard looking coolly to his right, of a mouth moving in gabble, of Godard looking coolly to his left, of another mouth, looking just like first mouth, moving in gabble. Cut to closeup of dwarf sitting in front row. His mouth moves in time, silently, with other mouths. Cut to woman in black, in audience. Her mouth looks just like first mouth.

She has her head held high. She looks at Godard with shining pride. Cut to closeup of Godard's face looking down at audience. His face shows no expression at all.

Intérieur: The rear of the auditorium. Last row. Two seats in near corner occupied by young couple, kissing coolly. They are seen from rear, profiles of heads in full-screen closeup. Young man's hair is long, straggly. He wears black turtleneck sweater. Girl's hair is cut in what used to be called Buster Brown style back in Carl Laemmle days. She wears black turtleneck sweater.

GIRL (*withdrawing mouth from boy's mouth and speaking in a monotone*): If Arthur Knight can be a California movie professor, then Andrew Sarris should be a California movie professor.

BOY (*studying her face and putting both of his hands over her Buster Brown bangs*): That is true. Andrew Sarris is as much a professor as Arthur Knight is a professor. (*He puts his mouth on hers.*)

Intérieur: The lobby of the auditorium. Panel discussion has ended. Audience is filing out of auditorium. Woman in black waits for Godard. He joins her.

WOMAN: Well, was it like *The Mask and the Pen?*

GODARD (*in the soft, expressionless voice*): The same. Quite the same.

FIN

❧❧ SWITCHED ON

Four days after seventeen-year-old Lynnell Bass, of Virginia Beach, Virginia, won the title of Miss American Teen-Ager, in competition with two hundred thousand other girls between the ages of thirteen and seventeen, in the sixth annual nationwide contest, held at Palisades Amusement Park, she arrived at the salesroom of Young Naturals, Ltd., one of many divisions of the Puritan Fashions Corporation, at 1400 Broadway, to collect one of her prizes, a Young Naturals, Ltd., wardrobe. All the dresses, skirts, sweaters, and pants that Miss American Teen-Ager won were part of a trademarked fashion movement initiated by Puritan Fashions and called Youthquake. On hand in the salesroom to greet the new title winner were Paul Young, who is thirty-five, the senior vice-president of Puritan Fashions, and the inventor of, and in charge of, the Youthquake Program; Terence Hooper, who is thirty-one, and the fashion director of the Youthquake Program; Kari-Ann Möller, an eighteen-year-old model for Youthquake; some Puritan salesmen; and half a dozen publicity people—one of them working with a still camera—who were going about their business of making expert use of Miss American Teen-Ager and her new wardrobe for Puritan Fashions. One man handed out typewritten sheets stating that the titleholder was five feet five inches tall, weighed a hundred and five pounds, had blue eyes and blond hair, had earlier been a finalist for the title of Miss Thom McAn Teen Queen (at twelve), and had won the titles of Miss Ocean View (at thirteen), Best Dressed Teen-Ager of Virginia Beach (at fifteen), Platter Princess of a local radio station (at fifteen), and Peanut Bowl Festival Princess (at sixteen), and that her father was a civil-service employee at the Little Creek Amphibious Base, in Norfolk, Virginia. Miss American Teen-Ager wore her blond hair long; it reached to her shoulders. She arrived dressed in a non-Youthquake two-piece outfit consisting of a school-girl navy-blue skirt and blouse, with a matching beret and high-heeled navy pumps. Her skirt reached to just below her knees.

"Thank you, sir," Miss American Teen-Ager said to Mr. Hooper, who, like Mr. Young and Miss Möller, is from London, and who was wearing his hair very much in the style of Ringo Starr's and had twice as much of it. Mr. Hooper raised his eyebrows at the "sir." He had handed her a small red-covered brochure entitled "Youthquake Lingo (For Salespeople Only)," and he handed one to Miss Möller, too.

"I don't want it," Miss Möller said coolly, handing it back. "I don't need it." Miss Möller, who is very thin and very beautiful, had a lot of makeup around her eyes, and she was wearing her hair, which is dark brown, cut in the Ringo Starrish style of Vidal Sassoon. She had on white Courrèges-type boots and a boyish shirt dress of camel-colored English wool, which came to four inches above her knees. She was smoking a cigarette, and she blew the smoke out in the direction of Miss American Teen-Ager in a rather impatient manner. Mr. Hooper and Mr. Young, who were both wearing dark suits of English cut and both looked handsome, stood side by side for a moment examining the new titleholder.

"That," Mr. Young said, indicating the brochure that Miss American Teen-Ager held, "will tell you about Youthquake, the new fashion beat of London. It's the name of the daringly different young clothes by the English designer Mary Quant. Have you heard of Mary Quant?" He spoke very softly, and he gave the new title-holder a sympathetic look.

"Oh, no, sir, but it sounds very interesting," Miss American Teen-Ager said. She smiled, and held the smile for quite a while, showing perfect teeth.

"Yes," Mr. Young said, somewhat dryly, as Mr. Hooper turned away to talk to Miss Möller. "And you can learn the Youthquake Lingo from it."

"Oh, yes, sir!" Miss American Teen-Ager said eagerly, flashing the smile again. She opened the brochure and read aloud, " ' "Super" is the British way of saying O.K. All these Youthquake fashions are very much super, meaning O.K. "Smashing" is the English word for "great," meaning the most exciting. And it's a great word to use for the entire Youthquake collection. A "flakeout" is so bad it's really awful. "Miss Fox"—a sexy kind of girl.'" Then she said, "Oh, yes, sir, that sounds very interesting!"

" 'Cooling it' means getting it down to great," Mr. Hooper said, turning back to her.

"Mr. Hooper was in the Beatles' first movie," Mr. Young said encouragingly. "His wife, Prue, who is another one of our models, was in the movie, too. She played the girl on the train." He gazed at Miss American Teen-Ager expectantly, but she looked blank. "Did you see *A Hard Day's Night?*" he asked.

"Oh, I missed it, sir," Miss American Teen-Ager said. "But I want to see it."

"Good," Mr. Young said. "And what are you planning to do, now that you've won the contest?"

"My crown is a stepping-stone to a well-planned career in dramatics," Miss American Teen-Ager said immediately, sounding much surer of her ground. "I got a lot of prizes. I got an all-new, stunning Dodge Dart convertible. It's called the Go-Go Car for Go-Go People." She smiled.

Mr. Young, Mr. Hooper, and Miss Möller looked unimpressed.

One of two salesmen who were standing on the periphery of the group asked Miss Möller what kind of car she drove.

"I don't have a car," she said, drawing deeply on her cigarette. "I ride a bike, a Moulton."

The publicity people led Miss American Teen-Ager off to a rack of Youthquake clothes and started pulling out some of her prize wardrobe.

"And didn't you win a trip to Hollywood?" a publicity woman asked the titleholder, motioning to Mr. Young, Mr. Hooper, and Miss Möller to come closer.

"Oh, yes, ma'am, I got a trip to Hollywood and a role in a *Dr. Kildare* TV show with Richard Chamberlain," Miss American Teen-Ager said.

"Would you like to go to Hollywood?" the publicity woman asked Miss Möller.

"No," Miss Möller said, and left it at that.

Miss American Teen-Ager gave her the smile.

"No?" the publicity woman pursued.

"I like being in London," Miss Möller said.

"Kari-Ann is the star of our Youthquake movie," Mr. Young said. "It was directed by one of those people who worked on the film of *The Knack*. It's a wonderful movie. Have you seen it yet, Kari-Ann?"

"I saw it only on a crummy little screen in London," Miss Möller said.

Miss American Teen-Ager and a couple of publicity women, carrying Youthquake dresses, adjourned to a dressing room. Mr. Young, Mr. Hooper, and Miss Möller stood around in the salesroom, waiting.

"She's a Dolly," Mr. Young said to his companions and to the two salesmen. "Too much froufrou. Too schooled. Too trained. She's not free."

"They ought to cut her hair off," Miss Möller said, tossing her head so that her hair swung freely about and then settled back neatly in place.

"She's a boosted teen-ager. She's not typical of the American teen-agers we've seen," Mr. Hooper said. "We've just come back from a six-week fashion-show tour of America," he went on, addressing the salesmen, who looked rather rumpled and tired alongside the Youthquakers.

"We went as far south as Atlanta, as far west as Dallas," Mr. Young said. "Everywhere we went, we found pent-up demands for the Mod look. Which was started by Mary Quant five years ago. Teen-agers here are clamoring for the Mod look. They want to be with it. It's a new type of geometry. Short hair. Short skirts. Sculptured lines as opposed to froufrou or the Dolly look. It relies on a clever use of seaming, it relies on clarity of line, to emphasize the prettiness of a girl. And very little jewelry. The enamelled target circle pin, and that's all. It shapes up a girl's prettiness."

The salesmen looked intimidated. "But the French," one of them said. "The French use of seaming . . ." His voice faded.

"The French have been switched off for four and a half years," Mr. Hooper said.

"Courrèges?" the other salesman asked.

"But what more can he do?" Mr. Hooper said. "His geometry is perfect, but what more can he do?" He raised his eyebrows at the salesmen, who said nothing. "Young Naturals is the most switched-on division of Puritan, and the most switched-on in the country today," Mr. Hooper continued. "The crowds at our fashion shows! The teen-agers turned up by the thousands. Because we showed the clothes the way the kids want to wear them! Without any tacky fashion-show commentaries. We showed the models doing things. And with their own music forms. Dancing to our Youthquake song, sung by The Skunks. The whole bit. You should have seen the kids go for the clothes in Akron. Akron! Akron!" He seemed to be singing.

One of the salesmen asked Miss Möller if she had done any modelling before she joined Youthquake.

"I worked for Mattli's for a month, but I couldn't stand it," she said. "All those tacky fashion-show commentaries! Then I just smooched around for a bit. I went to the Ad Lib one night. Dancing," she said, observing the salesman's unspoken question. "It's a discothèque. In Soho. And that's how I met Mary Quant."

"We have the two top names—Mary Quant and Tuffin & Foale—designing for Puritan," Mr. Young said, "and now other manufacturers are watching us and trying to get on the gravy train. Imitators think that anybody can do it."

The salesmen looked alert.

"Youthquake had been on my mind for three years," Mr. Young went on. "Three years ago, I knew that 1966 would be the key year in America, because I'd done some research, and I'd learned that by 1966 half the American population would be under twenty-five. Everything in England had started cracking right after the Second World War. There had been a tremendous surge in England. There was a tremendous pent-up consumer demand, coupled with a gigantic need for consumer goods, and the postwar generation were looking for identity. They wanted to be important. They had suffered a traumatic shock. To exist, they cocooned together. They are really scared, but they have group freedom. I call it a Queen Bee society. And in England they've been able to find expression early. They leave school early, because the colleges are too full, and, because of the loss of the Empire, they feel they want to be important. Do you know what I mean?"

The salesmen looked at each other as though they were trying to think. Mr. Hooper and Miss Möller exchanged looks of their own.

"They had been raised matriarchally," Mr. Young continued, speaking as softly as ever. "Their fathers had been killed in the war or had committed suicide—you know, in the depression. The mothers indulged their children. Permissiveness," he said slowly. "Did you ever hear of John Dewey?"

The salesmen looked for help at the racks of Young Naturals, and, not finding it, continued to listen.

"In London, suddenly, it all went *clonk*," Mr. Young said. "But why wasn't it happening in New York? The American teen-ager was still in school. The teen-agers still had to account to their parents for the way they spent their money; they had to explain their purchases. Five years ago, when I started doing research, I found that the American teen-ager had no identity symbols. Then President Kennedy came along, and there was great interest in Jacqueline. The teen-agers had an identity symbol in her. And now it's cracking here. We're in the midst of a social revolution. We're going to see a change in socio-buying patterns."

The salesmen looked deeply relieved as Miss American Teen-Ager came into the room wearing a Youthquake dress, designed by Mary Quant, that was short-sleeved and simple in its lines, reached to a couple of inches above her knees, and had one hip pocket.

"This one is called the Hipster," Mr. Young said as the publicity people told each other the dress was pretty cute and one of them said to Miss American Teen-Ager, "Atta girl! 'At's it! Very lovely! Very lovely!" Then the still photographer started photographing.

Mr. Young turned his attention to Miss American Teen-Ager. "Have you ever thought," he began in a kindly way, "why some people say that short dresses are disgusting?"

"Oh, yes, sir! That's *true!*" Miss American Teen-Ager cried out. "People wear bathing suits, don't they, and *that's* not disgusting." She looked at Mr. Young for approval.

"It's something new," Mr. Young said. "Some manufacturers resist anything new or radical. Do you think it's difficult to accept something new?"

"Oh, no, sir, I don't think so," Miss American Teen-Ager said, and put a hand, tentatively, over her hip pocket. The salesmen looked as though they were cooling it.

Miss American Teen-Ager retired, to put on another sample of the Youthquake.

"I personally *like* young people," Mr. Young said to the salesmen. "If teen-agers are enthusiastic about something, they give everything to it. Don't you agree?"

Again the salesmen looked at each other, and this time they said they agreed.

"I've just started a new division at Puritan, which I've named Daphne," Mr. Young said. "Daphne will be the division for junior dresses. I saw her as whimsical, as a person, and I've just written a description of her, advising everybody, 'You'd better be ready for Daphne; she has a different wave length.' "

The salesmen nodded overenthusiastically.

"Daphne is a new dimension," Mr. Young said.

Mr. Hooper stepped up to Mr. Young and told him that Miss American Teen-Ager had put on another Youthquake dress. "But they're photographing her wearing pearls!" he said. "Pearls!"

"No! No! No!" Mr. Young said, going over to the photographer and the titleholder but not raising his voice. He didn't have to raise it, for everybody else was silent. "*You'd* never wear it with pearls, would you?" Mr. Young said softly to Miss American Teen-Ager. "That little strand of pearls looks so incongruous, doesn't it?"

Miss American Teen-Ager gave a smile, first to the photographer and the publicity people and then to Mr. Young, and waited, saying nothing.

"Of course not," Mr. Young said, and removed the pearls. Then he stood back and regarded Miss American Teen-Ager, and said, "*Smashing!*"

Following are the dates of The New Yorker issues in which the stories in this book appeared:

MOVEMENT—April 16, 1960
ANNIVERSARY—August 20, 1960
GELBER—July 9, 1960
THE VINYL SANTA—December 8, 1962
LIFE LINE—August 6, 1960
DAME EDITH—January 21, 1961
SYMBOL—April 8, 1961
AMBASSADOR STEVENSON—January 28, 1961
FIRST REHEARSAL—September 3, 1960
SIMON—February 18, 1961
RIPPLES—March 4, 1961
PLAYWRIGHT—May 9, 1959
HENNY—March 18, 1961
BEFORE THE FÊTE—May 6, 1961
ALBEE—March 25, 1961
THE SOUND—April 22, 1961
MR. KENNETH—May 13, 1961
1650 BROADWAY—May 27, 1961
THE ATTORNEY GENERAL—June 24, 1961
SUNNY HILL—July 15, 1961
COFFEE WITH COWARD—July 22, 1961
LEARNING—July 1, 1961
DAG HAMMARSKJÖLD—September 30, 1961
THE FIRST ONE—October 28, 1961
ON BRECHT ON BRECHT—June 16, 1962
PIONEERS—June 30, 1962
REALISM—July 28, 1962